Encountering
the Impossible

THE SUNY SERIES
HORIZONS OF CINEMA
MURRAY POMERANCE | EDITOR

Encountering the Impossible
The Fantastic in Hollywood Fantasy Cinema

❦

Alexander Sergeant

Cover: *The NeverEnding Story* (1984). Dir. Wolfgang Petersen. © Warner Bros. Credit: Warner Bros./Photofest.

Published by State University of New York Press, Albany

© 2021 State University of New York

All rights reserved

Printed in the United States of America

No part of this book may be used or reproduced in any manner whatsoever without written permission. No part of this book may be stored in a retrieval system or transmitted in any form or by any means including electronic, electrostatic, magnetic tape, mechanical, photocopying, recording, or otherwise without the prior permission in writing of the publisher.

For information, contact State University of New York Press, Albany, NY
www.sunypress.edu

Library of Congress Cataloging-in-Publication Data

Name: Sergeant, Alexander, author
Title: Encountering the impossible : the fantastic in Hollywood fantasy cinema / Alexander Sergeant, author.
Description: Albany : State University of New York Press, [2021] | Series: SUNY series, horizons of cinema | Includes bibliographical references and index.
Identifiers: ISBN 9781438484594 (hardcover : alk. paper) | ISBN 9781438484587 (pbk. : alk. paper) | ISBN 9781438484600 (ebook)
Library of Congress Control Number: 2021939444

10 9 8 7 6 5 4 3 2 1

Contents

List of Illustrations	vii
Acknowledgments	xi
A Note on Terminology	xiii
Introduction	1
1 What is The Fantastic?	11
2 Continuity and Cathexis: Character, Space, and Time in the Classical Hollywood Fantasy Film, 1930–1945	33
3 The Wonder Film: Postclassical Fantasy Cinema and Phantasies of Introjection, 1946–1975	79
4 High Fantasy Blockbusters: Alternative Worlds and Phantasies of Projection, 1976–1991	129
5 Interpreting the Fantastic: Contemporary Fantasy Cinema and Symbol Formation, 1992–2018	175
Conclusion: The Fantastic *Beyond* Hollywood Fantasy Cinema?	219
Notes	225
Bibliography	237
Index	245

Illustrations

Figure 1.1	The magical faun seems to appear and disappear (*Pan's Labyrinth*, 2006)	27
Figure 1.2	Ofelia dies a tragic death	28
Figure 1.3	Ofelia arises to become Queen of the Underworld	28
Figure 2.1	The *Alice in Wonderland* (1933) cast transformed into Lewis Carroll's beloved characters	39
Figure 2.2	Alice meets the Dodo	41
Figure 2.3	Alice is scolded by her governess	45
Figure 2.4	Alice meets Humpty Dumpty	47
Figure 2.5	Dorothy is greeted by the Munchkins with a lavish parade (*The Wizard of Oz*, 1939)	52
Figure 2.6	Dorothy opens the door to the house to peek into the world of Oz	54
Figure 2.7	Oz appears in all its emotive glory	54
Figure 2.8	Dorothy marvels at being in a magical space	55
Figure 2.9	The magical space threatens to subsume Dorothy	55
Figure 2.10	Oz dominates the screen, the camera leaving Dorothy behind	58
Figure 2.11	Munchkinland is revealed in all its glory	58
Figure 2.12	The camera returns to Dorothy to remind us of Oz's emotional impact	59

Figure 2.13	Dorothy realizes that she is not in Kansas anymore	59
Figure 2.14	Dorothy stands in front of an empty field	62
Figure 2.15	The Scarecrow seems to magically appear in the field behind Dorothy	62
Figure 2.16	The twinkling stars embody angels (*It's a Wonderful Life*, 1946)	68
Figure 2.17	George promises Mary he will lasso the moon for her	73
Figures 3.1–3.4	Elwood talks to empty screen space throughout *Harvey* (1950)	88–89
Figures 3.5–3.8	Elwood is given a moment to explain Harvey to Miss Kelly and Dr. Sanderson	96–97
Figure 3.9	Veta explains the difference between "mechanical" photographs and paintings filled with dreams	98
Figures 3.10–3.13	Mary's magic is almost always mediated through the astonished faces of the Banks children (*Mary Poppins*, 1964)	104–105
Figure 3.14	The bird woman appears in a quasi-hallucinogenic manner	109
Figure 3.15	Live-action collides with cel animation	113
Figure 3.16	The presence of a pro-filmic, photographed ship's mast is highlighted (*The Golden Voyage of Sinbad*, 1974)	119
Figure 3.17	The previously photographed ship's mast becomes animated	119
Figure 3.18	The climactic battle	123
Figure 4.1	Conan traverses various spectacular frontiers (*Conan the Barbarian*, 1982)	137
Figure 4.2	The title card of *Conan the Barbarian*	141
Figure 4.3	Bastian reacts viscerally to the events taking place within the book of *The NeverEnding Story* (1984)	147

Figures 4.4–4.5	Through a close-up on Bastian's eyes, the film travels into the fictional world of Fantasia	153
Figure 4.6	Atreyu looks into the magic mirror gate to see Bastian reading the eponymous novel	155
Figure 4.7	Peter peers through the ripped bedsheet in *Hook* (1991)	163
Figure 4.8	Framed from Peter's perspective, a small hole provides access to Neverland	163
Figure 4.9	That world is revealed fully	163
Figure 4.10	Peter stumbles lost around the world he left behind	164
Figure 4.11	Peter Banning/Pan does not believe he can fly	64
Figures 4.12–4.13	Peter learns to have the imagination to start a food fight	169
Figure 5.1	Gandalf offers Frodo some advice (*The Lord of the Rings: The Fellowship of the Ring*, 2001)	187
Figure 5.2	Gandalf battles the Balrog	191
Figure 5.3	Doodles and drawings appear over the opening credits (*Where the Wild Things Are*, 2008)	195
Figure 5.4	Max is introduced to Ira's Hole	199
Figure 5.5	Max is introduced to Bob and Terry	200
Figure 5.6	A wild rumpus ends	202
Figure 5.7	A magical threat detector displayed in *Fantastic Beasts and Where to Find Them* (2016) closely resembles the real-life terrorist alert signal used in many countries	207
Figure 5.8	Grindelwald addresses his followers (*Fantastic Beasts: The Crimes of Grindelwald*, 2018)	209
Figure 5.9	Grindelwald's spell fills the room with WWII-esque imagery	209
Figure 5.10	The spell echoes real-life atrocities, including the Holocaust	209

Figure 5.11	Nuclear war is evoked	209
Figures 5.12–5.15	Jacob enters Newt's enchanted briefcase and encounters a menagerie of magical beasts (*Fantastic Beasts and Where to Find Them*, 2016)	213

Acknowledgments

This book is indebted to a series of educators, without whom it could not and would not have been written.

To Gill Sergeant for reading a copy of L. Frank Baum's *The Wonderful Wizard of Oz* to me. To Rob Sergeant for renting me the movie. I'm sorry I've yet to get a proper job.

To Nigel Matthias for giving me a copy of Philip Larkin's *The Whitsun Weddings* and showing me the awesome potential the interpretative arts offers to the world. Thank you for not dismissing my absurd reading of the poem "Water."

To Martin Pumphrey for transforming an apathetic undergraduate student reluctantly and forcefully into a film scholar. Thank you for turning my Monday morning film classes into something more than an excuse to get out of another lecture, or to avoid the four-story climb up to the History Department.

To Sarah Cooper for your unflinching support as my PhD supervisor. Despite my choice of subject matter, your expertise, professionalism, and compassion were by far the most magical experiences I had the pleasure of witnessing throughout some formative years during my time at King's College London. I will be forever grateful for that.

To the AHRC for their generous financial support of this research in its early stages, my reviewers for providing useful feedback and to the editorial staff at State University of New York Press, especially Murray Pomerance. Thank you for taking the project under your wing and helping to steer it (and me) toward publication.

To my colleagues and peers at Bournemouth University, King's College London, London Metropolitan University, the University of Portsmouth, and beyond. To Andrew Asibong, Tom Brown, Jane Chandler, James Fair, Austin Fisher, Hannah Hamad, Lilly Husbands, Edward

Lamberti, Aaron McMullan, Lawrence Napper, Jeff Scheible, Deborah Shaw, Irini Tendall, Ben Tyrer, Catherine Wheatley, Christa Van Raalte, and Candida Yates. Christopher Holliday deserves a particular mention for letting me rant about things a little more often than he should.

To everybody who has assisted this book to its completion, whether in the form of a supportive critical voice or a shoulder to cry on in times of need. To Dan, Emma, Harry, Harvey, Holly, Joe, Liv, Kat, Matt, and Rhi. To Natalie, with all of my love. To give proper justice to all of you would be to fill the pages of an even larger volume, so please accept this volume as it stands.

To my family, my friends, my teachers.

A Note on Terminology

I make a distinction throughout this book between two words, *fantasy* and *phantasy*. When I am discussing fantasy, I am referring to a genre label used to describe a particular kind of storytelling, that is, the fantasy genre or concepts of the fantasy film. When discussing phantasy, I am referring instead to a mental process that is much harder to describe but alludes toward ideas of dreaming, creativity, and the imagination. This distinction between fantasy and phantasy is admittedly something of an artificial construct. Within psychoanalytic discourse, the two terms of *fantasy* and *phantasy* are often used interchangeably depending on the author and/or translator of the specific work in question. Embracing the *ph* spelling of phantasy in this instance—as well as derivatives such as *phantasize* and *phantasizing*—is designed to clearly distinguish on the page between psychoanalytic definitions of phantasy and alternative definitions of fantasy fiction. The distinction also acknowledges a broader tradition of avoiding the word *fantasy* spelled with an *f* in order given the connotations of whimsy or triviality that often surround such a term within the wider public discourse. Quotations from authors using either "fantasy" or "phantasy" will be left unchanged so as to preserve the integrity of their original prose, meaning that, on occasion, the alternative spelling of fantasy/phantasy may appear in the book in contrast to the definitions previously outlined. It is hoped that in such instances, the context of the discussion will be enough to guide the reader toward which version of fantasy/phantasy is intended.

The term *spectator* is also a crucial one in this book. In line with previous academic work on this subject, I do not utilize this term to refer to a living, breathing audience member but to a theoretical construct. Yet, for the sake of style, it seems sometimes necessary to personify such a term through the use of pronouns. In such instances, I have adopted conventional terminology that suggests gender fluidity and plurality as opposed to binaries of gender (we/they/their/them rather than he/she/her/his/him).

Introduction

Fantasy exists, regardless as to whether or not we choose to believe in it. Fantasy is all around us, permeating our existence, influencing our thoughts, and informing our worldview. It is part of our culture, deep-seated and ubiquitous, constructing our society, and distributing our wealth. Every day, every hour, we imagine. We imagine a world that exists and a world that does not. We imagine things for ourselves and we imagine things for other people. To exist outside of fantasy is to exist outside of reality, and to live in the real world is to live in a world full of dreams.

This is a book about fantasy. More specifically, it is a book about two different kinds of fantasy. It is a book about *fantasy cinema*, a genre that is responsible for some of the most enduring images throughout film history from Dorothy's (Judy Garland) arrival into Munchkinland in *The Wizard of Oz* (1939) to the entrance into the Great Hall of Hogwarts in *Harry Potter and the Sorcerer's Stone* (2001). Fantasy films have informed our collective memories and expectations surrounding the cinematic experience and have provided a global film industry historically based within the hills of Los Angeles with some of its biggest commercial successes. But this is also a book about *phantasy*. It is a book about how we use our capacity to imagine to experience the world around us without credence to ideas of rationality and logic, and how our ability to phantasize allows us to forge relationships with stories we know are not real and cannot be true. *Encountering the Impossible: The Fantastic in Hollywood Fantasy Cinema* explores a particular kind of cinematic experience that liberates us from our everyday responsibility to find meaning in things based on our capacity toward empiric knowledge and objective understanding, and the freedom that comes from engaging with scenarios that we know are neither accurate, nor realistic, nor natural. This book is about the experience we associate with the Hollywood fantasy film, and why that experience matters.

What Is a Fantasy Film? Film Genre and the Problem of Classification

In the words of David Orr writing in the *New York Times*, we are currently living in a "high time for high fantasy."[1] The commercial success of franchises such as The Lord of the Rings (2001–2003), Harry Potter (2001–2011), The Chronicles of Narnia (2005–2010), Pirates of the Caribbean (2006–2017), and the Marvel Cinematic Universe (2008–) has not only seen the fantasy genre dominate Hollywood's production cycles over the past few decades but also has resulted in the word *fantasy* becoming a seemingly ubiquitous category of narrative filmmaking used within all manner of popular cinematic discourse. *Fantasy* is a term used by newspaper and magazine journalists to categorize new releases. It is utilized by theatrical chains like AMC Theaters to provide their customers with a more efficient means of searching for the types of films they want to see. Online forums like IMDb dedicate numerous pages to the discussion and celebration of fantasy cinema, apps such as Rotten Tomatoes and Letterboxd allow their users to find out what film journalists/critics have already said about different examples of fantasy cinema, and streaming services like Netflix, Amazon Prime, and Disney+ allow users to easily access the latest or best examples of fantasy filmmaking through a designed filtering device embedded within their website coding. The notion that there is a stable and recognizable genre of filmmaking known as fantasy cinema is a prerequisite assumption for many to participate in large sections of the landscape of popular film culture, operating as a useful and effective means of film classification across the globe.

So what exactly is a fantasy film? Given the popularity the genre enjoys, it seems almost bizarre that such a question needs asking and, even more bizarre, that it is very difficult to answer. Audiences and producers should surely have a very clear idea of what a fantasy film is if they are to use the term in the promotion and discussion of cinema. Indeed, it is not difficult to think of an example of fantasy filmmaking from the menagerie of dragons, dwarfs, ghosts, goblins, munchkins, mome raths, ogres, orcs, pirates, pixies, trolls, titans, witches, wizards, and warlocks that have emerged from Hollywood over the past century. Yet, finding an essential ingredient that unites all these disparate quests, spells, and creatures together is an altogether more difficult matter, a problem not helped by what Frances Pheasant-Kelly refers to as the "scant scholarly attention" the genre received within film and media scholarship prior to the turn of the twenty-first century.[2] Some fantasy theorists have tried to classify the genre according a certain narrative criteria, suggesting that all fantasy stories are required to contain an element of "magic" (Alec Worley) or else a kind of "ontological rupture" (Katherine A. Fowkes) that sets them apart from other stories that seek to represent or mirror reality within their fictions.[3] Yet, although these definitions offer some clarification, they are muddied by the inherent subjectivity of the terms they evoke. For some audience members, a film like *King of Kings* (1927 and 1961) may offer a complete and self-conscious departure from their sense of reality in that it depicts the death and rebirth of Jesus Christ. For others, though, *King of Kings* represents a vivid confirmation of a preexisting worldview in that it tells a story that is the basis for the Christian faith. A definition of fantasy as a story that breaks from reality, then, relies first and foremost on a shared definition of what a story based on reality might look like, an issue that gets us into often contentious territory. Using these definitions alone, it becomes very difficult to state with any certainty what is one person's fantasy and another's philosophy or theology, where one person's fabrication ends and another person's realism begins.

It is for these reasons, alongside a lack of standardized terminology across different languages (*fantastique* in French, *fantastika* in Russian, *fantezi* in Turkish, *fantaji* in Japanese, each with their own subtle distinctions about the relationship between fantasy and reality), that what is referred to in Anglophonic circles as fantasy cinema has proven to be one of the most difficult categories of cinema to pinpoint and define among both critics and academics alike. Scholars like David Butler and James Walters have gone so far as to suggest that fantasy is not a genre but a wider storytelling mode or impulse, with the latter arguing that fantasy is as likely to occur in a "story about an escaped convict as it is in a story about a mythical kingdom."[4] But these attempts to broaden out the parameters by which we might analyze the form and function of fantasy onscreen are fraught with their own problems. From elaborate pratfalls to choreographed song-and-dance numbers to last-minute dashes through airports, popular cinema is littered with situations that are unlikely to occur in real life, moments that we might say showcase a wider impulse toward fantasy onscreen. This does not mean, however, that is either necessary or even useful to consider films like *The General* (1926), *Singin' in the Rain* (1952), or *Love Actually* (2003) as works of fantasy, even if they do contain moments that seem to push the boundaries of credulity onscreen. Moreover, if we try to make sure we include everything that might be a fantasy in a definition of what fantasy is, then we have to acknowledge the fact that, when we sit down to watch a group of highly paid and extremely famous actors pretend to be journalists, accountants, or downtrodden janitors for our viewing pleasure, we are often very aware that we are delighting in things we know are not real. So, it might indeed be argued that *all* films are fantasy films, which is akin to saying none of them are when it comes to assessing the viability of a recognizable and well-used category of genre filmmaking.

Perhaps the difficulty in assigning an adequate definition for what constitutes a fantasy film comes not from the fact that fantasy is unable to be defined but that we are asking the wrong kinds of questions in pursuit of that definition. As Raphaëlle Moine argues, the dominant "classificatory or analytical logics" of contemporary film genre scholarship are useful in that they identify recurring thematic and stylistic traits that help to shape a formal understanding of what constitutes a film genre.[5] Yet, as Moine also states, a focus on these formal characteristics alone is in danger of bypassing the "functional dimension of genre" as a process that gives shape and meaning to the film experience itself.[6] Fantasy cinema functions as an effective means of classifying particular film releases for many individuals across the globe, even if it does so while operating in imperfect or flawed terms. This is not necessarily proof of the invalidity of fantasy as a film genre label but a symptom of its status within popular culture. Cultural theorist John Fiske once famously argued that one of the determining characteristics of popular culture is that it is full of contradictions and imperfections.[7] It almost has to be that way if anything is to achieve the level of popularity it needs to resonate within the age of mass media. Popular films rarely dictate a singular meaning to a mass audience but provide platforms for a variety of often contrasting and contradictory meanings to be formulated. Their formal and stylistic specifics are permitted to be stretched and bent by the demands of different national and regional cultures across the globe, and this allows them to function as examples of popular cinema. As such, popular culture does not have to be defined or articulated; it does not have to make sense or be consistent. It simply has to work in practice.

To quote Stanley Fish's reflections on the wider performative function of academic writing, genre theory is sometimes guilty of not just providing information to its readers but asserting "the power of an interpretative community to constitute the objects upon which its members . . . can then agree."[8] By writing books attempting to define different genres, scholars implicitly tell the individuals they address what films they should or should not classify according to different labels. In this way, we indirectly scold audience members for getting genres "wrong," for describing films like *Star Wars* (1977) and *Back to the Future: Part III* (1990) as science fiction films when we know they bear a more striking resemblance with the semantic/syntactic structure of the western, or else chastise them for daring to think that animation is even a genre at all, when really it is a cinematic technique. Through this model, genre labels are in danger of operating as top-down, authoritative devices analogous to Pierre Bourdieu's notion of a cultural nobility on taste.[9] They try to dictate the terms by which examples of cinema can operate and exclude audiences themselves from any part in the decision making in an act of cultural imposition. This act of imposition can happen as a result of efforts made by Hollywood due to the forces of pure capital (industry, commerce) or else as a result of the imposition of either academic (duration of schooling) or cultural capital (knowledge of art's history, theory, codes, and conventions). Yet, it remains an act of imposition that tells audiences what a particular genre is, regardless of what they might think in response. I could tell you that a film needs five hobbits, six trolls, a magical talisman, and a talking animal in order to be considered part of the fantasy genre. But, whether you agree with this definition or not, this makes very little difference to the seemingly more pertinent factor of why you might choose to watch a film in the first place because you know it is a fantasy.

I therefore propose an alternative. Instead of telling audiences what fantasy films *are*, why not ask what fantasy films *do*? Why not try to define the experience that lies at the heart of the various plot tropes, character archetypes, and thematic paradigms that are so often articulated within genre theory and consider how films often labeled under certain popular categories produce similar reactions and responses that help to assert their identity as film genres? If genre theory can articulate what a genre *does* rather than what a genre *is*, then it ceases to be an exercise that dictates the meaning of film labels to a filmgoing public. Instead, it becomes a way of adding value and meaning to those existing categories, allowing audience members to decide for themselves whether a particular film generates the kind of experience that is attached to certain genre labels, and to use that rationale as the basis for classifying films into categories.

Indeed, historically, genre analysis has often strayed into such territory to answer basic questions about other popular categories of filmmaking. Studies of film comedies have helped us understand some of the reasons why films make us laugh. Studying horror has helped us understand what it is about films that scare us. Yet, despite all that has been written about such so-called "Body Genres,"[10] despite all that has been thought about why action excites or thrillers thrill, we are still bereft of a comprehensive theory of the experience fantasy cinema offers. Without such a theory, we are left only with an understanding of fantasy as a form of classification, rather than as a cinematic experience.

What Do Fantasy Films Do? The Fantastic and Spectatorship Theory

At its most basic and most self-evident level, the term *fantasy cinema* seems to exist because certain films allow spectators to engage in an imaginative experience of phantasy. Defined by Jean Laplanche and Jean-Bertrand Pontalis as "a purely illusory production which cannot be sustained when it is confronted with a correct apprehension of reality," phantasy (often spelled with a *ph*) is a term evoked by psychoanalytically informed thinkers to describe a set of psychic activities that include dreams, daydreaming, and the wider ability human beings have to imagine situations beyond the physical constraints of the world surrounding them.[11] Fantasy cinema takes its name partially from this namesake activity and, as such, has been and continues to be associated with the act of phantasizing as a key component of its generic identity. And, yet, as much as it might seem rather obvious to some that the unique appeal of fantasy films resides in their ability to offer spectators opportunities to experience film fiction in a more imaginative or more obviously "phantastical" manner than either everyday life or other film genres that seem to be aiming for a naturalistic or realistic register, explaining why that is becomes so complicated that it will take up the entirety of what follows. This book tries to explain how and why fantasy and phantasy are related.

We spend so much of our lives trying to make sense of the world that surrounds us, and making sense of the world seems to provide us with both some of our greatest pleasures and our greatest anxieties. When we discover new things about reality, we are often shocked, amazed, affirmed, and gratified; while, when we feel like our grasp of reality is slipping away, we find ourselves at our most anxious, scared, confused, or irritated by the world's failure to match up to our expectations about it. Vast amounts of research within the area of clinical psychology support this idea that humans are designed to make sense of a world we believe to be real, and that the appeal of fictional narratives more broadly is found in their ability to operate as essentially intensified versions of the way we unpick, unlock, and understand everyday life.[12] Yet, at least within the realm of literary theory, it has become an almost commonsense notion to suggest that the pleasure of reading fantasy fiction comes from its appeal to the imagination, the genre's pleasure arising from what Gary K. Wolfe terms the "desire and longing arising out of the promise of other worlds or states of being."[13] This idea might seem perfectly natural given what many might already associate with the fantasy's genre uniquely imaginative register. Yet, it should also strike some as rather unnatural given what we claim to know about the way both our minds and our emotions operate in relation either to the world, or within the context of cinema.

Given all we invest in making sure we get reality "right," given all the emotional and intellectual attachments we make with a world we have come to know, understand, and believe in gradually as we grow from infancy to adulthood, it seems instinctively strange to think that we would devote equal amounts of attention to the pursuit of deliberately getting reality wrong, actively trying to comprehend ideas and information that we know to be false. Yet, when we talk about a pleasure associated with using our imaginations, that is in essence what we are assuming. We take for granted that the act of willfully and deliberately avoiding the hard-earned truths we have gleaned from reality provides some innate sense of respite, relaxation, and fun without often thinking about why that might be. This poses a particular problem when trying to understand the place of phantasy in fantasy fiction. Perhaps we need to reconcile these two strands of thinking between the rational pleasures of narrative and the irrationality of imagining by arguing that, despite any superficial difference, the role phantasy plays in our understanding of fantasy fiction is no different from other narrative forms. If such a reconciliation feels unsatisfactory, it is because it suggests that fantasy fiction operates like other genres whose pleasures reside in their appeal to our rational, cognitive selves, albeit in a more intensified manner. Or, we have to find a way of speaking to the unique role the imagination plays in our experience of the fantasy genre that operates outside some of the assumptions we make about how both phantasy and reality operate in our everyday life. Either fantasy is just like all other forms of storytelling, or nothing like them whatsoever.

If the problem of how we square the circle to understand why we enjoy stories that demand a phantastical triumph of the emotional over the logical were not difficult enough, an additional problem in understanding fantasy filmmaking comes in articulating the uniqueness of such a reaction in the context of cinema. It is not too difficult to see a place for the imagination when we sit down to read the outlandish and otherworldly scenes described by writers like Lewis Carroll, J. M. Barrie, or Ursula Le Guin. As readers, we are required to take their words and imagine something altogether abstract and unbelievable in our minds, giving fantasy literature a quality of what I. R. Irwin calls "mental play."[14] Yet, when we watch a fantasy film, the experience seems to be far more reactive than proactive. Rather than letting us imagine fantasy scenarios into being, we are required to experience them onscreen in a way more akin to the way we might see things in everyday life, making the place of the imagination far more difficult to pinpoint and describe. Within the realm of film studies, the study of the imagination has not often been a subject of interest in and of itself but has instead fallen under the wider rubric of spectatorship theory, a branch of film analysis that E. Deidre Pribram defines as a consideration of "the relationships between individuals and filmic processes."[15] Noted spectatorship theorists throughout film history from Hugo Münsterberg (1916) to Laura Mulvey (1975) to Todd McGowan (2007) have all described the appeal of watching films by evoking the medium's appeal to our imagination, arguing, in their own respective ways, that films allow spectators to construct an elaborate world of illusion through their ability to forge intense relationships with the images onscreen as if they were every bit as real as everyday life despite the fact they are not.[16] This sense that film's imaginary power lies in its ability to feel real is so pervasive that it feels almost an insult to describe a film as implausible, unbelievable, or unrealistic. Yet, that is exactly what fantasy films are, or at least what they pertain to be.

What we need, then, is not just a theory of fantasy cinema but a theory of the role phantasy plays within the act of watching cinema that acknowledges the rather obvious but no less provocative idea that, despite the fact that films look and feel a lot closer to everyday life than books, some films are still not designed to be believed by their spectators. Preoccupied with the arresting perceptual realism that cinema can achieve, we do not let ourselves think about a form of imaginative experience that is brazen and unapologetic, self-conscious and fully aware of the fact it is making things up, that is nevertheless perfectly possible within the experience of narrative cinema. Instead, we prefer to think that the experience of being a film spectator is essentially an extension, embellishment, or intensified version of what it means to witness everyday life. We have therefore constructed detailed theories as to how films invite us to use our imaginations in order to make them seem real, but we know very little about what happens when we phantasize in relation to films that declare themselves to be unreal. And, so, the space of both the fantasy genre and phantasy as a spectatorial act within both Hollywood's history and its theory remains partially unarticulated.

By offering just such a theory of the experience of Hollywood fantasy cinema, this book hopes to not only avoid some of the problems surrounding the classification of fantasy cinema given the "fuzzy set" of formal criteria that emerges when one tries to define the genre according to any strict definition of typical narrative or iconography,[17] but to address the reluctance we have in discussing the role of the imagination in experiencing films that offer themselves as alternatives to reality. This experience, which I label as *the fantastic*, is not only fundamental to our understanding of a particularly popular film genre like fantasy but offers a fundamentally new way of understanding the role the imagination plays in the act of watching films more generally. While other Hollywood genres typically strive for a quasi-naturalistic mode of address, fantasy films require a rejection of naturalism as a fundamental part of the way they communicate as works of fiction. Instead of trying to make cinema conform to the standards and expectations of reality, fantasy cinema encourages us to forge new relationships and new experiences, to find value in what we are watching precisely because it does not match up with the reality that we know or believe in. It is precisely this lack of belief that characterizes the experience of the genre, and yet also makes the experience so difficult to articulate or explain. Why do we like encountering the impossible? What is pleasurable about experiencing situations that we know cannot be real? How can disbelief be exciting, and why can incongruity feel good? This is the story of the fantastic in Hollywood fantasy cinema.

1

What is The Fantastic?

I F THE ENTIRE HISTORY OF FANTASY fiction were to be told, the story would not begin with a sentence or an image but a feeling. Where that feeling began is uncertain, but it is recognizable in each and every one of us. From Plato's *Republic* to Martin Luther King Jr.'s "I Have a Dream" speech, humanity has displayed a consistent tendency to use its cognitive abilities to recognize how the world operates in tandem with its creative powers to imagine an entirely different one. More so, it is often our attraction and fascination with the different worlds that we are able to create that compels us to keep imagining, otherwise we would have no such desire to dream. In that sense, we have always known what fantasy does. We have just not always had the right words to describe it.

The response fantasy cinema seeks to produce is a consequence not only of these deep-seated tendencies ingrained within the human psyche but the genre's origins in medieval and early modern Europe, to which most contemporary fantasy fiction owes a considerable degree of debt. In other cultures, the relationship between the imagination and reality is often far too intertwined to necessitate an entirely separate category of storytelling of fantasy within popular culture. Yet, European intellectual society created the necessary conditions for a fantasy genre of storytelling to emerge due to its historic struggle with the problem of what to do with the imagination when it comes to art. This problem began in antiquity, first with Plato's infamous ban on poetry within his ideal state in his *Republic* and then with Aristotle's declaration that art, when functioning at its most noble, should operate as form of mimesis (representation).[1]

Aristotle's theory of mimesis was not an acknowledgment that art must replicate the surrounding world as a necessity but an argument against doing anything else, suggesting that to give in to the desire for fantasy that seems embedded within our psyche was akin to giving in to lesser, baser instincts. The history of fantasy storytelling has been a sustained reaction against that idea.

Denied the ability to create or innovate within the strict orthodoxy demanded from a Catholicism influenced by Platonic and Aristotelian ideas alike, medieval European folklore created a vast unofficial network of oral storytelling that sought to provide reassurance to its audiences that the world that they imagined outside of the Christian doctrine did indeed exist. The etymological origins of the word *fairy* of the fairy tale include traces of the Latin word *fatum* (meaning "fate") and the Anglo-Saxon verb *fegan* (meaning "to agree").[2] The fairy tale can be understood as an attempt *to agree with fate*: to reconcile its listeners to the paradoxes and contradictions of the surrounding world through stories that posited the existence of powerful, magical forces beyond their control. After the European enlightenment, writers such as E. T. A. Hoffmann in Germany and George MacDonald in Britain drew from the iconographies and stories of such folklore to provide an artistic reaction against the so-called age of science and rationalism. Just as the intellectual culture of the time repeated the same Aristotelian sentiment of the right of reason to dominate over all aspects of cultural and artistic life, writers who remained attracted to the culture surrounding folklore co-opted its iconographies to create a form of fiction that did not necessarily seek to offer alternative explanations for the world but a different set of values and principles for appreciating the world as it was.

Slowly, out of this reaction against the rise of realism and rationality during the eighteenth and nineteenth centuries, three distinct types of stories emerged. In their attraction to their own imaginations, some writers chose to vilify, almost as if they were scolding themselves for indulging in such fanciful tales. Telling stories designed to scare audiences with all that was impossible and unknown, these works harnessed the powers of the imagination to create monstrous beasts and demonic forces that threatened reality with their abject impossibility. The label of horror was subsequently attached to these kinds of stories. Others tried to rationalize their dreams, offering logical explanations as to how we might one day achieve something as outlandish as traveling to the center of the earth or forward in time to the world's end. *Science fiction* became a label to describe these kinds of narratives. And then there was a third kind of storytelling, a kind in which the impossible was not made abject, nor was it explained, but enjoyed for what it was. To this kind of storytelling, the label *fantasy* was eventually given. All three genres asked their readers to go on far-fetched journeys in which they encountered stories, situations, and characters that were purposely designed by their authors not to seem as if they would or could happen in everyday life. But fantasy fiction required something extra. It asked us to enjoy these impossible creatures, celebrate and find comfort in the magical and the illogical, and find something in that experience that other equally impossible genres did not and could not provide.

Many theories have been offered to articulate the appeal of this form of storytelling, the most popular of which have since been co-opted into widespread explanations of the appeal of fantasy cinema. When audiences talk about the thrill of suspending one's disbelief (an idea taken from the writings of Romantic poet and philosopher Samuel Taylor Coleridge) or losing oneself in the detail of a rich and dense secondary world (an idea advanced by Middle-earth's own J. R. R. Tolkien), they are paraphrasing the arguments of writers who sought to defend fantasy fiction from the same accusations of triviality that it has been met with since its earliest incarnations.[3] These theories are no doubt compelling, but they were constructed more as defenses of the fantasy genre than as detailed explanations of how the genre works. Within more recent academic circles, the study of the techniques utilized by authors working in this style of writing is often labeled as the study of *the fantastic*, a term that is used to describe both a broad category of literature that presents impossible situations (into which fantasy, science fiction, and horror would all fit), as well as to describe a particular experience such a presentation of impossibility might provoke within the reader. Brian Attebery, one of the world's leading experts in the history of literary fantasy fiction, describes the fantastic as "the mode" which fantasy fiction looks to contain, formulate, and regulate into a coherent genre.[4] I too will use the term *the fantastic* as a means of describing the underlying experience that I believe spectators search for and find in works of fantasy that gives the genre a unique identity as a cinematic experience, and it is therefore in direct reference and with a certain amount of gratitude to this heritage of scholarship that I too adopt the term. Yet, as I will make clear, the way I use the term is also in partial contrast to the way it has been employed within almost a century of literary criticism, and it is therefore worth making clear what exactly my version of the fantastic entails before we apply it to works of Hollywood fantasy filmmaking.

In setting out this theory, I think it is worth starting with an influential and yet idiosyncratic theory of experiencing impossible stories through fiction that set the precedent for a century's work of literary criticism, namely, Tzvetan Todorov's *Introduction à la littérature fantastique* or, to refer to it by its English title, *The Fantastic: A Structural Approach to a Literary Genre*. This book is not about fantasy fiction, at least not explicitly. The term *fantasy* does not appear in his study once, and the majority of the texts Todorov selects for analysis would be better described as works of supernatural horror, although he does make more than occasional references to early works of science fiction and to examples of folklore. Yet, despite it not being about the fantasy genre, Todorov's *The Fantastic* manages to construct a theory of the reader's experience of the supernatural in fiction that partially looks back to Romanticism's initial interest in the imagination as a force that exists in parallel with the human capacity toward reason, while at the same time being mindful of the far more complex picture of human psychology that emerged since such early writings on fantasy were constructed. *The Fantastic* therefore has a great deal to say about the experience of fantasy fiction, even if that usefulness emerges more as a by-product of the ideas that are presented rather than an intended consequence of the original theory Todorov proposes.

In this study, Todorov examines what he refers to as a genre of writing produced within a finite historical period, which he argues began with the publication of Jan Potocki's *Saragossa Manuscript* (1815) and ended with the writings of Franz Kafka.[5] Surveying this period of writing, Todorov observes a recurring narrative trope in which the protagonists of such stories become uncertain as to whether the strange events they are experiencing are really occurring or else can be explained as a series of hallucinations, delusions, or coincidences. Todorov's theory of the fantastic is based upon the idea that this presentation of events that are known to be impossible by their readers provokes a response that he chooses to classify as a kind of *hesitation*. As he argues:

> In a world which is indeed our world, the one we know, a world without devils, sylphides, or vampires, there occurs an event which cannot be explained by the laws of this similar familiar world. The person who experiences the event must opt for one of two possible solutions: either he is the victim of an illusion of the senses, of a product of imagination—and the laws of the world remain what they are; or else the event has indeed taken place, it is an integral part of reality—but

then this reality is controlled by laws unknown to us. Either the devil is an illusion, an imaginary being; or else he really exists, precisely like other living beings—with this reservation, that we encounter him infrequently.

The fantastic occupies the duration of this uncertainty. Once we choose one answer or the other, we leave the fantastic for a neighboring genre, the uncanny or the marvelous. The fantastic is that hesitation experienced by a person who knows only the laws of nature, confronting an apparently supernatural event.[6]

If a text resolves the ambiguity it sets up within its narrative to offer a rational explanation for the impossible event as a delusion experienced by the central protagonist, then it can be classified as belonging to a separate genre of literature that Todorov labels as the uncanny. An example of such a text would be Poe's "The Fall of the House of Usher" (1839), in which the reader is left to assume the protagonist has merely imagined the events displayed within the text rather than them actually existing within the context of the fiction. Alternatively, if the event in question is revealed to be really happening, and thus though impossible to the reader seemingly permissible within the fictional story taking place, then the event falls into the literary category of the marvelous. Todorov includes fairy tales within this genre, as well as works such as Hoffmann's "The Nutcracker and the Mouse-King" (1816), in which the circumstances depicted are not ultimately explained according to a preexisting rational schema but are instead accepted as part of an alternative fictional world in which such things are possible. The fantastic, therefore, is defined by Todorov as an experience of hesitation provoked by certain works as a result of encountering an impossible event. Such moments of the fantastic are designed by writers to contradict either the rules established within a fictional world, or contradict some of the basic principles of everyday life. Nevertheless, they are built on a fundamental disjunction between what is said and what is believed, creating a complex response within the reader as he or she struggles to find a way of relating to the event as a result.

Attempts to apply Todorov's ideas on the fantastic to the realm of cinema have focused almost exclusively on the study of horror, considering works such as *Vampyr* (1932), the early films of David Cronenberg, or Neil Jordan's *The Company of Wolves* (1984).[7] To an extent, this makes a great deal of sense given the fact that these films replicate cinematically some of the strategies Todorov argues are necessary in order to generate the experience of hesitation he theorizes, creating a quality that Amaryll Beatrice Chanady describes as "bidimensionality" between two alternative explanations for the narrative taking place.[8] *Vampyr*, for example, generates tension by interspersing seemingly objective shots of the mise-en-scène with subjective shots framed from the protagonist's point of view, blurring the lines between whether what the spectator is being asked to consider is a fictional reality, or simply a character's subjective phantasies. Likewise, both *The Company of Wolves* and *Videodrome* (1983) often frame their moments of fantastic disruption onscreen through the perspective of their characters, presenting them simultaneously as subjective phantasies dreamt up by fictional characters and as real events within the context of the fiction, allowing the ambiguity as to their true nature to form part of their function as works of horror. But the experience of the fantastic both on and off the screen need not to be confined to this narrow Todorovian definition, nor does it necessitate a discussion of fear or anxiety in order for it to be understood. Instead, the notion that the fantastic consisting of an experience of hesitation provoked by encountering an impossible fictional event (impossible either in the context of the fiction itself, or impossible in the context of everyday life) can provide the basis for unlocking some obvious truths about fantasy fiction that we seem either unwilling or unable to accept.

If we think of the experience of fantasy cinema as reliant on the spectator's suspension of disbelief in a fictional circumstance that contradicts the logical principles that govern reality, we are constructing a somewhat false dichotomy between belief and disbelief that not only does exist in everyday life but seems to simplify greatly the process we are asked to go through when engaging with such stories. It is as if, when we are experiencing an impossible circumstance like the appearance of a dragon, monster, or other magical figure, we are making a choice to believe in things that we know completely contradict our understanding of reality, which would suggest that our capacity toward logic and rationality were such an easy impulse to switch off that we could simply choose to do it whenever we see fit, or whenever it felt advantageous or pleasurable. But our belief in reality and its governing principles is not something that can be so easily disregarded. As any evolutionary psychologist, cognitive therapist, or psychoanalyst will attest, our brains are fundamentally structured around our own, perhaps begotten, desire to understand the world as a reality. We are dependent on those structures to keep our thoughts ordered and rational, to allow us to communicate with others and to find pleasure and satisfaction in the world. This is not something that can just be abandoned depending on what fictional circumstance we happen to be experiencing. However, viewing the experience of impossibility in fantasy as a process of hesitation, one that does not require us to reconcile our desire to enjoy a fictional story with our ability to understand the world according a set of preestablished, logical principles but one in which the very essence of the experience relies on the discrepancy between those two impulses, means that we are able to start to complicate a picture that is far too often made simple by those who wish to either romanticize or criticize the fantasy genre for its refusal to conform to the recognizable standards of reality.

More so, seeing the experience of the fantastic as a form of hesitation allows us to recognize something fundamental about fantasy fiction. What makes it unique is not how it makes us believe in its reality but how it makes room and allowances for our disbelief. It is not scared of letting us notice that it is not real, or that it does not make sense. In fact, it encourages it because its storytellers seem to have faith in the fact that the act of not believing in things does not necessarily amount to dismissing them, or finding them uninteresting. After all, what we choose *not* to believe in our everyday lives is often as important in forming our understanding of the world around us as the things we choose *to* believe in. I do not believe in lots of things. I do not believe in Father Christmas (which, to any unlikely readers under the age of ten, is of course foolish). I do not believe in fairies, despite the existence of a number of social media platforms dedicated to reports of their sightings. I don't believe that Brexit will lead to a brighter, better, global Britain (despite what my current prime minister insists) and I do not believe that the narrative of *The Sound of Music* (1965) tails off somewhat after the wedding (as my father maintains). These things that I do not believe in all still matter to me in some way. They are still ideas and concepts that I have to encounter, to process, and to engage with. Not believing in them does not equate to not understanding them, or having no emotional or intellectual relationship with them whatsoever. It does not even mean I am not attracted to or pleased by the idea of some of them. It simply requires a different set of emotional and intellectual mechanisms in order to understand them as objects of disbelief, rather than as objects like those we experience in a world we define as reality.

Living in the sociocultural environment in which I do, believing in the world that I currently believe in, I am predisposed to believe some things are real and not to believe in others based on the values I have partially inherited and forged independently through my own capacity to think rationally and critically about the world around me. I happen to think this is a healthy approach to life. I do not think it wise or prudent for people to suddenly start believing in fairies just because they might like the idea of them existing, nor do I think it is the sign of a healthy mind to start believing in fairies just because you see one presented in a fairly convincing, photo-realistic manner on a screen. And, yet, as a fan of fantasy cinema, I also enjoy seeing fairies. When I watch the various incarnations of *Peter Pan* that exist throughout cinema's history—my favorite is the 2004 adaptation, although I also have a soft spot for the 1924 silent version—and get to the moment where Peter asks his audience to clap along if they believe in fairies in order to save Tinkerbell's life, I am compelled to put my hands together, not because I actually become temporarily convinced that fairies exist but because not to clap along with Peter would be to resist the films' attempts to offer a pleasurable, valuable, and meaningful experience through the display of fictional circumstances onscreen. Not clapping, or at least not wanting to clap, would amount to abandoning the film. By engaging with fantasy fiction, I invest my energies not in trying to get myself to a point where I can believe in the world presented to me fully, nor do I invest energy in dismissing the film for making me disbelieve in that world either. Instead, I hesitate between what the film presents and what I and its filmmakers know to be true, a reaction that allows for certain imaginative possibilities that I would not have had access to if I insisted on treating the film as I might treat such a circumstance in reality.

Filmmakers, film academics, and film enthusiasts who try to describe the pleasures of fantasy cinema as offering a chance to *escape reality* or *believe in the impossible* often occupy a position akin to one of the most famous lines from one of the most famous examples of the genre. Like the exasperated wizard (Frank Morgan) about to be revealed as a fraud in *The Wizard of Oz* (1939), they think that what fantasy needs is for its audiences to "pay no attention to the man behind the curtain," as if the only way to appreciate the genre is to somehow ignore or conceal the fact that it is a manipulated illusion. But they forget that this famous line occurs itself in a fantasy film, and that the revelation that the wizard is a fraud is actually perhaps his most redeeming quality. As a wizard, he is scary and threatening. Dorothy and her friends tremble at the very sight of him when they think that the apparitions that he conjures before their very eyes are real, much in the same way as we might be tempted to react if we witnessed just a small number of the events occurring in most fantasy films happening in everyday life. If I ever encounter a fairy,

I am going to have to make some pretty severe changes in my attitude toward life. But what we end up liking about the wizard is that he does not exist. He is all the more lovable when we know that he is pretending, when we are paying attention to the man behind the curtain. Because it is in dealing with self-conscious illusions that our imaginations are at their most explicit, brought to life by the hesitation we feel in the gap between seeing and believing. The question is not whether or not we believe in fantasy films. The question is, how does an experience of the fantastic in fantasy cinema encourage us to disbelieve, and what are the consequences of this hesitation as the spectator struggles with the faux-reality of the fiction and is forced to reconcile with the fact that what they see is not what is real?

Phantasy: The Imagination, Hesitation, and Responding to the Impossible

To truly understand the fantastic, we must develop a better understanding of the nature of our own imaginations, as well as the role they play in our experience and appreciation of works of fantasy fiction. We are helped in this regard by a rather convenient coincidence that provides the starting point for just such a discussion. The year 1900 saw the publication of two key texts that, in their own way, would go on to shape our current understanding of the human imagination, namely, L. Frank Baum's *The Wonderful Wizard of Oz* and Sigmund Freud's *The Interpretation of Dreams*. The coincidence of these two publications emerging in exactly the same year demonstrates all too well how closely the interests of psychoanalysis mapped with the aesthetic concerns of the experience of the fantastic first expressed by Todorov. Both the literature of the fantastic and psychoanalysis emerged out of the same cultural inquiry into the limits of rationality and reason taking place during the nineteenth century. Yet, while psychoanalysis sought to understand the way the human mind was influenced by areas beyond its propensity toward rationality, the fantastic (as a literary mode and as an experience) became part of a creative attempt to articulate how we sometimes find ourselves unable or unwilling to experience the world purely on rational terms. Ever since that date, the fantastic and psychoanalysis have shown themselves to be somewhat natural bedfellows. Freud frequently discussed fairy tales, folkloric imagery, and works of supernatural horror as part of his attempt to theorize the existence of the unconscious domain of the human mind, while key theorists indebted to Freudian theory such as Carl Jung and Jacques Lacan have all felt similarly compelled to refer to myth, fantasy, science fiction, and horror in their attempt to offer new understandings of the role of phantasy in the human psyche.[9] Yet, despite the areas of productive overlap, the insight psychoanalysis provides in understanding the fantastic is made somewhat complicated by the excesses those working within the discipline have often engaged in when it comes to applying psychoanalytic ideas to the interpretative arts, with critiques surrounding the pseudo-scientific nature of psychoanalytic theory offered by individuals like David Bordwell and Noël Carroll.[10] Instead, alternative conceptual models like cognitive psychology and phenomenology have been embraced as seemingly better working alternatives to psychoanalytic theory, each offering certain correctives to the dominant and often totalizing effect psychoanalysis once had on critical understandings of the cinema medium during the 1970s and 1980s, and allowing for new avenues of exploration beyond those available within the previous theoretical model.

Beyond these concerns over the appropriateness of psychoanalysis as a discipline, there is another potential stumbling block to overcome in applying what might otherwise be a very useful set of ideas to the study of fantasy fiction. Regardless of the scientific or scholarly merit in psychoanalysis, it just feels instinctively wrong to compare the pleasure we get from reading *The Wonderful Wizard of Oz* (or watching its beloved film adaptation) with the experience articulated within infamous Freudian notions such as unconscious repression, oedipal anxiety, and the death drive. When we think of stereotypical psychoanalysts and their patients, we do not necessarily picture an experience that comes even close to watching films like *The Wizard of Oz* or *The Lord of the Rings* (2001–2003). However, this mismatch between the kind of imaginative experience associated with fantasy fiction and the kind of understanding of phantasy thought to be practiced within psychoanalysis is not so much a misconception as it is a misunderstanding. It is certainly true that, within psychoanalysis, the overwhelming emphasis is often placed on the negative role the imagination can play in our experience of the world. But this is partly an occupational necessity. For Freud, whose work primarily focused on the irrational origins of negative human emotions and behaviors, phantasy is a kind of thought-activity rooted in early infancy, functioning chiefly as a series of "reality-testing" exercises that include play and daydreaming that help children to construct a coherent picture of reality as their conscious mind develops.[11] Encountering it often in patients who are suffering from a trauma or disorder rather than experiencing life in a functioning, healthy manner, the imagination is often represented in his writings as a force to be tackled and ultimately conquered in the treatment room through the process of transference. The picture he paints is of psychoanalysts doing battle with phantasy on a daily basis, trying to temper its more wild potential and tame it into a force we can use to progressively understand the world around us.

However, while Freud's own famous account of phantasy informs a lot of both popular and scholarly attitudes toward psychoanalysis, other theorists have offered alternative theories of the imagination that are far more in keeping with the experience that is often associated with the fantasy genre. Most notably, the work of Melanie Klein and D. W. Winnicott provide a very different picture of the role of the imagination in both human life and in psychoanalytic treatment from one popularized by Freud (and latter Jacques Lacan, a key influence on applied psychoanalytic thought in the humanities). Although altogether less famous, Klein and Winnicott are two theorists and practitioners who are nevertheless incredibly influential in shaping the contemporary sphere of psychoanalytic thought. In the UK in particular, Klein and Winnicott are as frequently cited in psychoanalytic journals as Freud himself, and their pioneering ideas toward both the human mind and clinical practice have shaped a lot of treatment rooms around the globe. In such therapy, phantasy is not the tortured symptom that it might seem to be in its Freudian incarnation. In the Kleinian and Winnicottian mode of psychoanalytic treatment, phantasy is as much a tool for well-being as anything else. Their patients are encouraged to dream, to phantasize and to play their way through their mental insecurities and illnesses to find a way of reclaiming a world understood rationally through a self-conscious celebration of the imagination.

Both working as practicing therapists in London during the early to mid-twentieth century, Klein and Winnicott developed ideas on phantasy as part of a branch of psychoanalysis commonly referred to as object relations theory. Taking shape within the work undertaken at the British Psychoanalytical Society (of which Klein and Winnicott were both members), object relations psychoanalysis focused its attention on "individuals' interactions with external and internal (real and imagined) other people, and to the relationship between their internal and external object worlds."[12] This broad set of interests meant their focus was not in continuing Freud's project of articulating the irrational behind the rational veneer of everyday life in order to provide treatment to those who self-identified as being sick or infirm; it was to evolve Freud's project into a more nebulous understanding of how humans come to understand the world both intellectually and emotionally. Both Klein's and Winnicott's contribution to this approach to psychoanalysis was to place an emphasis in each of their respective theories on the important role that phantasy plays in such a process. Both were interested in the role phantasy played in our childhood development from infancy to adulthood, as well as the role phantasy then played as a tool for meaning-making in adult life. In fact, their works positively celebrate this fact, developing, extending, and evolving Freud's initial theories of phantasy into a comprehensive psychoanalytic understanding of how we use our imaginations to understand the world not only rationally but emotionally.

Sharing a productive professional and personal relationship with one another, Klein's and Winnicott's respective visions of phantasy, though differing somewhat from one another, collectively offer a corrective to the Freudian vision of phantasy as an expression of trauma and mental instability. Their understanding of phantasy is neither utopic nor simplistic; they acknowledge the often anxious and unstable role our capacity toward the imagination plays in our everyday lives as children and as adults. Yet, nevertheless, both Klein and Winnicott offer a partially celebratory take on phantasy in that they each recognize the need and necessity for an active imagination in a healthy human individual, and they do not see the stimulation of their patients' phantasies as mere symptom of psychological distress. Instead, phantasy is showcased as both an inevitable and enviable part of being alive, articulating the psychoanalytic basis for a range of creative activities that have since been applied to a rich field of media and cultural studies, used to understand everything from smartphones to museum galleries.[13] It is also Klein's and Winnicott's acknowledgment of the role phantasy plays in our well-being that provides the tools by which we understand the fantastic in relation to the affirming capabilities of fantasy cinema.

Focusing her theoretical analysis on the early relationships established between infants and the objects and/or persons they encounter, Klein's work develves Freud's own concerns with phantasy as both a preconscious and unconscious mode of expression most prominent in infancy and yet influential in determining the psychic structures that govern the human mind in adult life. Crucially, Klein does not talk of phantasy as either a pathological symptom or a disturbance to conscious thought but instead as an important contributor to "our happiness and mental strength," tracing the role phantasy plays in early and later life not just as a tool to understand reality but as a way of expressing and understanding the inner emotional life of the individual.[14] Her key contribution to the field is therefore to carefully map the way phantasy develops in childhood, to provide a series of taxonomies for different types of imaginative activity children are likely to experience, and to work on how these different types of relating to the world through phantasy influence our experiences in later life. Winnicott's psychoanalytic work both overlaps with and develops Klein's theories of phantasy in order to examine how ideas of creativity, art, and culture might be productively considered through a psychoanalytic examination of phantasy. As such, Winnicott's contribution to psychoanalysis provides perhaps the richest psychoanalytic basis for the creative life of the adult subject. Creativity becomes a psychic force rooted in phantasy that manifests itself in the everyday experience of the subject, revealing itself most explicitly in acts of artistic expression or appreciation but also bound up in any individual's attempt to negotiate the delicate psychological balancing act between living in a world of objective characteristics, and expressing yourself in that world subjectively.

Both Klein's and Winnicott's ideas can be mapped onto what we know about the fantastic thus far, and they begin to help explain what might be going on inside us when we react to fantasy fiction in a positive manner that distinguishes it from other genres. The experience of hesitation associated with the fantastic gives it a quality akin to what Lucie Armitt describes as the "interrogative drive" between reality and phantasy that psychoanalysis seeks to explore.[15] Faced with an event that does not match with their understanding of reality, the reader's ability to phantasize is suddenly detached from their ability to understand the text as a reality. This mismatch requires the reader to solve the hesitation by constructing a new way of experiencing the fiction that allows their experience of phantasy and reality to be realigned once again. In the context of cinema, hesitation becomes a way of allowing what is shown on the screen to be considered and engaged with without having to make those events fit within a preexisting understanding of reality, offering instead a way of processing and considering the images onscreen that is more in line with the kind of phantasy activity explored in Kleinian and Winnicottian modes of thought. Instead of trying to make cinema conform to the standards and expectations of reality, the fantastic allows for an approach to film fiction in a manner more analogous with objects of childhood play or adult creativity proposed in psychoanalytic theories of phantasy, whereby the object's lack of reality becomes a tool to explore often unexpressed aspects of the human experience that are either denied or deemed irrelevant when trying to approach the world as a coherent reality. These embedded impulses toward phantasy are then coaxed out or revealed through an experience of hesitation, as the spectator shifts from engaging with the fiction as a reality to engaging with it as an impossible figure of the imagination.

This is what the fantastic is, at least in theory. But speaking about the fantastic in generalized, abstract terms like this is likely to create more uncertainty about the nature of the experience behind a genre like fantasy than it is to illuminate that experience. Readers may well wonder at this point whether the vision of the fantastic that I offer here is suitably specific, or whether or not I am fully divorcing myself from Todorov's original definition. In truth, what I am proposing is not a clear separation from his central idea of hesitation but an extension and broadening out of such a concept, evolving it into something far more useful that speaks to the issues we have faced already in articulating the specifics of fantasy cinema. If we cling to some basic insights about what happens to us when we experience impossible things in both fiction (as Todorov details) and in life (as psychoanalysis informs us), then our understanding of the fantastic can be shaped according to the specific demands of different texts and, indeed, different genres. In horror fiction, the detachment from reality caused by the fantastic is a source of doubt and uncertainty. It is the cause of the fear we feel as we look upon things that do not make sense and yet are apprehended in such a manner that we find ourselves unable to dismiss them. In science fiction, our desire to reclaim a sense of certainty in the face of the fantastic causes us to engage in an act of imaginative speculation. We intellectualize the gap between seeing and believing to offer rational explanations for the schism between reality and fiction that are fueled in part by our imaginations. We look beyond the reality in front of us to find a new reality that can make sense again. In fantasy, however, we embrace the gap. We are encouraged by the genre's writers and filmmakers to let that sense of reality go, to let go of even bothering to try and make sense of events as a reality that needs coherence, causality, and agency to be understood, and to embrace a partial alternative wherein the impossibility we encounter acts as a source of liberation from the restrictions of rationality itself. Fantasy asks us to see the hesitation we feel in response to impossible events not as a source of confusion but a source of celebration. To examine how it does this, we must consider the fantastic not in theory but in practice. A case study is therefore needed, one that will not preempt the journey in Hollywood fantasy cinema we will shortly undertake but one that helps establish the stakes of that journey before it commences.

The Fantastic in Fantasy Cinema: *Pan's Labyrinth* (2006)

Pan's Labyrinth utilizes the spectator's capacity toward disbelief in interesting and nonconformist ways, as well as being a usefully illustrative example in establishing the specific kind of fantastic experience offered by the fantasy genre. Described by popular newspaper and broadcast film critic Mark Kermode as "a *Citizen Kane* of Fantasy Cinema,"[16] the film is a celebrated example of fantasy filmmaking that replicates many of the same narrative techniques Todorov analyzes in his original literary study. Set in 1944 during the immediate aftermath of the Spanish Civil War, the film tells the story of a young girl named Ofelia (Ivana Baquero) who, along with her pregnant mother (Ariadna Gil), relocates to live with her stepfather, the fascist Captain Vidal (Sergi López). Vidal and his accompanying squadron have been tasked with finding and arresting a local band of communist rebels, and Ofelia and her mother arrive into his care and thus into this war-like scenario. The film therefore intertwines two narratives. In one storyline, Ofelia must contend with the harsh discipline and brutality of Vidal, conceal her friend Mercedes's (Maribel Verdú) involvement with the communist resistance, and attempt to deal with her mother's increasingly deteriorating health as complications emerge as a result of her pregnancy. In the other storyline, Ofelia discovers a vast labyrinth, at the center of which she meets a faun (Doug Jones) who informs her that she is the long lost princess of a subterranean kingdom. While Vidal mercilessly and violently hunts down the local rebels, Ofelia must engage in a number of different tasks involving encounters with monsters and quests to retrieve lost artifacts to prove her worth to the faun and regain her throne.

In establishing two parallel storylines, one a historical narrative that seems to make a claim to represent the world as it was in 1940s Spain and the other entrenched in the legacy of fairy tales, the film seems to be composed of two diametrically opposed narratives, with two contrasting modes of address to the spectator. In one storyline, we are asked to accept the events as though they were really happening, to suspend our disbelief and process the information onscreen like we might process those same events in everyday life. In the other storyline, we are made aware of the presence of creatures that are not part of everyday life and self-consciously incongruous within the historical fiction otherwise established. Yet, slowly, these two worlds and aesthetics begin to blend together to reveal common themes across both stories, celebrating disobedience over obedience as both the communist rebels and Ofelia are ultimately rewarded for their refusal to act against their own sense of ethics and do what they are told by the authorities that govern them. Beyond these thematic concerns, the film's function as an example of fantasy cinema is also concerned with this blending together of realistic and fantasy storytelling. After first introducing the character of the faun, the film begins to make various suggestions to the spectator that the creature might be a product of Ofelia's imagination by interspersing subjective shots from Ofelia's point of view with seemingly objective shots of the camera. In perhaps the most obvious example of this technique, Ofelia is at one point seen by Vidal and, through a shot of his point of view, we witness the little girl appearing to talk to thin air. The spectator is invited to consider the faun not as magical creature but as a delusion the young girl has dreamt up in order to deal with her increasingly oppressive environment (fig. 1.1). The question of whether the faun is real becomes increasingly important as the film's narrative plays out, positioning the spectator to consider the precise nature of what is and is not part of the diegetic reality presented onscreen, and what consequences such a decision holds for the rest of the story.

At its conclusion, the film presents two endings to its parallel stories. In one ending, Ofelia is shot by Vidal for the attempted kidnapping of his newborn son—her half-brother—leaving her body to be discovered by the victorious local rebels. In another, her act of sacrifice serves as final proof of her divinity, and she descends into the underworld to take her place alongside her lost father and mother. Both endings are placed in parallel without any sense of which is the true explanation for the series of events on display (figs. 1.2 and 1.3). Spectators are therefore invited to speculate on the nature of these two events, and to form their own conclusions as to which part of the film is "real," and which part is just a "phantasy." Inviting doubt and suspicion as to the authenticity of the scenarios presented, the film seems to require the spectator to accept one of two uncomfortable realities. Either the film's conclusion represents nothing more than the final dream or hallucination of a dying child, or else the faun really exists, in which case the final scene reveals that everything we have watched up until now is just a phantasy, including the moment of false hope at the film's conclusion where a small band

Figure 1.1. The magical faun seems to appear and disappear (*Pan's Labyrinth*, 2006).

of communist rebels are able to defeat fascism, sitting as they do on the wrong side of history.

If the experience *Pan's Labyrinth* manages to generate were simply a hesitation between these two endings, then the film might leave many of us feeling somewhat dissatisfied. If we choose to believe that Ofelia has imagined the faun into existence, perhaps in a quasi-Freudian manner to help shield herself from a reality that is too traumatic for her to wish to comprehend, then we seem to rob the mise-en-scène of all its beauty, turning what otherwise would be fully realized fantasy creatures into harmful delusions, and a narrative full of wonder and quests into a story of unhelpful distractions from a complex and troubling reality. If, however, we accept her worldview that the faun is real, then this seems to deny Ofelia her heroism and tragedy as she suffers at the hands of Vidal as well as some rather basic truths, namely, that there were no fauns in 1940s Spain. We either deny the emotional investment we have made in

Figure 1.2. Ofelia dies a tragic death.

Figure 1.3. Ofelia arises to become Queen of the Underworld.

a little girl's fantasy world, or we deny our capacity for reason, rendering the choice we have to make somewhat unhelpful either way. However, given all the emotional and intellectual energy we have invested in both storylines, it would seem that the greater indecision we are faced with at the end of the film is not which narrative to accept as the film's true ending but whether we have to choose at all. The more compelling option is to choose neither, keeping both stories partially alive and refusing to accept either one as fully representative of the experience of the film. If we do this, the film ends on a bittersweet, hesitant note, expressing the reality of the phantasy of Ofelia assuming her rightful place as Princess of the Underworld, and phantasizing a reality in which a band of communist rebels are not defeated by Franco's forces moments after the credits roll. It is in that in-between world between these two storylines that much of its affecting poetry lies.

In the context of *Pan's Labyrinth*, hesitation is not a scary or destabilizing experience. Quite the contrary, by hesitating with the film's formal properties, the spectator is allowed to have their cake and eat it too, using the disbelief provoked by the impossibility of the film's ending to enact new ways of comprehending the film fiction that they might be otherwise unable to access. If something is believable, it has to make sense. It needs to at the very least be perceived as being logically consistent and well reasoned based on the objective characteristics of the external world and the behavior of the people who inhabit it. But if an event is unbelievable, such a criteria is no longer necessary. The meaning we find in it can be deeply emotionally affecting—it can annoy us, anger us, or charm us in its lack of believability—but it does not have to conform to reality's rules or conventions. Trying to understand a faun as a believable object is an exercise in futility. Trying to understand the faun as an object of the fantastic is a far more worthwhile and rewarding exercise, as well as being a far more complex one than simply dismissing it as not real. To dismiss is to reject any opportunity to engage with the creature. To hesitate is to find in its lack of logic, credibility, and believability a vitality that cannot be ignored, despite how hard the rational side of our brains tell us to do so.

Psychoanalytic theories of phantasy inform us that our imagination often finds it hard to battle with the demands of logic and reason. Faced with an event we can either believe in or can phantasize about, it is likely that we will choose the former and be reluctant to do the latter. Freud states in his own case studies that "it is only with hesitation that [the patient's] phantasy is confessed to."[17] Likewise, in Winnicott's account of using game-play and phantasy as a therapeutic tool, he describes a moment in his own treatment room wherein he offered a child patient a spatula to play with, only for the child to first reject and then ultimately embrace the object after undergoing a "period of hesitation."[18] We are often afraid of our own capacity to dream. We think it will unsettle us, lead us astray, and block out our attempts to understand the world rationally. But the fantastic empowers us to do just that. It prevents us from making sense of fiction as a quasi-believable experience, as something that reflects or requires meaning-making strategies like those that we use in everyday life. Instead, the fantastic becomes a means of coaxing out and revealing the unconscious phantasies that underpin the subject's relationship to the world around them by bringing phantasy into the conscious domain as a part of the reader's attempt to make meaning out of the fiction presented.

The hesitation provoked by *Pan's Labyrinth* therefore rests not solely in a trait of narrative ambiguity within the film's construction. Rather, the hesitation at the heart of the film comes from the film's failure to be adequately processed through techniques of meaning-making that are often articulated within both film spectatorship theory and within wider popular conceptualizations of the way we understand the film experience. When we talk of films seeming believable as if that were a mark of quality, we demonstrate the deep-seated influences Aristotelian thought still has on contemporary cinema culture. We gravitate toward discussing films that present fictional scenarios that might exist in everyday life, or else praise films that are able to make even the most far-fetched scenario seem realistic and believable. But fantasy films are not constructed in this way. The genre's moments of impossibility function like Winnicott's spatula, daring the spectator to let go of their search for conscious, rational meaning in favor of another mode of meaning-making that has been with us all since birth but rarely surfaces unless we permit it. We can chose to reject that invitation, refuse to see the spatula as anything more than a functional tool. But, if we choose to accept it, we give ourselves license to watch a film like *Pan's Labyrinth* in a way that rejects the search for rationality as an inappropriate method of making meaning out of the fiction, and transcends into a far more creative, playful engagement with the screen. The worlds onscreen become not faux realities that need understanding but phantasies that need experiencing.

I began this chapter stating that the history of fantasy storytelling might be best summarized as a feeling. The fantastic is that feeling, albeit one that might produce different emotions depending on the kind of story being told. Put as simply as possible, the fantastic is an experience of impossibility that can only happen when encountering fiction that gives license to the spectator to experience a story through a different mode of meaning-making than that which traditionally governs our typical way of thinking. So much of our capacity to understand the world around us is almost synonymous with our desire to make things make sense according to a consistent set of principles and logic. Whether it is something as obviously intellectual as learning the countries of the world so that we might recognize them on a map or at an airport or learning how to say the word *butter* so we might use it in conversation, the human mind is desperate for, even obsessed with, things that make sense. We are so concerned with this that we must make our popular art forms make sense, and we find pleasure in our ability to decode fictions in the same way we decode everyday life.

And, yet, in life and in the cinema, things are often at their most profound when they do not make sense. When we play with our children by making silly faces, when we doodle on a notepad to alleviate our boredom, when we send Snapchat photos using filters that make us look older or younger, or stick dog's noses on our faces, we are playing with life in a way that does not require it to be logical or sensible but is still profoundly meaningful. We are expressing deeply felt emotions through a language and thought process that is no longer concerned with whether what we are saying or doing is consistent with the world's values and take a great deal from those experiences that overtly violates the world's logical restrictions and impositions. In a society dominated by rationalism and reason, we are taught not to value these experiences, at least not out loud. Instead, we ghettoize them into a leisure time in which we are able to "switch our brains off" (which of course we can never do), and to talk about that time only through how it relates to the world of reality.

The fantastic liberates the spectator from this mindset. Through its sheer impossibility, it challenges the spectator not to watch the images onscreen like they were reality. A certain component of the audience will try to rationalize what is presented onscreen according to preexisting law, or by creating new laws applicable to the reality of the fiction. But as much as one can plot the historical and cultural trajectory of a dragon in the context of a particular fiction, you cannot ignore the fact that it does not actually exist. Some audience members might seek to trivialize fantasy as not meaning anything, rejecting the genre entirely so they can remain in the comfort of things that make sense. But even these people will often succumb to the occasional work of fantasy, even if it is simply to nostalgically remember a childhood text. The impossibility of fantasy fiction is enthralling because it is safe and yet it is challenging. It is impossible and so cannot harm us because it does not exist. And, yet, it is there: we are able to see, hear, and comprehend, and that act of perceiving without believing seems to challenge us to search for its meaning. That search for meaning, when successful, offers up a joyous, affirming experience that fans turn to again and again, and it is that experience that the Hollywood film industry desperately tries to bottle and release in their latest work of fantasy. Every potential genre trope or narrative cliché. Every genie, monster, orc, or goblin. All of these elements are attempts to quantify and codify the experience of the fantastic, and every single one of them accounts for the success and popularity of the fantasy genre. They just need to be found.

2

Continuity and Cathexis

Character, Space, and Time in the Classical Hollywood Fantasy Film, 1930–1945

THE STORY OF FANTASY CINEMA is almost synonymous with the story of cinema itself. It is sprawling and nebulous, far too large for a single volume, and begins as far back as the late nineteenth century with audiences queuing up to watch pioneering director/producers like Georges Méliès adapt popular fairy tales such as *Cinderella* (1899), *Red Riding Hood* (1900), and *Gulliver's Travels* (1902). The story of the fantastic in Hollywood cinema, however, is linked inexplicably to the development of narrative filmmaking, something which occurred within the US with particular force and alacrity thanks to a number of market conditions that transformed a cottage-like industry producing films like Edwin S. Porter's adaptation of *Jack and the Beanstalk* (1902) into a mass entertainment industry capable of producing the kind of fantasy cinema we have come to demand and expect from the latest release. Like it or not, the conditions in which Hollywood fantasy cinema is manufactured have set the global standard for what audiences want from the genre at large, whether that be at the level of technical sophistication we assume from the latest special effects in order for them to seem arresting enough to entertain us, or from the broader expectations we have about the way fantasy stories are typically told onscreen.

Yet, if Hollywood has proven itself to be particularly good at making popular works of fantasy then, we, its audiences, have proven ourselves to be equally bad at describing or explaining *why*. This difficulty in appraising Hollywood's role as the world's most popular producer of fantasy cinema is not necessarily all our own fault, but is in part a result of Hollywood's own efforts to promote itself through the near century it has been in existence. Over that time, Hollywood has largely relied on two broad strategies to promote its particular brand of filmmaking. On the one hand, it sells itself as a "Dream Factory," a phrase first coined by cultural anthropologist Hortense Powdermaker in 1950 that has since been appropriated by the industry as a useful moniker to describe Hollywood's capacity to incite the passions and imaginations of its spectators through cinema.[1] Supposedly, Hollywood movies appeal to our hopes, dreams, wishes, and phantasies, allowing spectators to retreat temporarily from the pressures of the real world into an entertainment industry whose style of popular filmmaking grants us relief and solace from reality. At the same time, we are also told frequently by Hollywood's own practitioners that the secret to their particular brand of storytelling is that they get us to believe in the events as if they are really happening. As Lea Jacobs has already explored, Hollywood filmmaking utilizes techniques adapted from the naturalistic staging techniques of 1920s quality theater.[2] Its mise-en-scène is organized around the principles of renaissance painting to give a realistic impression of depth and coherence, its characters act and behave in a way that feels like authentic representations of real life, and its stories follow a narrative logic of cause and effect that, by and large, avoids a reliance on coincidences or deus ex machina interventions. These contradictory and competing identities of Hollywood as both the dream factory and a believability machine encourage us to think that fantasy cinema is a mere extension or exaggeration of Hollywood's powers of make-believe, as if its secrets lay not in its uniqueness from other film genres, but how similar it is. In doing so, we are taught not to value fantasy films for what they offer in contrast to other types of filmmaking, often normalizing and explaining away their power to show us things that are not real, would never be real, and cannot be real.

A theory of the fantastic in classical Hollywood fantasy cinema is therefore needed to broaden out both film theory's and, more widely, film culture's currently restricted view of the role the imagination plays in the spectator's experience of Hollywood's popular style of narrative cinema. To do this, I find it necessary to begin at the moment in Hollywood's history where many of the formal and stylistic conventions that are now deemed to be standard practice in terms of narrative filmmaking were first cemented, the era of classical Hollywood. As the standard narrative of this era suggests, the type of cinema implemented during this period commonly referred to as classical continuity established a filmmaking style that sought to move cinema away from its presentational and theatrical origins into a mode of film production more in line with the practice of quality theater or the great American novel. David Bordwell, perhaps the world's leading authority on classical continuity, argues that the Hollywood feature typically presents itself as "'realistic' in both an Aristotelian sense (truth to the probable) and a naturalistic one (truth to historical fact)."[3] But, as well as being the era in which Hollywood perfected this continuity style of filmmaking that has since become the standard for narrative cinema across the globe, classical Hollywood was also the era of lavish monster movies like *King Kong* (1933), Mother Goose pantomimes like *Babes in Toyland* (1934), and orientalist fantasies like *A Thousand and One Nights* (1945). The period saw the production of frequent adaptations of popular texts from the heritage of fantasy literature and theater (*A Connecticut Yankee in King Arthur's Court*, 1931; *A Midsummer Night's Dream*, 1935; *A Christmas Carol*, 1938), while supernatural romances (*Lost Horizon*, 1937; *The Enchanted Cottage*, 1945; *The Ghost and Mrs. Muir*, 1947) and comedies (*Topper*, 1938; *I Married a Witch*, 1942; *The Canterville Ghost*, 1944) made up a significant number of the productions released by the studios at the time. An audience research survey conducted in 1942 selected "Fantasies" as one of the eighteen choices available on a questionnaire designed to investigate audiences' favorite types of narratives and over half the people interviewed agreed that they "liked improbable happenings" in films.[4] It seems those conducting the survey did not inform its participants that, in theory, they were not supposed to notice which films were fantasies and which were not, as Hollywood's improbable happenings had been filtered through a narrative system that made things believable and natural as part of its mode of address to the spectator.

Taking this discrepancy between the regularity by which fantasy cinema was made during the classical era and the virtues we tend to associate with the filmmaking style perfected among the Hollywood studios as my starting point, I wish to suggest that, despite what we are often told about the success of continuity filmmaking, there is nothing innately naturalistic about the experience of Hollywood's system of narration that blocks or prevents our ability to appreciate Hollywood films as impossible works of fantasy. Rather, it is simply that the theories that are currently available for describing our emotional and intellectual relationships to Hollywood storytelling do not tend to emphasize this potential, given that they have been developed largely to discuss other film genres that pertain to some kind of naturalistic or realistic tone. Within psychoanalytic theory in particular, the conventions of continuity filmmaking have been used as the basis for a consistent thread of explanations as to how cinema creates what Richard Allen describes as an "impression of reality."[5] It gives us characters we can identify with as we might people in everyday life, spaces we can perceive as three-dimensional and objective, and a sense of time that feels functional, progressive, and orderly, much like the temporal progression we feel as we go about our day-to-day lives. However, if we accept that fantasy cinema does not want us to understand it as a reality, that it derives a huge sense of its cinematic identity and purpose through its lack of reality, then we need alternative ways of understanding the process by which spectators might forge meaningful relationships with the characters, space, and narrative time as presented onscreen, not as objects in reality but as objects that exist as overt and self-conscious figures of phantasy.

A fruitful concept for describing just these kinds of relationships that can exist between an individual and external objects/people is that of *cathexis*, a term that has its origins in Freudian theory but which was developed most prominently through the work of Melanie Klein and D. W. Winnicott. The term *cathexis* originates within James Strachey's English translations of Freud's writings, taken initially from the German word *Besetzung* (literally, "to occupy" or "to take possession of") but was seized upon by Klein especially as something of a catch-all term used to describe the ways humans are able to forge relationships with external objects as figures of the imagination rather than as objects belonging to an external reality. Born into the world without the innate ability to relate to its objects and beings in a rational, conscious capacity, our first task as humans is not to understand the world logically, but to process it emotionally. To do this, we need a mechanism that forges some sort of link between the inner world of the psyche and the external world that surrounds us, that allows us to first recognize things *as things* before we start to understand them according to a set of rational principles and fixed laws that govern reality. Cathexis describes that process. It is a psychological bridge forged between external and internal life, a bridge that exists prior to any of the conscious associations we might bring onto the world, and a relationship forged with objects that allows them to start to develop the capacity to affect us emotionally as well as intellectually.

The existence of this process of relating to the world prior to our ability to understand rationally calls into question the assumed primacy or exclusivity in which we treat other psychological mechanisms of understanding fictional narratives we have within theories of Hollywood film spectatorship. We are told repeatedly, that is, by making things seem believable that meaning is forged, that it is the spectator's ability to make Hollywood fit within the order of reality through an act of phantasy that allows it to work its spell. But, in both early life and again in later adult existence, we often forge relationships with the people and objects that surround us not by engaging with the world rationally but by responding to it imaginatively and creatively. Imagine the difference, for instance, between using a pen and pretending that a pen is a wand. In the first instance, the object is understood as part of a functioning world of pre-ordained principles, one where each object has a predetermined use that we understand and adhere to as part of the relationship we forge with it. I understand that a pen is an object that allows me to write down words permanently, and I use it to fulfill a task. In the second example, however, pretending that a pen is a wand allows us to enjoy certain aspects of the object you might not otherwise appreciate—allowing us to hold it differently, use it differently, and respond to it differently. And, yet, we do this not by believing a pen is a wand, but by using the pen as a vessel through which our subjective world and the objective world is fused together in an act of phantasy. This is what is meant by an act of cathexis. As Klein describes, it becomes a way of imagining "good" objects out of certain situations, people and objects we encounter that bring us joy and satisfaction and "bad" objects for those situations that block or frustrate our instinctual desires.[6] Fantasy cinema provides just such conditions, offering an experience of the fantastic that challenges the spectator to think and feel about the narrative events differently from how they might otherwise given the impossibility with which they are presented.

Using selected fantasy films from the classical era as my guide, I will demonstrate how, and to what effect, Hollywood fantasy films make themselves available to this process of cathexis. Focusing on the three fundamental elements of Hollywood continuity filmmaking as my guide—namely, its depiction and usage of character, space, and time—I wish to systematically deconstruct the reliance on realism we currently have within contemporary film culture, and offer alternative ways of understanding how fantasy films can be both stylistically adherent to many of the principles of continuity filmmaking but offer a completely different experience as a result. In *Alice in Wonderland* (1933), I wish to examine the experience of cathexis in relation to character, offering an understanding of the pleasures available when the process of identification is superseded by a desire to relate to unreal people and characters. In *The Wizard of Oz* (1939) the relationship the spectator forms with space will be examined, considering how the film encourages an experience of the fantastic that makes Dorothy's (Judy Garland) fantasy land seem unreal, serving both its function as a work of fantasy and its thematic treatment of home. With *It's a Wonderful Life* (1946), I will consider how time takes on an unrealistic quality within the film and explore the emotional value of such an impossible experience as part of the film's thematic and experiential goals. In doing so, I wish to correct the mistakes of the past that insist on describing fantasy films as if they were works of realism and offer a more diverse vision for the kinds of experiences Hollywood's style of filmmaking makes available to its spectator.

The Fantastic and Character: Object Cathexis in *Alice in Wonderland*

Paramount's *Alice in Wonderland* is as appropriate place as any to start to observe the different kinds of experiences available within the classical Hollywood fantasy film in comparison with other genres produced at the time. Adapted from Lewis Carroll's popular novels *Alice's Adventures in Wonderland* (1865) and *Through the Looking Glass and What Alice Found There* (1871), the film represented the evolution of a commercial strategy Paramount Studios had been pursuing since the silent era, during which time it had established its reputation as a leading industry player partially by adapting well-known works of fantasy such as *Peter Pan* (1924) and *A Kiss for Cinderella* (1925). These lavishly staged works showcased the rich technical and financial arsenal of what was then known as the Famous Players-Lasky Corporation onscreen, an arsenal that, within the classical era, the studio was keen to extend further by producing a fantasy film suitable for the age of the talkie. Carroll's novels were famous for their wordplay and witty dialogue, and Paramount sold the film heavily on its links to the original novels, casting up-and-coming stars such as Cary Grant, Gary Cooper, and W. C. Fields to take on the roles of some of the more famous inhabitants of Wonderland in an attempt to bring together the studio's signature production values with Carroll's verbose fantasy. A series of full-page adverts taken out in *Variety* showed off the vast array of famous characters taken from Carroll's novels and sold the film as "The World's Greatest Story! With the World's Greatest Cast!"[7]

The anticipated pleasure in seeing Hollywood's stars perform the already iconic roles of creatures such as the Mad Hatter (Edward Everett Horton), March Hare (Charles Ruggles), and Cheshire Cat (Richard Arlen) is established in the film's opening credits sequence. The film begins with an unseen reader flicking through the pages of a book called *Alice in Wonderland*, a device it uses to introduce its famous cast one-by-one. As each new page is turned, an image of a character from Carroll's original novel transforms into an image of the actor performing the role, as a series of fade edits are used to give the impression of actors transforming into their respective roles, a feature that then manifests in the film that follows (fig. 2.1). Loosely structured around a set of episodic encounters between Alice (Charlotte Henry) and the different characters she meets, the film establishes a precedent for future adaptations by picking and choosing liberally from the various inhabitants from both Carroll's

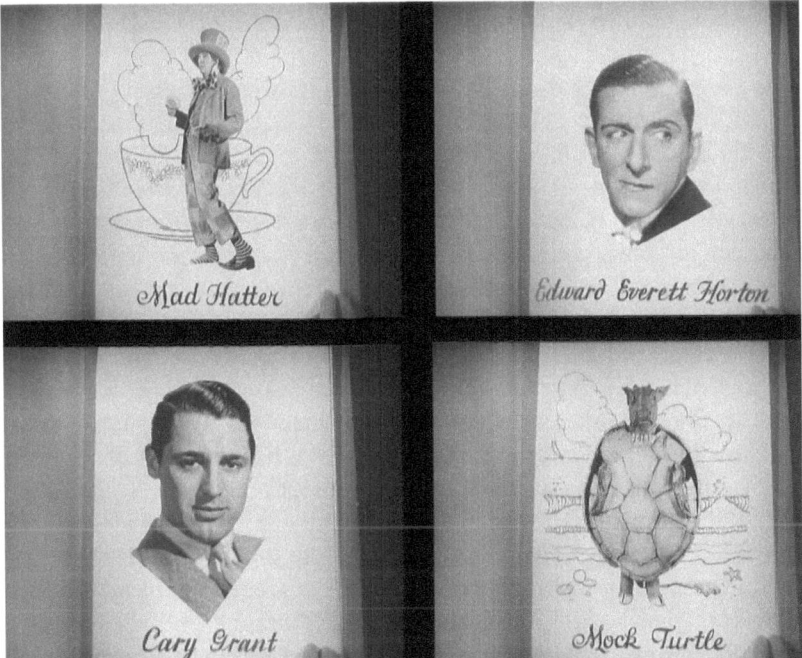

Figure 2.1. The *Alice in Wonderland* (1933) cast transformed into Lewis Carroll's beloved characters.

novels, giving little rhyme or reason as to why the next creature appears onscreen other than seemingly which one happened to be favored by the scriptwriting and production design team. As such, although each individual sequence possesses a degree of internal logic as Alice tries to surmise a particular piece of information out of the creature in question, collectively, the episodes add up to very little in the context of the overall narrative. Alice does not learn a lesson or pursue a particular goal; she does not learn why a raven is like a writing desk. Instead, she wanders haphazardly around her Wonderland, enjoying some of its inhabitants while finding others rather frustrating as the film pauses to take in each one sequentially in a veritable parade of different exotic characters.

The net effect of this dynamic is to create a film with a vastly different set of priorities to the standard Hollywood feature, particularly in terms of the relationship it asks spectators to forge with its characters. The typical Hollywood feature relies on a narrational strategy referred to by Bordwell as "character-centered causality."[8] Characters are the driving force of the classical Hollywood film, their decisions dominating the narrative logic so that the causality of stories relies upon the clear expression of their inner psychology and personality. Deviations from this general principle can occur from time to time depending on the genre in question. Donald Crafton, for example, has explored the vaudevillian logic of early sound comedy, in which the primary motivation of the filmmaking in any specific moment can often be given over to the demands of a comedic skit (rather than to the demands of narrative).[9] However, *Alice in Wonderland* takes an even greater step away from the typical logic underpinning classical narration by undermining not only the dynamic of character-based causality through the kind of story it tells but the very fundamental relationship between characters and spectators offered through such a process. Taking its cue from Carroll's original novel, the film not only gives over vast swathes of its running time to the presentation of different characters that Alice meets rather than establishing a clear psychological through line of rational action but, in the words of Christine Roth, it utilizes its heroine as the "chief butt and victim of its jokes."[10] From the moment Alice decides to step through the looking glass in her drawing room to enjoy the delights that lie on the other side, screenwriters Joseph L. Mankiewicz and William Cameron Menzies use Alice more as an anchoring point rather than a classical heroine, making her a vessel through which the spectator can experience the famous characters that populate Carroll's original books rather than as means of watching a character with established personality traits pursue her goals and desires.

Take, for example, the re-creation of the original novel's "The Pool of Tears" sequence, in which Alice is suddenly shrunk to a fraction of her original size and finds herself swimming in a sea created by her own tears, populated by a number of talking animals. When this moment appears onscreen, it is shot largely from Alice's perspective, the filmmaking employing a series of mid-angle shots framed tightly around her body alongside frequent close-up shots that help to showcase both her initial distress at the scene's beginning, followed by her utter confusion at what follows. In this sense, the framing of the scene is typical of the standard Hollywood feature, providing the means for spectators to watch the unfolding events from the perspective of the characters onscreen (fig. 2.2). Yet, despite this stylistic adherence to classical Hollywood filmmaking technique, the desire to see things from Alice's perspective seems only a small part of the dynamic established in the scene that follows. As Alice eventually swims up to the riverbank and meets the Dodo (Polly Moran), what follows is not an attempt to help the spectator understand the exchange that follows by mediating it through Alice's desire to get dry. Instead, the very essence of the pleasure

Figure 2.2. Alice meets the Dodo.

offered in the exchange between Alice and the Dodo comes through the ability of the Dodo to break the narrative chain of causality previously established and offer itself up as an impossible and illogical creature of fantasy storytelling. Not only does the Dodo seem unable to help her on her quest—the bird thinks that homonyms are synonyms and so believes that reciting "dry" historical facts will in turn assist a person in getting "dry"—it also seems uninterested in even trying. Instead, the scene becomes very quickly superseded by an overwhelming focus on nonsense and wordplay, with Alice's desires either largely left forgotten, or ignored. The Dodo is neither Alice's antagonist nor is it a useful or functional character in terms of her story. Instead, it seems to exist entirely outside the character-centered causality established within the narrative thus far, creating a sense of the fantastic that emanates partially from the creature's physical impossibility (the fact that the Dodo's species is well known to be extinct plays an important role in establishing this dynamic), and partially from the position it occupies within the narrative as an impossible character through the way it acts.

The fact that, as a character, the Dodo does not seem to allow the spectator to enter into the same relationship they might with a character like Alice is important to recognize if we are to pinpoint one of the key differences through which *Alice in Wonderland* functions as a fantasy film as opposed to a more standard Hollywood feature. Typically, when we think of our ability to form emotional and intellectual ties with fictional characters onscreen, we imagine ourselves to be involved in a process commonly known as identification. Defined by Freud as the ability of the subject to form "an emotional tie with another person,"[11] identification has been at the forefront of both psychoanalytic and broader theoretical attempts to explain the way Hollywood's system of communication makes it possible to encounter and understand characters as one might do in everyday life. Christian Metz describes cinema's ability to get spectators to identify with both its camera and its characters as the primary weapon in its "psychic machinery," providing the basis from which we forge meaningful and affecting relationships with its content.[12] However, while it is certainly possible to partially identify with Alice (we can identify with her desire to get dry, and her distress at being in a place she feels she does not understand), our relationship with a creature like the Dodo is far less certain. Not only are we not provided with the information necessary to understand the creature's perspective—is it either ignorant or willfully defiant of her request for explanation or justification—but the only thing we have to recognize and begin to forge a sense of who the Dodo is happens to be the one distinguishing feature we know about the bird's species: it does not exist.

When we identify with people, we need two parallel components of meaning-making to operate simultaneously, one located in our conscious minds and the other in our sense of imagination. Consciously, we have to make a series of logical postulations about what a person might be feeling or thinking at any one moment based on our own experiences and the observable evidence in front of us. If they are smiling and laughing, we might assume they are happy and enjoyed our joke. If they are crying, we might equally assume they are upset, either as a result of our actions or some other external consequence, making it our role to comfort them. All of this activity takes place at a rational level as part of our ability to make sense of the world as an objective force bound by logical criteria, and thus represents exactly the kind of cognitive activity that a theorist like Murray Smith has focused on in the past in his attempt to explain the process of spectatorial identification in narrative cinema.[13] However, underpinning these logical attempts at guesswork is a far less conscious and far more primal act of phantasy. For identification to function on an emotional level rather than a purely intellectual level, it is not enough to simply recognize the emotional state of another human being. An individual must somehow fuse the objective with the subjective to create a sense that they are somehow inhabiting that same emotion. They must feel upset on another's behalf, an act that requires not a logical framework of intellectual speculation but a cathexis of emotion from one person to another. Phantasy is used to bridge the gap between the objective and the subjective so that we cry as others cry, laugh as others laugh, and feel what others feel. This element of phantasy is always subservient to the logical demands of our attempt to understand and relate to people on a conscious level, but it is nevertheless a necessary and vital part of how we identify with both our fellow human beings and with characters onscreen.

The experience of the fantastic we might feel in response to a character like the Dodo works to undermine our attempts to speculate logically about what this creature might be thinking or feeling in any given moment. Despite the Dodo's anthropomorphized nature, we are not provided with a coherent-enough picture of the creature's likely emotional state, nor are we able to forge firm guesses about how it might be feeling. Our intellectual capacity to identify with the Dodo is therefore compromised, helping to generate a feeling of hesitancy as we become aware that we cannot hope to know or even guess what it is like to be the Dodo, a dynamic which is compounded by our knowledge that such a creature does not and could not exist. However, though it may be impossible to identify with the Dodo, it is still perfectly possible to forge those primal, imaginary attachments with the creature through cathexis that I described earlier. As an act of phantasy, cathexis does not rely on the principles of logic in order for it to be meaningful. Dreams occur when we are able to dream, not when it is logical to do so, and phantasies take place in life not when it makes sense for them to appear but when there is an emotional as opposed to an intellectual need for them. This makes cathexis alone a largely useless device for understanding an objective reality, which is why it is often subordinated to other conscious processes like identification. However, cathexis rises to dominance in our habits of meaning-making precisely when we are given license through external circumstances, or give ourselves license through internal factors, to express our inner emotions outside the confines of logical thought. When we play with objects, for example, we do not seek to identify with their status or purpose in reality. We simply use them to express any reaction we wish, so long as it is feels emotionally cathartic to do so. Likewise, when I call my boss an ogre or my best friend an angel, I am not constructing fully realized pictures of them as people with whom I identify. I am using them as vessels to express my own inner, imaginative life. My boss becomes a "bad" object for my frustrations, my friends become "good" objects due to the affection I have for them, and life is simplified not to alter what reality is but to articulate my response to it. The creatures in *Alice in Wonderland* operate on a similar basis. Because they announce their impossibility through the way they rupture the established chain of causality, the concern we might have in making sure we understand them as if they were living, breathing people ceases to be important. Indeed, it is precisely because we cannot identify with them that we are given license to engage with them purely through the imagination.

The emotional impetus cathexis requires in order to operate without the need for further intellectual support through processes such as identification is evident most clearly in its usage in early life. When infants first begin to experience the external objects that surround them, they do so not out of a conscious desire to understand the world but because of the sheer force of emotion they feel in response to it. They are acutely frightened, frustrated, or angry, and thus create phantasy objects as a way of coping with the unbearable tension of being in a world without meaning. In Paramount's *Alice in Wonderland*, a similar kind of emotional impetus is also offered within the context of the story. Beginning in the real world, Alice's journey into Wonderland (which in the book is established in just a few short paragraphs) takes place first and foremost because she is seen, at least on some level, to *want* to go there. She begins the film in her nursery, trapped inside on a snowy day and unable to go out and play. She therefore proceeds to walk around the stuffy room, picking up objects and playing with them haphazardly, all under the disapproving glare of her stern governess (Ethel Griffies). Continuity techniques are used to highlight the emotional status of both characters. Alice's boredom is clearly etched on her face, as is her delight as she starts to play with the objects around her, while the governess's tuts and sighs of frustration at Alice's behavior are also captured clearly onscreen (fig. 2.3). Two ways of approaching the world and its objects are therefore dramatized neatly and effectively through the interaction

Figure 2.3. Alice is scolded by her governess.

between child and guardian, one favoring emotional reality over objective reality, and one concerned with behaving properly rather than behaving in a manner one wishes.

The scene works to secure the spectator's preference toward Alice's way of relating to the world, juxtaposing it with another form of object relations that is embodied by her governess. Watching on disapprovingly, her governess begins to scold Alice for her playful exchanges, accusing her of saying things that are "untrue," a phrase Alice responds to by arguing that what she was saying was not untrue "exactly." For Alice, the phantasy objects she creates are "true" to her because they are born out of the reality of her interior world. Her boredom necessitates her need to stop focusing on the practical or worldly use of objects surrounding her, and to use them instead as vessels to stimulate an emotional satisfaction. While we can therefore identify with both of these characters' positions—Alice's boredom, and the governess' desire to have Alice learn practical skills as opposed to engaging in acts of play—it is Alice's position that seems the more compelling given the narrative scenario we are watching unfold. If we follow the governess's logic, the film that will shortly take place will not only cease to make sense, but it will be far less enjoyable than the one Alice has in store for us. We therefore identify with Alice's position more strongly, and this in turn allows us to feel the same emotional need for cathexis as a form of meaning-making.

It is here where Alice's role within the unfolding narrative becomes most vital in the spectator's ongoing attempts to forge relationships with the impossible creatures she encounters. Despite the fact that Alice does not seem to have the same grasp over her own story as other classical Hollywood protagonists, the fact that she acts both as a visual reference point of familiarity during these encounters with strange and impossible creatures, and mediates them emotionally so that we get an insight into her own responses to them, provides a schema through which the spectator is provided with the necessary emotional impetus to cathexis the figures of Wonderland as objects of phantasy. For example, in Alice's encounter with Humpty Dumpty (one of my highlights of the film thanks largely to the oddness of the costume design and the droll performance given by W. C. Fields as Carroll's perhaps most eloquent practitioner of nonsense), her role is vital in helping the spectator ascertain some important information about the talking egg. Presented in a manner typical of classical Hollywood convention, Humpty Dumpty first appears onscreen through a shot taken from Alice's viewpoint, the two characters framed closely so that the spectator is given a clear view of his body mediated through the presence of the film's protagonist (fig. 2.4). The shot in question achieves

Figure 2.4. Alice meets Humpty Dumpty.

two things simultaneously. First, it allows the spectator to take in the physical object that is Humpty Dumpty and perceive him in all his glory. Second, it creates the impression that the creature is already being seen by another, that his impossibility is not merely an aberration or distortion onscreen but something with consequence to the story unfolding.

If the spectator were tempted to dismiss Humpty Dumpty as a mere special effect, the presence of Alice reminds them that, like it or not, this is a character in a story, albeit an impossible one who stimulates a reaction in Alice that serves to highlight the hesitancy we might feel in experiencing and understanding such a creature. Yet, just at the moment we might feel equally as inclined as Alice does to reject the creature for its confusing and illogical impracticality with an otherwise logical narrative structure, her reaction shows us the negative emotional consequences this will have on our experience of the film. Her attempts, or indeed failures, to identify with Humpty Dumpty as if he were a real person quickly means that he becomes a somewhat aggravating presence who frustrates and blocks her attempts to establish a causality or reason behind the situations she encounters in Wonderland through his persistent use of wordplay. Responding to this dynamic, we can either choose to be like Alice and ostensibly be right about Humpty Dumpty without feeling good, or we can learn to see her failings in dealing with the creatures in Wonderland like she, in turn, used to view her governess's warnings to treat things properly. Alice, in effect, teaches us what not to do. Instead of choosing rationality, we choose the realm of phantasy, enjoying the creature not for what we can learn from him, but how it might it feel if we fuse our own subjectivity with his.

In this way, Humpty Dumpty's famous question to Alice ("which is to be the master, you or the word?") resonates beyond the ramifications the exchange has within Carroll's original novel. In the novel, such nonsense-laden exchanges are utilized, as Kamilla Elliot argues, in order to alert readers to "the instability of language" as a system that creates meaning out of the world.[14] Onscreen, Humpty Dumpty's sheer physical presence alone alerts the spectator to the broader instability of reality as something influenced first by phantasy. The assault he makes is not simply on the faux-logic surrounding language, but on perception itself. We may like to think that it is our intellect that governs the attachments we make with the world. But when creatures as vivid as him are placed onscreen, shot through a close-up that emphasizes their pro-filmic features and forces us to look at them despite the fact we know that there is no credible substance to what it is we are seeing, it becomes difficult to do so. When we are placed in dialogue with a character like Alice, with whom we identify intellectually, but ultimately do not wish to feel what she feels, then what is left is not to force our emotions to go with our minds, but to allow for a fusion of subjective and objective in a manner that amounts to a celebration of perception over cognition. In the case of Humpty Dumpty, seeing is not believing; it is something far more primal and exciting than that.

The pleasure in relating to characters in this way is found throughout *Alice in Wonderland*. Whether this be the Cheshire Cat (who seems to delight in the ability to exist beyond physics), the Queen of Hearts (May Robson) (who rages against reason and rationality), or Humpty Dumpty (who seems to enjoy speaking so much without having anything to say), each inhabitant of Wonderland relies on an imagined relationship forged through cathexis that fuses the subjective with the objective in a binding act of phantasy. These characters are all plucked from the original novels and largely exist to fulfill similar functions as they do in the book. Yet, onscreen, the pleasures of Carroll's famous dialogue combined with the specifics of costume design, performance, and a framing style adherent to classical Hollywood principles encourage the spectator into a willful act of imagination in defiance of logic and reason. "Good" objects like the amusing Mock Turtle with his terrible jokes, delivered with a comedic desperation by Cary Grant, can in turn make us feel good, while "bad" objects such as the grotesque pig baby deliver a feeling of the abject onscreen without a need for the complexities and nuances of a fully rounded identity to emerge at the same time. Cathexis is not identification. It makes no claim about the external object's character, function in the world, or objective identity. On the contrary, cathexis is merely an attempt to fill something perceived to have no objective reality with an emotional resonance. Like the beginning of a game or the self-conscious awareness of phantasy required on the part of the subject to begin a creative act, it signals a temporary displacement of the rules of reality, triggering a way of experiencing the world in which the image of a talking egg can be considered if not fully understood.

By encouraging this approach to its characters, *Alice in Wonderland* offers spectators an alternative way of experiencing characters onscreen that differentiates it from other examples of Hollywood filmmaking. Yet, judging by the film's poor commercial performance at the time and the fact that Paramount's adaptation has largely failed to resonate with subsequent audiences since its initial release, it seem that the invitation it extends is still fraught with anxiety, despite the film's own attempts to offer a pleasurable solution to its own impossibility. Reviewers at the time criticized the film's lack of narrative coherence, pointing out its episodic nature as evidence of the adaptation's lack of success in transferring Carroll's novel to the big screen.[15] However, the awkwardness articulated in such reviews suggests not an incompatibility of subject matter and form between Carroll's novel and cinema, but a fundamental schism between how the film asks its spectators to experience its characters and the standard relationship offered by the typical Hollywood feature. As I move onto a far more famous and successful fantasy film, *The Wizard of Oz*, I wish to examine how this attempt to infuse fantasy storytelling devices within continuity practice was developed in this era, helping to create some of the most beloved narratives and cinematic moments of all time by trying to integrate rather than compete with continuity style, creating films that did not seem real but were worth forging relationships with, nonetheless.

The Fantastic and Space:
Phantasy and Spatial Cathexis in *The Wizard of Oz*

Over eighty years since its original release, *The Wizard of Oz* occupies the enviable status of perhaps the world's most well-known classical

Hollywood film. Its influence on popular filmmaking is so ubiquitous that it is impossible to fully quantify, nor could one hope to list the seemingly endless number of pastiches, allusions, and references to the film that exist within popular culture. The esteem in which the film is held by audiences is matched by the attention it has received within scholarly circles. *The Wizard of Oz* has been subjected to an astonishingly wide range of critical analyses, examined as everything from a coming of age film, a road movie, a lesbian fantasy, a meditation on Aristotelian virtue, an expression of the dominant isolationist spirit of pre–World War II US culture, to a demonstration of Jean Baudrillard's concept of the symbolic exchange.[16] I myself have already had one attempt at understanding the film's mesmerizing appeal by exploring how, through its contrasting relationship between Kansas and Oz, the film enacts a hesitation within the spectator somewhat similar to Todorov's own theory of the fantastic in narrative (an attempt I draw from but evolve here).[17] Yet, aside from demonstrating a preexisting theory or offering itself as available to a variety of interpretations, *The Wizard of Oz* is also a fantasy film, perhaps *the* quintessential fantasy film. It is therefore a crucial film to analyze in order to understand exactly what it offers spectators that other films produced at the time could not, and why indeed the film has gone down in history as one of Hollywood's most beloved classics.

Produced by MGM partially as a response to the success of Disney's *Snow White and the Seven Dwarfs* (1937), *The Wizard of Oz* was an attempt to recreate in live-action the same vivid fantasy spectacle that had proved so popular in the animated feature. This involved a huge creative and financial investment from the film's production team, employing the latest advancements in costume, prop, and production design in the hope of delivering one of the first truly cinematic retellings of a best-selling fantasy novel. L. Frank Baum's *Oz* books had been adapted numerous times for the screen during the silent era, including a few efforts produced by his own ill-fated production company (*The Patchwork Girl of Oz*, 1914; *His Majesty, the Scarecrow of Oz*, 1914; *The Magic Cloak of Oz*, 1914). However, these earlier versions tended to borrow liberally from their source texts in accordance with both the technical capabilities and commercial considerations of the time, creating a number of adaptations that were more vaudevillian than they were fantastical in their effect. *Wizard of Oz* (1925), for example, not only reduces the reliance on built sets in favor of less expensive, real-life locations by shifting the majority of the action from the world of Oz to the Gale farm in Kansas, but it also utilizes the characters from Baum's novels largely as the basis for a series of slapstick vignettes, providing an early role for Oliver Hardy in the process. With the 1939 version, MGM resolved to stick much closer to the path already trodden down the yellow brick road within Baum's source novel. This meant not only mustering up the considerable resources to try and recreate some of the book's iconic locations in a way that matched the detailed set design audiences had grown accustomed to while watching other classical Hollywood productions. It also meant paying close attention to how Baum presented his fantasy narrative in order to create what critics referred to at the time of its release as a film of a "fairy-book tale" shot in a "fairy-book style" (*New York Times*), and one that should "settle an old Hollywood controversy: whether fantasy can be presented onscreen" (*Time*).[18]

This desire to replicate onscreen what Baum had achieved within literature was no small task. Fantasy historian Brian Attebery describes *The Wonderful Wizard of Oz* (1900) as one of the most influential books in the history of US fantasy fiction, largely because of the innovative way the novel uses and presents space as part of its storytelling.[19] Prior to its publication, US fantasy fiction largely offered what Attebery refers to as an "atmospheric" sense of magic.[20] Baum's predecessors, such as Washington Irving ("Rip Van Winkle," 1819), James Fenimore Cooper (*The Last of the Mohicans*, 1841), or Nathaniel Hawthorn (*The Marble Faun*, 1861), wrote fantasy stories set within a romantic vision of early colonial North America or the Europe it had left behind. Baum, on the other hand, broke with this convention toward a historicized, romanticized experience of the fantastic to offer his readers a far more clearly demarcated schism between reality and fantasy on the page. His Oz was not part of our world, but all the more vibrant because it separated itself from it, a trait that seemed to capture the public's imagination by presenting a sense of magic that was not found in the everyday or forgotten but in a self-conscious break from the physical restrictions or historical conventions that govern everyday life.

By adapting this quality, MGM was blessed in that Baum's spatialized vision of magic would seem to lend itself somewhat naturally to the demands of cinematic storytelling. If cinema (as is often said) is a machine for capturing moments in space and time, then *The Wizard of Oz* would need to manipulate both its pro-filmic and onscreen space in such a way as to replicate Baum's contrasting relationship between Kansas and Oz. To achieve this task, *The Wizard of Oz* draws from a number of different techniques designed to give Kansas and Oz a remarkably different look and feel from one another. Most obviously, Kansas is shot in sepia and Oz in Technicolor, an iconic feature of the film that has the effect of giving both Kansas and Oz remarkably different textures and tones onscreen. But the contrasting representation of space between Kansas and Oz does not stop there; it permeates the design of each set or each choice of location, the blocking of movement within the pro-filmic space, and the way the action is filmed. Kansas is presented as a sparse and desolate world, a feature exemplified both in the opening shot of the film—which displays a long road framed by empty fields as the solitary figure of Dorothy travels further away into the background, seeming to strip the frame of all life and movement—right through to the numerous empty establishing shots of farmland that seem to proliferate every movement from one location to the next. Oz, in contrast, is often lively and cluttered. Each location presents a throng of activity, both in terms of the number of characters ready to interact with Dorothy and the sheer number of things to look at within the frame, whether this be Munchkinland—where Dorothy first arrives to be greeted by a crowd of well-wishes who fill each shot with multiple planes of activity (fig. 2.5)— or the moment the Emerald City's large green gates swing open and a briskly paced tracking shot gives the spectator a long-awaited glimpse at the seemingly endless sea of activity waiting on the other side. There is no empty space in Oz: everything is colorful, significant, and vibrant as

Figure 2.5. Dorothy is greeted by the Munchkins with a lavish parade (*The Wizard of Oz*, 1939).

the film utilizes techniques to both emphasize and celebrate the difference between this world and the one Dorothy leaves behind.

The juxtaposing representations of space offered within Kansas and Oz help the spectator to differentiate not only between the two locations within the narrative, but between two competing fictional spaces whose identities are derived partially from being placed in contrast with one another. Oz's magic is so firmly established because it is offset against the banality of Kansas, the Technicolor dazzling precisely because it is preceded by the sepia tones that, in turn, seem dull and gray when compared with the iconic shots that follow on from them. More than simply offering two contrasting representations of space to serve a narrative purpose, *The Wizard of Oz* also uses this sense of juxtaposing space to provide the stimulus for the spectator to engage in an experience of the fantastic. In presenting Kansas, the film offers a vision of a kind of narrative space that can nominally claim to be representing reality. Space seems to look and feel onscreen like it does in everyday life. The space in Oz, however, is designed to create a sensation of being over the rainbow, used to create a feeling that looking at Oz onscreen is akin to leaving behind reality's physical laws and restrictions and to entering into a new realm of possibility.

The key instance in which this experience of the fantastic is enacted onscreen—the moment Dorothy opens the door of her sepia house and steps out into the Technicolor world of Oz—is also perhaps the most well-known sequence in one of the most widely seen films ever produced. And, yet, the strange effect it has in creating a sense of encountering a new form of space onscreen is often taken as something of a given, or else as an obvious side effect of the lavish set design. In actuality, something far more complex is taking place in this iconic moment that is worth pausing on and analyzing. The moment in question is characterized by a set of contrasts and juxtapositions that help cement the feeling of spatial dislocation that is at the heart of *The Wizard of Oz*'s fantasy narrative. The camera travels from a closed, claustrophobic frame in which Dorothy opens the narrow door to a large, open vista, the graphic composition of the shot shifts from a fairly sparse décor of plain wooden panels to a complex foliage of lush plants (figs. 2.6 and 2.7) At the same time, an almost silent soundscape that emphasizes Dorothy's shuffles and yelps within the house is replaced by heavy, nondiegetic orchestration, with music used to generate a rush of delight and excitement at seeing Oz for the first time. In keeping with the overall focus on space as the source of the film's sense of impossibility, the first few shots of Oz focus largely on the physical attributes that immediately greet Dorothy as she makes her first steps into the magical world (figs. 2.8 and 2.9). The set design is certainly elaborate, decorative, and, to even

Figure 2.6. Dorothy opens the door to the house to peek into the world of Oz.

Figure 2.7. Oz appears in all its emotive glory.

Figure 2.8. Dorothy marvels at being in a magical space.

Figure 2.9. The magical space threatens to subsume Dorothy.

a casual observer blessed with the hindsight of a century of filmmaking innovation, artificial, but no more so than any classical Hollywood musical or melodrama produced during this period. The Munchkins have yet to appear, the Lullaby League has yet to start singing, and the horse of a different color remains unknown. But, still, in the exact moment Dorothy steps out into Oz, something feels profoundly different.

What changes in this moment, then, is not the introduction of a clearly impossible object or character, but a realignment in the way the imagination is used to process and understand space onscreen. The film's relationship with the spectator shifts from a fairly typical one established through the classical continuity style to one in which those same filmmaking techniques are used to achieve a different experience unique to *The Wizard of Oz*'s status as a work of fantasy. Classical Hollywood filmmaking typically positions the spectator in such a manner that their perception of the space onscreen matches the way in which space is perceived in everyday life. Space is meant to feel objective and fully realized, each frame positioned and the action blocked in such a way so as to give the impression of a world beyond the limitations of a single shot or set. Despite the decision made to alter Baum's original narrative and turn Oz from an ostensibly "real" magical world into Dorothy's dream, Oz is largely shot within the continuity style, giving the world a sense of autonomy and independence from its heroine that other dream sequences in films like *Spellbound* (1945) or *Vertigo* (1958) do not offer. As James Walters argues, the spectator gets the sense not of being inside Dorothy's dream but of existing within a "dreamed world."[21] However, making Oz feel autonomous does not amount to making it feel naturalistic or realistic. Instead, despite both Kansas and Oz seeking to orient the spectator to a clear understanding of the pro-filmic space in which the action operates, the values and characteristics of their mutual spaces are remarkably different. In Kansas, space was organized onscreen in such a way that stressed its objective and intersubjective function within the narrative. Each location was introduced in a manner economic and pertinent to the story, using clear establishing shots to orient the spectator quickly to the physical site of the action in a manner typical of the wider patterns of classical narration. As Stephen Heath states, "The classical economy of film is its organization thus as organic unity and the form of that economy is narrative. . . . What is sometimes vaguely referred to as 'transparency' has its meaning in this narrativization."[22] The space is narrativized onscreen so that it serves a function within the story, and this provides necessary conditions for the spectator to imagine each individual frame not as a singular unit but as part of a single, cohesive whole.

The opening moments of Oz abandon this dynamic. It is not just that the space in Oz looks different to that of Kansas; the spectator is immediately asked to treat it differently as well. Leaving its protagonist Dorothy behind for a few moments after having entered Oz at her side, the camera proceeds to float out over Munchkinland, gliding over the sights slowly and effortlessly in a protracted tracking shot. Instead of a sense of narrative economy in which space is highlighted onscreen only to orient the spectator to the physical environment in which the story takes place, here space seems to take on a value in and of itself (figs. 2.10 and 2.11). The shot is beautified by the accented lighting, allowing the river's waters to sparkle and shimmer onscreen, and the shots of Oz become something that are offered to the spectator to be appreciated for what they are rather than what purpose they serve to the storytelling (figs. 2.12 and 2.13). As the sequence comes to an end and finally returns to Dorothy to allow her to utter her now famous line, "Toto, I have a feeling we're not in Kansas anymore," the understatement feels acute. Dorothy is right. This is a different world not just because of what it is, but how it feels to be there.

The experience of the fantastic evoked in this sequence therefore encourages the spectator to forge an entirely different imagined relationship with the physical properties on display. By narrativizing space to the point of obscuring it, classical Hollywood treats space in terms of its form and function, much in the same way we often treat space in everyday life when we are going about our day to day lives. As we move from A to B, space is something we use rather than something we appreciate, viewing it as we do as a largely objective force whose value is determined by what we do in it rather than what it is. But this is not always how we see space. When we choose not to walk down a dark alley, or smile peacefully as we step onto a deserted, tropical beach, we are doing something else entirely. We are imagining space has certain qualities and values through a process of cathexis. Space can make us feel happy or scared just by being in it, whether it be the pleasure of arriving home after a long day or (in my case certainly) the feeling of dread associated with walking into a shopping mall. In such moments, we do not just understand space; we fuse our subjective feelings with the objective properties of space, making darkness frightening and sand relaxing, despite the fact that, faced with the cold harshness of logic, neither of these statements seems to have any value.

In *The Wizard of Oz*, the impossible quality of space is achieved thanks to Oz's ability to take on a quality that is far more in keeping with space's role within both early object relations and within the imaginative, creative life of the individual. Infants are not born knowing

Figure 2.10. Oz dominates the screen, the camera leaving Dorothy behind.

Figure 2.11. Munchkinland is revealed in all its glory.

Figure 2.12. The camera returns to Dorothy to remind us of Oz's emotional impact.

Figure 2.13. Dorothy realizes that she is not in Kansas anymore.

that there is an objective world surrounding them. Instead, the sense of objective space that permeates throughout our conscious lives is something we are required to learn, having first forged relationships with the physical world that surrounds us through cathexis. As Trevor Pateman argues, "The infant's early explorations of the outside world in looking, crawling, and toddling are very much *spatial* explorations."[23] An understanding of space is forged first and foremost through phantasy before it is understood rationally, explaining why small children often show little to no awareness of how surrounding spaces might be considered to be related to one another but associate different spaces (the bedroom, the bathroom) with contrasting emotions and activities.[24] While we partially abandon this primarily emotive way of relating to space in later life in order to understand space as part of a functional, external reality, there are countless moments where we retain our ability to relate to space primarily through cathexis through more overt acts of creativity. As we play games with one another, we fill space with whatever we feel like filling it with, pretending that there are monsters under our beds or fairies at the bottom of our garden. Space becomes not objective but, in the words of Winnicott, "potential."[25] We can use it to express pleasure and satisfaction, to rage at or vilify, its meaning defined not by its status as an objective force but for what its external qualities might be if we were to fuse them with our own imaginations.

Once space takes on this primarily emotive quality in *The Wizard of Oz*, locations within the story begin to have value in excess and at the expense of the narrative causality being presented in any one moment. It is how space resonates once its objective characteristics are fused with subjective feeling that makes the world of Oz matter, a dynamic that the film uses to both interrogate its protagonist's psychology and direct the spectator's appreciation of the Land of Oz onscreen. Turning Oz into Dorothy's dream allows the film to foreground the emotional as opposed to physical value of the space that surrounds her. The spectator is encouraged to experience Oz as an egocentric world, one which kowtows to her wants, needs, and emotions as opposed to blocking or frustrating them, and one which has ties back to reality through the elements Dorothy chooses to bring with her (her dog Toto, for example, and her friends Hunk [Ray Bolger], Zeke [Bert Lahr], and Hickory [Jack Haley], a feature emphasized through the emphasis on their faces in the costume designs of the Scarecrow, Tin Man, and Cowardly Lion). Rather than being fully autonomous, Oz is a world you can fill with phantasy, a world into which you can bring emotions and ideas, and it will shape itself accordingly.

In this sense, Dorothy is more than just the main character in Oz; she is its lifeblood. Upon her arrival, Dorothy is instantly heralded as the savior of the Munchkins, greeted enthusiastically by representatives of the Lollipop Guild and the Lullaby League who seem to have simply been waiting for her arrival with a dance already prepared, and is entertained on a village square that seems custom-designed solely for that purpose. She sets out on the yellow brick road that starts precisely where she is standing and ends precisely where she needs to get to and, when she arrives at a crossroads and contemplates which way to go, an unknown voice off screen is instantly available to give her advice on the matter. The character of the Scarecrow is introduced, appearing in a field that was previously empty not because of any narrative reason, but because, it would seem, if Dorothy is not there to notice him, then he does not exist (figs. 2.14 and 2.15). As the duo form a partnership and merrily continue onward, they dance from one potential path to the next, without any sense of trepidation as to where each might lead but simply allowing the rhythm and flow of the music to direct which way they will go. It is as if, whichever way they choose, Oz's space would simply modulate to fit their desires. If none of these moments seems at odds or incongruous with the fantasy story taking place, this is not because what appears onscreen is not impossible. If anything, it is the fact that the space in Oz *is* impossible that makes it permissible for all the frequent simplifications, disruptions, and alterations to the way space should actually operate to occur. Like Dorothy, the space can be used by the spectator as a vessel onto which phantasy can be placed, a quality that demarcates Oz's imaginative potential in comparison with the fixed and orderly Kansas.

The emotional benefit of such an experience of space is rooted in the way cathexis both tries, and often fails, to function in everyday life. The reason my emotional experience of space is always of secondary importance to my conscious experience of it is not because I necessarily wish it to be. Ask a group of marathon runners thirteen miles into their race whether they would like space to be different from how it is in their current moment, and it is likely that their fatigue and agony will yield a positive answer. However, the reason they keep running as opposed to merely wishing themselves over the finishing line is because they know that, despite whatever values they might wish space to exhibit, it will remain cruelly and often sadistically objective. Winnicott refers to this as the trauma embedded within the "object's capacity to survive."[26] We learn when we are very young that no matter how loud we scream or how hard we kick, sometimes wanting something from the world is not

Figure 2.14. Dorothy stands in front of an empty field.

Figure 2.15. The Scarecrow seems to magically appear in the field behind Dorothy.

enough to get it. We therefore channel our emotional energy into conscious processes that help us to mediate and solve the world's attempts to block and frustrate our desires, and we find meaning in the functional as opposed to the emotional value of space. Oz has no such reality. By being impossible, it lacks the capacity to restrain our desires, and it is this aspect of the magical world that represents perhaps its fundamental flaw that means it can only be maintained in a narrative system such as this. While we can enjoy being in Oz, we cannot imagine living in Oz. The place does not possess that crucial capacity to survive that we both hate and love in reality itself, and thus it seems inevitable from the moment Dorothy opens the door and steps into the Technicolor that, at some point, she will have to go back to the ordered land of sepia. As much as we might like the idea, staying in Oz with her new friends is just not a viable solution to her problems, nor is it ultimately a satisfying ending as the spectator watches on while a little girl wishes herself over the rainbow to reject the world of reality in favor of a realm of impossible fantasy.

Contrasting the excitement of experiencing a space like Oz with the objective normalcy, even dullness, offered in a world like Kansas, then, allows *The Wizard of Oz* to match its narrative and thematic concerns with its experiential concerns, merging its identity as a fantasy film with its identity as a work of classical Hollywood cinema. *The Wizard of Oz* is a film based on a seemingly irreconcilable contradiction. It is a film that teaches us there's no place like home, while at the same time showing us a world over the rainbow and asking us to delight in how much brighter and better it is than the grays of Kansas. Scholars have therefore struggled with this seemingly inherent paradox embedded within the heart of this beloved classic. Elizabeth Bronfen's work on the film even goes so far as to suggest that it is this unresolved dichotomy that explains the very reason for its enduring popularity, as viewers struggling with its thematic denouement rewatch the film to "regulate its ideological message."[27] However, as a fantasy film, the film is reliant not on setting Kansas and Oz as antagonists in a fight between the value of physical reality and the emotional value of dreams but on the fusion and interaction between the two possibilities. The fantastic is not, after all, an experience that denies the presence of reality. It is an experience in which the spectator's inability to make sense of a fiction as reality allows for new approaches that transcend—as opposed to avoid—the more rational impulses we feel toward everyday life. Likewise, Oz is not a rejection of Kansas. It is a realm that transcends Kansas, a place Dorothy and the spectator can experience differently to Kansas, and a place that, when returning to Kansas, offers new ways of appreciating the space the film has temporarily left behind.

It is therefore in the film's treatment of and engagement with the concept of home that has proven so contentious for so many that the film attempts to match the spectator's experiential concerns with enjoying a pleasurable and imaginative relationship with space, with the narrative concerns of understanding Dorothy's journey from seeing Kansas as her house to seeing it as her home. The two impulses are, in a way, one and the same, at least in the way they play out with the film's narrative. Home is, after all, both a real place that provides us with essential protection and stability within the world, as well as a highly imaginative place wherein, as Gaston Bachelard famous describes, we comfort ourselves with "the illusion of protection."[28] It requires us not only to understand its objective form and function, but to fuse the emotions and memories we might forge in response to being inside it onto an imagined understanding of being inside home as space. It is therefore a crucial site where our two ways of approaching space through phantasy meet and collide, requiring an equally imaginative approach to the setting in which a rational and an emotional understanding of the world come together to give a home its proper form and function.

Dorothy's struggle to find that sense of home throughout the film is a struggle to combine two overlapping ways of approaching space together that, through its fantasy narrative, the film forces her to prize apart. In Kansas, the house she lived in, though functional as a space, was never able to provide her with a feeling of security. It was a place of narrative action, invaded immediately in the opening of the story by Miss Gulch (Margaret Hamilton) threatening to take Toto away from her because the very demands of classical continuity cannot afford Dorothy the luxury to simply enjoy being in a space. Her dream world of Oz, by rupturing that sense of economic, spatial organization and narrative function, offers her that opportunity to approach space differently and enjoy the feeling of being in different locations, arenas, and lands as she wanders from one place to the next as part of a rich fantasy adventure. Yet, her ability to use space as an emotional vessel comes at a cost. Because Oz is impossible, it also cannot provide her with the objective sense of stability that she craves. Oz is a not lived-in world. It is a realm whose delights lie precisely in its sense of newness, providing a visual pleasure in the arrival into new locations but not a pleasure in familiarity and security. So Dorothy, like the spectator, is essentially trapped throughout the film between two ways of existing in the world. She can either live in a world like Kansas, one of order, rules, and regulation but one that seems to provide her with little to no opportunity to enjoy the space she is in, or a place like Oz in which to enjoy the space is all she has, because space has no fixed order and meaning. Straddling these two impulses, Dorothy learns to construct a sense of home by fusing the way she learns to see space in Oz with the way she sees space in Kansas. Focusing primarily on her emotional attachment to her Auntie Em (Clara Blandick)—one that is given a visual manifestation in the scene in the witch's castle, which in turn echoes an earlier encounter with Professor Marvel (Frank Morgan) where Dorothy expresses for the first time her desire to return home to the Gale farm—Dorothy learns to take the emotional attachments she has with the world, attachments she has found it easier to focus on in a world like Oz, and fuse them with the objective reality of her farmhouse. In this sense, her journey toward appreciating her house as a home is not unlike the journey we all experience in life as we learn to appreciate the world around us. We find things in life we like—even love—and those attachments then allow us to see the world differently as a result.

It is not just Dorothy that goes on this emotional journey. By being encouraged to participate imaginatively in a similar journey through space throughout the narrative, the spectator assigns Oz with the same emotional qualities as Dorothy throughout her journey. The film lets spectators enjoy the thrill of being in spaces that are defined largely by their emotional quality as opposed to physical reality, whether in the form of the seemingly inherent euphoria of places like Munchkinland or the Emerald City or frightening spaces like the wild woods or witch's castle. And, yet, for those spaces to be available to the spectator, they must first dislocate themselves from the temptation to view Oz as reality. It is only, after all, through an experience of the fantastic that the spectator is given license to experience space primarily through an emotional cathexis in its alternative capacity. In this sense, *The Wizard of Oz* functions as a fantasy film both through the story that it tells and the way in which the spectator is positioned to perceive it. Its space becomes fantastic and, as such, there's just no place like it.

The Fantastic and Time:
Phantasy and Temporal Cathexis in *It's a Wonderful Life*

Like *The Wizard of Oz*, *It's a Wonderful Life* has earned a reputation as a cherished classic within the popular canon of classical Hollywood filmmaking. In the US in particular, the film seems to have become almost prescribed viewing for audiences around the festive winter period, shown endlessly on television schedules and rereleased in cinemas each year. Yet, unlike *The Wizard of Oz*, the film is not as often associated with the history of fantasy filmmaking, despite the fact that both films feature a protracted sequence set in a world that is not our own. While *The Wizard of Oz* was marketed by MGM as a film full of Technicolor delights that would marvel audiences with a display of different impossible circumstances onscreen, Frank Capra's film was instead largely promoted as a continuation of the director's successful prewar comedy-dramas such as *You Can't Take It with You* (1938) and *Mr. Smith Goes to Washington* (1939). Critics writing in *Variety* and the *Washington Post* made reference to the returning partnership of Capra and James Stewart after a wartime hiatus due to their respective involvements in the US military; however, they celebrated their return largely as an opportunity to replicate this preexisting formula rather than to provide an opportunity for them to extend their partnership into the world of fantasy.[29] Instead, the work to recognize the film's achievements as an example of fantasy storytelling has been undertaken by both genre fans and academics, meaning that, as Katherine A. Fowkes says, the film is now recognized as a "well-known" example of fantasy cinema.[30] *It's a Wonderful Life* is a fantasy film, perhaps one of Hollywood's best fantasy films. It is just a very different kind of fantasy film from some of the genre's more obvious examples.

It's a Wonderful Life is an example of what Peter Valenti has termed the "film blanc," a key subgenre of Hollywood fantasy cinema produced with some frequency during and in the immediate aftermath to World War II.[31] Exemplified in other productions such as *Beyond Tomorrow* (1940), *Here Comes Mr. Jordan* (1941), *A Guy Named Joe* (1943), and *Angel on My Shoulder* (1946), the film blanc delivered a lighthearted and optimistic take on the fantasy genre's long history of appropriating religious iconography, typically telling stories in which an unremarkable set of characters come into contact with beatific forces such as angels, guardian spirts, and, on occasion, devils. These characters were used to engage with notions of mortality and morality in a lighthearted manner, their success often attributed to their widespread appeal to audiences still suffering from an all-too-recent global trauma in which the specter of mortality had been dramatized on the world's stage. The film blanc therefore offered a vision of humanity in which amiable if unremarkable characters became supremely connected to a sense of the divine, their lives saved by forces beyond their control who ruled over them by a sense of celestial order and purpose all-too lacking during recent times.

It's a Wonderful Life is perhaps the most successful example of this fairly brief subgenre of filmmaking. It is certainly one of the few films made in this mode that has managed to transcend the sociocultural zeitgeist that initially made these films so popular and continues to offer audiences worldwide an experience that is both profoundly moving and affecting. Telling the story of George Bailey (James Stewart), the majority of the film's running time consists of a biographical account of a fairly unexceptional but likeable human being living in the small town of Bedford Falls. From an early age, George is shown to be an ambitious young man who dreams of leaving Bedford Falls behind and becoming an explorer, making his name on the covers of *National Geographic*. However, instead of fulfilling his ambition of traveling the world, George instead spends most of his days thwarting the efforts of local business mogul and property tycoon Mr. Potter (Lionel Barrymore), who seeks to either purchase or drive out of business the building and loan company George inherits from his father because of the opportunity it offers residents to avoid living in his notorious slums. One day, as George is threatened with bankruptcy after an important bank check is mislaid by his uncle Billy (Thomas Mitchell), he is driven to the point of such despair that he contemplates suicide, only to be saved by the arrival of a guardian angel named Clarence (Henry Travers). To convince George that his has been a life worth living, Clarence conjures up a vision of Bedford Falls as it might have been if George had never existed, a world ridden by poverty and fear where his friends, family, and wife Mary (Donna Reed) suffer at the hands of Potter. Graced by Clarence's divine intervention, George realizes the titular message of the film that a life need not be spectacular or even particularly noteworthy for it to be wonderful, just as long as the person living it has made a positive impact during their time on earth.

In trying to assess how *It's a Wonderful Life* functions as a work of fantasy despite its often humdrum or unexceptional settings, critics have often gravitated to the film's famous final act, perhaps the most obvious moment in the film where the spectator is presented with visions of objects and people onscreen that are quite obviously impossible. Robert B. Ray's analysis of the film, for example, argues that "the success of *It's a Wonderful Life* depended utterly on George's vision produced by Clarence."[32] Yet, such an analysis might do well to heed the film's central message of looking for the value in things beyond the most obvious or spectacular, and to find the magic in the everyday and unexceptional. Far from being the only moment in which the film enters into the realm of fantasy fiction, the final act is in fact only a culmination of a dynamic that has been established since the film's opening moments. Beginning with shots of the town of Bedford Falls, the camera proceeds to travel upward into the skies above, floating beyond the rooftops to provide a vision of the heavens themselves (fig. 2.16). A group of unseen angels begin talking, an act signaled through the twinkling of stars, and in this moment the film sets up clearly that the purpose of watching George Bailey's life is so that we might understand how he reached the point of despair where the story begins. What follows, then, is the story of George Bailey told not from an objective perspective but from the perspective of a group of on-looking angels who are assigned the task of both understanding George's character and assessing the quality of his life. As spectators, we are tasked with the important job of giving Clarence the necessary equipment he needs to perform his act of salvation.

This interjection of the heavenly presence permeates the film's presentation of George's life with a temporal paradox that the film then plays with as part of its imaginative appeal. On the one hand, the film draws on a number of strategies typical of classical Hollywood narration to tell George's life in a logical, chronological manner, jumping from one key

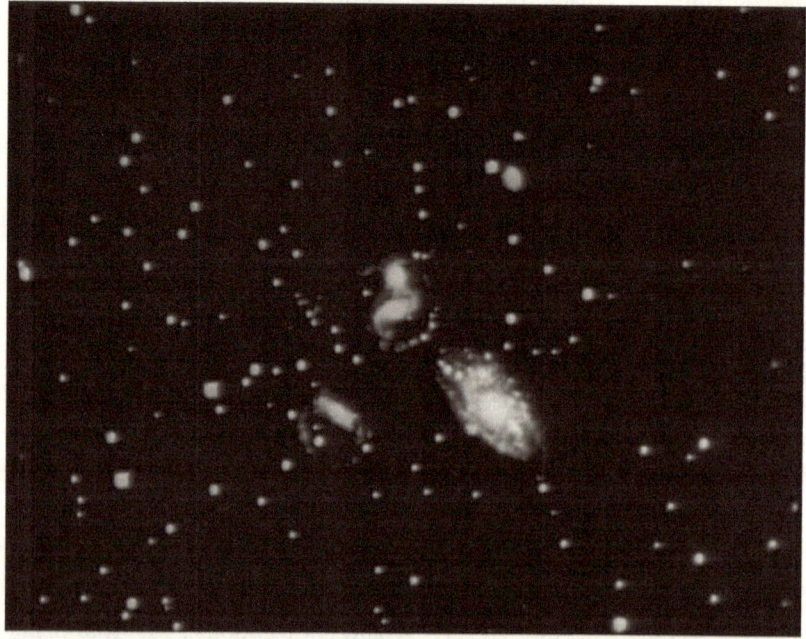

Figure 2.16. The twinkling stars embody angels (*It's a Wonderful Life*, 1946).

moment to the next much the same as a film like *Citizen Kane* (1941), which follows a similar unfolding flashback structure to Capra's fantasy film. Yet, while in *Citizen Kane* such devices are used to give a sense of time flowing logically from one scene to the next, *It's a Wonderful Life* uses its flashback structure to disturb this sense of naturalism. From the very first moment when the action snaps into focus onto a mid-shot of a young George Bailey and a voiceover begins to tell Clarence about his life, we are asked to accept the fact that what we are watching onscreen represents not something objective or natural but the manifestation of divine force. This is Clarence's viewpoint onto the mortal world, one possessed with an omniscient power that allows him and the other angels the magical ability to skip backward and forward across time, pausing moments to interject, comment, and evaluate their worth like they were operating some sort of celestial remote control. Sequences that would otherwise encourage the spectator to bypass or accept without thinking the passing of time from one scene to the next become moments of self-conscious deliberation and discussion, and assumptions and postulations the spectator would otherwise be encouraged to make implicitly as part of the process of comprehending a narrative unfold become part of the angel's off screen deliberations. Eventually, by being constantly alerted to the manipulation of time taking place onscreen, we are left with a rather explicit realization of something that is nevertheless true of other classical Hollywood fantasy films, but which we might not otherwise notice. We have both watched a life unfold over a series of decades (in terms of the amount of time as presented within the narrative) and watched a life play out over a single evening (in terms of the duration of both the film itself and the narrative events contained within it), and it is by cohabiting these two positions simultaneously that the film invites us to feel both distanced from and drawn into the narrative, as the position we have been asked to occupy as quasi-celestial beings throws us into a kind of temporal hesitation in which our relationship with the film's chronology and sense of time is thrown into question.

The experience of the fantastic offered throughout *It's a Wonderful Life* is therefore far less elusive than it might at first seem. Rather than offering us an impossible creature (as in the case of *Alice in Wonderland*), or an impossible space (as in the case of *The Wizard of Oz*), the film asks the spectator to occupy an impossible relationship with time, one in which the assumed naturalism of unfolding events within classical narration gives way to a celebration of a deliberately artificially reconstructed life onscreen. In his analysis of modernist narrative, Gérard Genette famously compares this experience of time in a story to that of crossing a road or field, felt only in terms of the movement from one place to another, an element that is replicated in the experience of continuity narration.[33] When I am running late to catch a train and decide to jog to the station, for example, I create a felt sense of time out of a series of temporal phantasies that make the events seem like a logical progression from A to B. I imagine what I did in the past (picturing myself taking too long to iron my shirt just ten minutes ago, which caused me to leave the house later than I should), as well as imagining what might happen in the future if I do not get to the station on time (i.e., that the train will pull away without me). These phantasies, when stitched together with a series of logical propositions, help me to generate a feeling that time functions as a linear, progressive force that helps me to understand my actions as a series of causal actions from A to B. Reproducing this kind of experience in the way it organizes its events onscreen, classical narration patterns typically encourage the spectator to relate to each moment onscreen through a similar sense of progressive time, allowing us to relate each scene to an imagined construct of what it might mean in relation to previous and future events. This not only gives time onscreen a naturalistic sensibility despite the fact classical narration often skips forward, jumps backward, or performs other acts of time travel onscreen; it also allows the spectator, in the words of Todd McGowan, "to take solace in the image of past (and future) satisfaction" that structures their viewing experience.[34]

As Bliss Cua Lim argues, in its desire to destabilize rational modes of engagement, the fantastic can invite us to not only think differently about the space or people we encounter in a narrative system, but it can also direct the spectator to think in "dis-accustomed terms about time."[35] To feel the impossibility of a narrative event is to be disconnected from the progressive through-line of action that tends to define our experience of both everyday life and narrative cinema, and instead be held in a moment of hesitancy. That hesitancy ruptures our desire to establish a chronology or causality of the event taking place and prevents us making predictions as to what might happen next, at least not any that we can hold with a particular conviction. Instead, the only way to experience time is to feel its impact, an impact rooted in the here and now, giving time an emotional as opposed to a logical quality. The way *It's a Wonderful Life* positions the spectator to experience the fantastic triggers a similar form of temporal displacement. Disconnected from our attempt to perceive time onscreen as a naturally progressive through-line from the past to the future, the hesitancy we might feel toward the narrative events as they play out alongside a sense of the divine and the heavenly helps us to view time somewhat differently, assessing each moment onscreen for what value it has *as a moment* rather than for how it might connect with previous or future events. Indeed, the film's sense of drama rests on that discrepancy. If we simply followed George on his journey, we would presumably be left to reach the same conclusion as him, given the unlikelihood of his eventual redemption from financial ruin. But that is not what the film asks us to experience. Instead, the tragedy of the film's second act comes from George's failure to recognize something that we can see so clearly, that his life is not simply a story of how he got from A to B but a series of moments that have allowed him to be part of the world rather than just travel through it. It is the moments that have given George's life a "wonderful" quality, a quality we are asked to recognize from the opening reel as we watch each sequence unfold onscreen, but one George himself has to wait until the film's closing moments to understand.

This sense of feeling one's self in time, rather than using time as part of an attempt to understand a logical series of events, is demonstrated in one of the film's most fondly remembered sequences in which George and Mary are reacquainted as young adults and walk home together after George has attended his brother Harry's (Todd Karns) high school senior prom. The moment is not necessarily the most overtly magical sequence in the film if we were sticking to an understanding of the fantastic as something expressed through either the display of character or of space. But, if one considers the way this scene plays with the relationship between phantasy and time, then the moment does take on a more imaginative and, yes, fantastical nature than it might otherwise appear. In this regard, what is particularly notable about the scene is how its sense of drama and romanticism is achieved not by appealing to the traditional narrative stakes at play within such a sequence. In other Hollywood romances, part of the tension a scene like this would typically create would be based on the spectator's ability to try to guess what is going to happen. However, in *It's a Wonderful Life*, we already know the answer to this. Mary has been identified as George's wife since the opening reel of the film—we heard her pray for him alongside the children they have together as part of the town's evocation to the heavens—and so what we are watching is not a sequence in which we are made to guess if this will lead to a romantic occurrence, but a sequence in which we have the pleasure of watching two people realize something we already know: that they love each other.

George and Mary begin the scene by evoking a series of temporal phantasies that they each have about their lives. They discuss their past,

George expressing his disbelief that the now adult Mary can be the same young girl he once chastised for not liking coconut on her ice cream, while Mary tries hard to suppresses her own delight within her body language that the boy she once solemnly declared her love for into his bad ear is now standing there, looking at her. Then, their conversation turns to the future. George begins to rattle off his "hatful" of wishes for what his life might hold, a list Mary resists because, notably, George's phantasies do not contain her, and so she throws a rock at the old Granville house in order to express her own wish for the future: that she and George will one day marry. Both characters are constructing phantasies about what the past and future might mean rather than being in the moment fully and completely, and it is for this reason that neither of them realize the truth of the situation that the spectator is waiting anxiously for them to see. Blessed with the knowledge of both hindsight and foresight, they know that George's wishes will not come true, that Mary's concerns about his future are ill-founded, and that, in essence, the sense of time that two characters are inhabiting is, in effect, impossible.

George and Mary's temporal prison is the same one the spectator usually occupies in their pursuit of following the logical flow of time. As Christian Metz argues, classical narration's desire to present time as causal and progressive has the effect of obfuscating the often dramatic leaps in chronology we are asked to undertake as we jump forward or backward in a film's attempt to tell a cohesive story, but it also separates the spectator from what he describes as "the fullness of [the] *here* and *now*."[36] By creating a framing device that disrupts that sense of logical flow, that makes that logical flow seem impossible, *It's a Wonderful Life* is able to return the spectator to the emotional richness of the present, a dynamic which is dramatized in this famous scene through its evocation of a series of spectators that do not share the central couple's temporal understanding. The first of these spectators is a local neighbor who, without knowledge of the phantasies that move the couple to inaction, watches on, exasperated at what is taking place. But it is not the fact that he is the only character watching this scene unfold that highlights this dynamic. As the scene progresses, George performs his fondly remembered soliloquy. "What is it you want Mary," George says, "Do you want the moon? Just say the word and I'll throw a lasso and pull it down" (fig. 2.17). Evoking the moon through poetic dialogue, George seems to also evoke the stars that he and Mary not only stare up at but, crucially, stare back down. Clarence's unseen presence is referred to indirectly, an idea that gathers further traction as George proceeds to describe the idea

Figure 2.17. George promises Mary he will lasso the moon for her.

of Mary "swallowing" the moon and letting the moonbeams "radiate" in her skin, as they are infused with the same transcendent power that the film seeks to bring to George Bailey's life as part of its function as a film blanc. George's words therefore enact metaphorically what is taking place onscreen through the interplay of two different temporal experiences offered to the spectator. Mary and George are "on earth," living life normally from one moment to the next. Yet, they are also being watched from the heavens and stars, creating two temporal realms that merge and cohabit onscreen despite the everyday visuals. The spectator becomes the moon watching down on George, charged with the light of celestial significance, and in witnessing this intimate moment they are allowed the privilege of watching two people fall in love.

The difference between the subjective value in time the film asks us to feel in such a moment—in which George's life can be celebrated for the individual moments of romance, charity, and kindness he offers us throughout his life—and the chronological understanding of time George is constantly blinded by as he measures himself against his hopes from the past or his fears of the future comes down to a difference between time's relationship to our ability to understand reality and time's function as a potential tool for cathexis. In everyday life, we largely focus on time's progressive qualities because these features allow us to participate in a world of intersubjective action, one in which our interaction with events effects our experience of the external world. Such a dynamic is no doubt useful, but it also keeps us from feeling the full emotional value of time in any given moment, a point that has been made from philosophers like Henri Bergson to psychoanalysts like Klein and Winnicott.[37] Children are not born into the world being able to tell the time. Instead, they feel time in accordance with their emotional status, fusing their inner phantasy lives with a sense of duration as moments become happy or sad in equal measure. The absence of a parent for a brief period can feel terrible and lengthy depending on the strength of emotion felt, while the return of the parent and the safety and security it brings can be both euphoric and all too brief as the child lives an experience of time that is never objective but always dependent on how time feels in a particular moment. This sense of time is not lost in later life. Expressions like "time flies when you are having fun" attest to this emotional quality time can have, even when this way of understanding time through a fusion of the subjective and objective is often subsumed within a wider process of making sense of reality. But in those moments where time is felt for its durative, moment-by-moment impact, it is not the case that my imagination is utilized as part of my attempts to make time feel rational. Instead, I link my emotional state to my experience of temporality through a process of cathexis.

By allowing this relationship with time to exist throughout its running time, *It's a Wonderful Life* becomes a fantasy film that gives spectators opportunities to fuse the sense of time presented onscreen with the emotions they wish to bring to it. Once we see the film as operating in this manner, it becomes much easier to see exactly what is nightmarish about Clarence's alternative version of Bedford Falls, and how it fits within the overall strategy of the film's evocation of the fantastic. Clarence's alternative world is impossible not because it has anything in it that could not happen physically or features characters that are not real. The Bedford Falls we see at the end of the film looks largely the same as the real town, aside from a few superficial differences, and the people in it are also the same, at least in terms of their physical appearance. Instead, Clarence's version of Bedford Falls is impossible because it does not match the temporal phantasies built up around the location and its inhabitants until this point. Characters become impossible versions of their former selves and the world becomes supernatural because the more "natural" Bedford Falls has a different history and, consequently, a different present and future. George's discomfort at being in the alternative Bedford Falls resides in the fact that, despite knowing where everything is, he no longer understands what it all means. Mary is no longer his wife but a spinster, and staring into her eyes and not seeing the Mary he knows looking back at him forces George to stare into an alternative present. With this in mind, it seems significant that Clarence's occupation in life was a clockmaker; his spiritual powers reside similarly in his ability to manipulate and construct time. Not only that, but the experience of this alternative Bedford Falls allows for a cathexis of the memories, attachments, and phantasies associated with the more "natural" Bedford Falls that are returned to George at the film's conclusion.

It's a Wonderful Life has achieved a cherished status among film audiences specifically for its ability to reaffirm and celebrate mortality, corporeality, and what it means to have a satisfying life. This beloved status is largely because of the way the film appeals as a work of fantasy, albeit a fantasy that shares little of the conventional focus on an act of impossible display onscreen that is typical of some of the genre's other famous entries like *The Wizard of Oz*. The film is not interested in showing us things that are impossible, but in presenting things in an impossible manner so that the mundane world of Bedford Falls feels somewhat miraculous and otherworldly. Representing two types of temporality, one possessing a progressive and another a durational quality, time itself becomes a force not simply to be experienced in the same way as in everyday life, but something to be given value and meaning through phantasy. The film is therefore not simply about the specifics of George's wonderful life, but the concept of how life is assigned a wonderful quality in the first place, a process that is forged first and foremost through phantasy.

Conclusion: Cathexis in Hollywood Fantasy Films

Fantasy cinema did not begin during the age of classical Hollywood, nor did it culminate during this age. However, classical Hollywood does serve as a pivotal moment not only in the history of the US film industry but in the history of popular narrative media at large, not least of all because it was in this era that a template became established that has since shaped the production of popular narration onscreen ever since. Classical Hollywood established the dominance of an industry whose commercial performance is still the envy of the world. It established a filmmaking style that is still viewed by practitioners and audiences as the most effective means of communicating narratives to audiences, and it established many of the popular genres that still hold sway in contemporary culture, from the romantic comedy to the domestic melodrama to the fantasy film. Works like *Alice in Wonderland*, *The Wizard of Oz*, and *It's a Wonderful Life* taught filmmakers and audiences alike the pleasure that comes from experiencing impossible characters, spaces, and times as they manifest onscreen, pleasures that studios involved in the production of fantasy to this day have been trying to reproduce ever since.

Classical Hollywood taught us to embrace impossible characters. Through the way it narrativized and presented its scenarios onscreen in the age of the talkie, spectators were required to forge relationships not just with believable people whom we could see ourselves in, but imagined creatures of impossibility with whom we found pleasure experiencing through moments of cathexis. We learned to place ourselves into scenarios, even when such scenarios were completely unbelievable, and to choose to relate to things imaginatively in open defiance of our sense of rationality. Ever since films like *Alice in Wonderland*, this desire to imagine impossible people has been an ever-present characteristic of fantasy filmmaking. In the 1950s and 1960s, films such as *Tom Thumb* (1958), *Darby Gill and the Little People* (1959), or the *7 Faces of Dr. Lao* (1964) built their stories around magical characters whose delight onscreen came through their ability to evade fixed classification and logical understanding, refusing to let us identify with them fully so that they might preserve their sense of magic and mystery onscreen. In the 1970s, comedies like *Freaky Friday* (1976) provided iconic material for actors who wished not only to perform roles that audiences could happily believe they were inhabiting but to play outside their age and physical boundaries, displaying impossible behavior traits that we enjoyed precisely for their evasion of credibility and believability. In the 1980s, family-friendly monster fare like *Gremlins* (1984) built successful merchandising campaigns by selling their eponymous creatures to a receptive public, allowing audiences to possess physically that which they had owned imaginatively through the process of watching them appear onscreen. Impossible characters continue to flood our fascination with the screen and will continue to do so as long as we are provided with sufficient opportunities to make the objective and the subjective one and the same.

Classical Hollywood taught us to be inside impossible spaces. Displaying lands onscreen so that we could comprehend them just as we might the naturalistic worlds that populated other Hollywood genres, and yet allowing us moments to appreciate them as vessels through which we might engage with an experience of the fantastic, the fantasy films told through the continuity style during this era established a key virtue of fantasy cinema that the genre has been trading on ever since. Future chapters will cover the rise of high fantasy blockbuster filmmaking during the 1980s to emphasize the specific experiential opportunities and narrative devices that make this such a cycle worthy of analysis as a separate phenomenon. But, at the same time, the debt to films like *The Wizard of Oz* these latter works would have is so apparent it hardly needs explaining. The MGM classic showed filmmakers how to physically manufacture and then shoot lands that would seem impossible and yet inviting to those who experienced them, and that ability to cathexis space emotionally has been part of our expectation and appreciation of fantasy cinema ever since. Films such as *The Wonderful World of the Brothers Grimm* (1962), *The Princess Bride* (1987), *Big Fish* (2003), *Bridge to Terabithia* (2007), *The Imaginarium of Doctor Parnassus* (2009), or *Beasts of the Southern Wild* (2012), each of which rely on making the spectator inhabit worlds that are demarcated as outside of reality within their stories, all owe considerable thanks to their classical Hollywood predecessors.

Classical Hollywood taught us to feel impossible time. It created a filmmaking system that could manipulate time onscreen in interesting and multifaceted ways. There have been films throughout Hollywood's history that have sought to do something other than simply use time as a progressive device in order to achieve the same mythical resonance within popular culture as *It's a Wonderful Life*. *Groundhog Day* (1993), perhaps the finest example, is another film whose sense of the fantastic comes primarily through a rupture in time, and the film utilizes the opportunities afforded to the spectator through this process of temporal cathexis to make time feel like an emotive force. Phil Connors's (Bill Murray) purgatory of living the same day repeatedly affords spectators a lot of fun in the comedic opportunities that come when one character's experience of time is different from another's, as the film interrogates a similar message of the value spent in moments as opposed to the problem in seeing time merely as a force for narrative progression. Likewise, *Ghost* (1990) offers a profoundly effecting emotional experience to many people. The famous scene in which Sam (Patrick Swayze) and Molly (Demi Moore) are reunited after death, and share a re-creation of a romantic moment on Molly's pottering wheel, is a celebration of time through an experience of the fantastic. The impossibility of these two characters being together in a moment, yet given that moment onscreen nonetheless, signals its emotional resonance. In presenting narrative systems that encourage spectators to forge deeply felt emotional and imaginative connections with circumstances they perceive to be impossible, fantasy films of the classical era provide the means for engaging the spectator's phantasies that the film industry has relied upon ever since. Continuity techniques are not, de facto, naturalistic techniques. In the hands of gifted fantasy filmmakers, they can be so much more than that.

3

The Wonder Film

Postclassical Fantasy Cinema and Phantasies of Introjection, 1946–1975

THE CLASSICAL ERA WAS RESPONSIBLE for the most sustained period of commercial stability in Hollywood's history. Yet, perhaps inevitably, that stability would not last forever. Within the postwar climate, Hollywood would be faced with a number of industrial and societal challenges that altered the commercial landscape of the US film industry. The Supreme Court's landmark ruling against Paramount Studios in May 1948 forced the major studios to sell off their domestic distribution networks, creating greater opportunities for independent producers to offer counterprogramming to their mainstream rivals. At the same time, the advent of television created a natural competitor to cinema that, coupled with the widespread relocation of US families from the cities to the suburbs, halved Hollywood's attendance figures within the space of two decades. Hollywood was therefore faced with an increasingly competitive and fluctuating marketplace and would spend the next few decades trialing a number of different creative solutions. The regimentation of the classical era was officially over, and a new postclassical era of industrial uncertainty and experimentation had begun.

Not surprisingly, these changes taking place within both the US film industry and the wider society at large were to have a fundamental impact on the kind of fantasy films Hollywood made. Within this volatile commercial landscape, fantasy cinema was recalibrated within Hollywood's wider industrial strategy to become not just one of many storytelling modes available to the arsenal of a stylistically consistent narrative cinema but as a way of selling the virtue of cinema as an experience in and of itself. Mythical epics such as *Prince Valiant* (1954), *Helen of Troy* (1956), and *The Magic Sword* (1962) provided studios with seemingly natural vehicles to showcase the latest developments in Technicolor and widescreen technology, while fantasy musicals like *The 5,000 Fingers of Dr. T* (1953) (with a screenplay penned by children's author Dr. Seuss), *Brigadoon* (1954), and *Doctor Dolittle* (1967) allowed a similar demonstration of the latest innovations in practical special effects, set, and costume design. These films met with mixed fortune at the box office, with some achieving pleasing financial returns for their backers and others leading to somewhat infamous flops. Yet, regardless of its effectiveness, the strategy pursued by the mainstream studios concentrated fantasy film production on a number of high-cost (and thus high-risk) releases designed to garner the attention of audiences through the sheer scope and scale of filmmaking on display.

As the major studios experimented with both the technical and experiential possibilities of fantasy filmmaking, a new generation of independent producers making inroads into the industry also brought fresh new ideas and practices to the genre. Inspired by a form of pulp literature popularized within magazines like *Weird Tales* (1923–1954) and *The Magazine of Fantasy and Science Fiction* (1949–), independent producers working in partnership with the majors through a series of distribution partnerships and coproduction deals brought to the big screen stories that were themselves first conceived as low-cost alternatives to the cinema in the first place. This cycle of "sword and sorcery" films struck a chord for the kind of innovative experience they offered to spectators. Films such as *The Golden Blade* (1953), *Jack the Giant Killer* (1962), and *The Magic Sword* (1962) sought to deliver fantasy set-pieces over detailed plot and characterization, providing a unique subgenre that differentiated itself from the mainstream norm. Influenced by a variety of sweeping industrial changes, the goal of producers working on both major studio releases and more esoteric fringe productions was to create a style of fantasy cinema that would dazzle spectators not just through the imaginative act of telling impossible stories onscreen, but by using such narratives as a relative breeding ground for special effects and spectacular experiences.

Postclassical fantasy cinema can therefore be considered as a partial return to the kind of commercial filmmaking favored in the first few decades of cinema. Instead of following on from the example set by classical Hollywood and continuing to perfect the art of telling fantasy stories using a continuity filmmaking style, postclassical fantasy films allowed increasingly for moments in their storytelling that reasserted a perhaps more primal relationship with the spectator that resembled the magic shows and early trick films of the late nineteenth century. This shift into an arguably more presentational form of fantasy spectacle need not necessarily be seen as a regressive step made by the industry. Rather, it can be viewed simply as an attempt to offer a different kind of cinematic experience. By using fantasy films as narrative platforms from which to entertain spectators with an impressive display of impossible circumstances onscreen, producers hoped to do more than just eradicate or ignore the specifics of their storytelling style. Instead, they wanted to punctuate, accentuate, and adapt fantasy cinema to provide greater opportunities for the spectator to engage in a somewhat ephemeral sensation that is often referred to in both popular and academic discussions as an experience of *wonder*.

As David Butler has previously observed, the term *wonder*, or *wonder film*, was initially a very popular descriptor used by promoters within both the silent and classical eras of Hollywood to describe a relatively niche but certainly popular cycle of filmmaking devoted to the presentation of special effects.[1] The term was not necessarily genre-specific in its usage but was instead applied to a variety of film examples in which the assumed pleasure the spectator would take from the film emerged from their ability to witness rare, unusual, or spectacular sights onscreen, whether that be the "wonder" in watching a giant gorilla burst through the iconic jungle gates of *King Kong* (1933) or the "wonder" of an elaborate action set-piece like the famous chariot race from *Ben Hur* (1959). As Hollywood incorporated more and more techniques involved in the production and distribution of the wonder film throughout the postclassical age, the term began to lose its currency as a useful marketing term, largely because a significant number of the mainstream productions had, in effect, become wonder films. This is particularly true of the fantasy genre. By the mid-1970s, the production of fantasy fiction became essentially a subgenre in the production of wonder cinema. Taking advantage of the perceived overlaps between what fantasy films offered spectators and what cinema more broadly might be able to offer if it prioritized visual spectacle, special effects and technology above all else, postclassical producers sought to drawn upon the harmonious relationship between the fantasy storytelling form and their desire to generate an imaginative thrill in seeing certain moments appear on onscreen. In doing so, postclassical

Hollywood created a vast subculture of special effects aficionados and at-home experts who expressed their enthusiasm for experiencing these moments of wonder onscreen through a mixture of scientific inquiry and quasi-mystic appreciation, as audiences struggled to decide whether they wanted to know how such moments were achieved, or whether to simply attribute the power of wonder to the overall magic of cinema.[2]

The decision made on the part of Hollywood's producers to create wondrous fantasy films was by no means ill-considered or miscalculated. The experience of wonder has been associated with fantasy storytelling since its earliest origins, forming not only part of the audience's attempt to articulate the unique pleasures available in their experiences of the genre but part of fantasy's critical vocabulary as well. Kenneth J. Zahorski and Robert H. Boyer describe the "feeling of awe and wonder" generated by fantasy literature as an essential characteristic that helps to distinguish it from other genres like horror or science-fiction,[3] while the term *wonder* was used frequently by the aesthetic philosophers of the Romantic movement, many of whom were early practitioners of fantasy fiction.[4] At its heart, wonder seems to be a potential consequence of what James Donald refers to as the propensity of fantasy imagery to encourage a "disorientation of perception."[5] Because fantasy images often disobey the laws of both logic and physics, they often possess a quality akin to something like a dream or a hallucination. Yet, at the same time, they are real images rather than subjective apparitions, requiring the spectator to notice that exciting (and sometimes bewildering) gap that exists between *seeing* and *believing* that seems to only really be possible within the context of the visual arts. Christian Metz has previously referred to this quality in the context of cinema as a "paradoxical hallucination."[6] Cinematic images are real in the sense that, unlike a dream or delusion, they do actually exist in the physical world. Yet, like a dream, the experience of cinema is able to present sensory scenarios with no physical substance or form, to which we react as if they were more than simply graphic illusions. Wonder articulates that experience of perceptual dissonance, offering itself as a potential response to the natural hesitancy we might feel when confronted with impossible images that we know cannot be real but are perceived as if they are. It is therefore a reaction wedded to the wider potential of the fantastic to offer new ways of experiencing both the world and fiction, and to access more imaginative, creative modes of perception than the kind we typically favor when experiencing everyday life.

Wonder is therefore as much about the way we approach the screen as it is a reaction to what is onscreen. The reaction is complicated and multifaceted, emerging in many forms and works and in many different ways depending on the circumstances in which it is deployed. Thanks to the efforts of Hollywood's advertisers, we tend to attribute the power of cinema to produce such an intense reaction of wonder to a mixture of technical precision and artistic vision on the part of filmmakers. We do not think, necessarily, of our own role in generating that experience of wonder through the imaginative powers we are able to bring to the screen. And, yet, wonder is not just something external, but something profoundly internal. It is located as much in a spectator's self-conscious recognition that *I am seeing something wondrous* as it is in any objective property that is wondrous onscreen. It therefore requires us all to do some imagining, just as it requires filmmakers to show us imaginative things, and this dynamic means that we participate with, create alongside and, ultimately, dream wonder into being as we process, experience, and enjoy Hollywood's varied magical sights.

In psychoanalytic theory, this type of imaginative activity is often labeled as "introjective phantasy." As the term implies, introjection is a type of phantasy that is inward-facing rather than outward-looking. It describes a range of actions that individuals take in their everyday life to understand life through a subjective lens, a process which requires a certain amount of imagination in order for certain harsh, or incomprehensible, truths to be avoided and an individual's emotional life balanced according to their everyday needs. The grandest of all these introjective phantasies is the notion of a stable and fixed identity, something that is so fundamental to our day-to-day existence and yet, as many poststructuralist theorists have been keen to point out, is as illusory a concept as any unicorn or monster we might dream up. As much as I might like to wish it, there is no *me*. I am not funny or clever. I am not irritable or anxious. I may at times display such characteristics (some more frequently than others), but there is nothing internal or external that I possess that requires me to be those things at any one time. And, yet, we all construct phantasies to some degree about who we are that then influence how we process the world around us. When I make my commute to work, I do not just process the raw sensory data around me as if I were a machine. Instead, what I perceive is as much a by-product of the ideas and values that I have developed over time after living in the world and taking on its values. Do I want to take the bus or the subway? Depending on my decision, I will likely notice more bus stops rather than I will subway stations. Do I like coffee? If so, the sight of a nearby café and the smell of a fresh pot is likely to stimulate my senses in a way that is different from other sights and sounds that might not. Do I prefer being too hot or too cold? Depending on the answer to that question, my walk to work will be a different experience if it is sunny or if it is snowing.

When asking such questions, I am doing more than simply trying to forge a picture of the world filtered through my own subjective desires and tastes. I am creating those very same characteristics at the same time. After all, it is only by seeing, smelling, and tasting coffee that I can decide whether I am someone who likes coffee or not. It is only by taking the bus and the subway once or twice that I can then decide which I prefer as an experience, and which is more likely to get me to work on time. The phantasies I conjure in response to these external stimuli I experience do not help me to simply understand the world. First and foremost, they help me to understand who I am. I build a picture of myself through different phantasies I create by a process of introjection, allowing external qualities perceived in the world to feel as though they belong to me. In the words of Melanie Klein, I allow the world to be "taken into the self."[7] This is what is meant by an introjective phantasy. It is this capacity of the subject to take in and process the experiences of the world, to make a bus stop into *my* bus stop and a collection of streets into a commute, that not only creates the necessary conditions for the growth of an individual's sense of identity but becomes a key aspect of their later creative and cultural life.

Applying this understanding of introjection to the context of fantasy cinema helps to shed light on the nature of the imaginative experience that might result in a positive embrace of wonder as the solution to the hesitancy we feel in the face of the fantastic. Fantasy images do not solely ask us to imagine something onto them; they asks us to take aspects from them. We can imaginatively consume the external qualities we perceive onscreen in a way analogous to the way we consume air or food, bringing them inside us to alter our perception of what we see in turn. In the case of postclassical fantasy cinema, if we think of the experience of wonder as an imaginative way of responding to the events taking place onscreen, then it is not enough to simply assign certain images a wondrous quality and assume that they naturally generate the reaction often articulated within discussion of special effects. Instead, we must also understand how the phantasies surrounding that perception of wonder are first encouraged by the film form, brought into the spectator through a process of introjection, and then brought to bear to understand and appreciate what is happening onscreen. In short, the sights of wonder that postclassical cinema conjures allow us to access a wondrous way of seeing.

To understand this process of introjection and how, in many cases, it may be key to the feeling of wonder fantasy films evoke, I wish to examine a range of postclassical fantasy films that, in their own way, demonstrate what is at stake in understanding such filmmaking strategies in terms of their potential to offer an experience of the fantastic. To do this, I wish to start with a perhaps unlikely and atypical case study, namely *Harvey* (1950), a studio film produced toward the beginning of this era that perhaps has more in common with our last case study in the previous chapter, *It's a Wonderful Life* (1946), as it does with the postclassical fantasy filmmaking that would follow it. However, despite not being a "wonder film" in the commercial sense of the term, I argue that what makes *Harvey* such an interesting fantasy film to analyze is that, without displaying anything particularly miraculous onscreen, the film encourages its spectator to forge a series of phantasies in relation to its fiction that fundamentally effects their perception of what is seen. It is a film whose potential to offer an experience of the fantastic derives entirely from the process of introjection it encourages. This feature of the film highlights the role of the fantastic within the more effects-heavy fantasy films like *Mary Poppins* (1964) and *The Golden Voyage of Sinbad* (1973) that followed in its wake. With each of these examples, I will consider how these films encourage introjective phantasies that influence how the spectator perceives the set design, costuming, and visual effects, and in what space the pleasure of wonder within such films resides. Most fundamentally, I will examine how the experiences such works offer spectators are distinguished from their classical Hollywood counterparts and establish a distinct identity for the postclassical fantasy film.

The Fantastic and Wonder: Introjective Phantasy in *Harvey*

If the Hollywood fantasy film can be broadly defined as a genre that presents circumstances onscreen that defy reality, then *Harvey* fails this particular litmus test. In contrast to the effects-heavy productions that would come to dominate the postclassical era of fantasy filmmaking, *Harvey* features nothing onscreen that might be considered to be impossible or contradictory to the laws of reality. Instead, through its comedic interrogation of prevailing notions of sanity and insanity, *Harvey* tells a rather down-to-earth narrative that, at first glance, would seem better located within a history of Hollywood farce than it would within a study of fantasy cinema. And, yet, despite its largely real-life concerns and locations, the film was consistently reviewed at the time of its release not as a social satire but as a "whimsical fantasy" (*Box Office*), a "compelling world of fantasy" (*Film Daily*), and as a "fable of an invisible, pixie rabbit" (*Variety*).[8] *Harvey* is therefore a surprisingly useful place to start to explore the function of introjection in the spectator's experience of postclassical fantasy cinema. If a film like *Harvey* could allow spectators to feel a quasi-sense of wonder, then that suggests something about the imaginative investment in phantasy such a sensation is reliant on creating that is worth examining if wonder's role in the special effects–laden cinema that would shortly follow is to be better understood.

Harvey tells the story of Elwood P. Dowd (James Stewart), a kind, amiable, and wealthy gentleman living in small-town America who just happens to believe that his best friend is a giant, invisible "pooka" rabbit named Harvey, from whom the film takes its title. In other fantasy films, this set up might be used to introduce a narrative wherein the protagonist's belief in such an outlandish notion is affirmed through the introduction of a real magic character into the narrative. Indeed, this is exactly the premise of *Francis* (1950), a film released in the same year as *Harvey* about WWII soldier Peter Stirling's (Donald O'Connor) relationship to a magical talking mule that served as the basis for a number of successful sequels. Yet, while Peter's belief in *Francis* is confirmed to be accurate within the context of the fiction thanks to a voiceover device used to allow a mule to seemingly speak onscreen, *Harvey* never once offers spectators similar assurances that Elwood's rabbit friend is anything more than a delusion conjured up by its protagonist. Instead, it is Elwood's seemingly mistaken belief in the invisible "pooka" that serves as the source of the film's dramatic and comedic tension. His wealthy sister Veta (Josephine Hull) and niece Myrtle Mae (Victoria Horne) are so tired of being ostracized from their community by Elwood's constant attempts to introduce Harvey to everyone he meets that they resolve to have him committed to the local sanatorium, a plot that begins a chain of mishaps and misunderstandings that propel the narrative forward. Along the way, Veta and Myrtle learn that, as much as they might find Elwood's belief in Harvey difficult to accept, it is ultimately Elwood's friendship with the invisible rabbit that is responsible for their relative's amiable nature and generous spirit. Instead of trying to cure him, the family resolve to accept Elwood for who he is—Harvey and all—and to see his belief in the invisible pooka not as a dangerous hallucination that prevents him from seeing reality properly, but as a useful tool that provides a way of viewing the world that they come to admire.

If the fantastic components of *Harvey*'s narrative consisted solely of its thematic celebration of faith over reason, then that might not be enough for audiences both at the time and since its release to demarcate the film as a work of fantasy. However, the film goes one step further than merely encouraging the spectator to sympathize with its delusional protagonist. Instead, *Harvey* offers the spectator a way of approaching its narrative events that matches own Elwood's magical way of seeing the world. Compare, for example, two small instances in the film where Elwood is seen to gesture toward the presence of his invisible rabbit friend onscreen, one toward the very start of the film and the other at its climax. At the start of the film, Elwood is seen walking out of his home to be greeted by a bike messenger, a moment which introduces the spectator to the idea of Harvey the rabbit. Performing a series of erratic, unexplained movements, Elwood's behavior is framed as being strange and unusual, a feature highlighted through the decision to shoot the scene through a series of asymmetrical frames that lend a sense of unease or imbalance to the otherwise mundane setting of a quiet neighborhood in small-town USA (fig. 3.1). The technique is repeated throughout the film, creating the impression of Elwood appearing to be speaking to thin air as the framing of each shot evokes an absence rather than a presence within the mise-en-scène (figs. 3.2 and 3.3). However, by the end of the film, very similar filmmaking techniques are used to denote something else entirely. In the film's final shot (fig. 3.4), Elwood places his arm around nothing and walks off into the sunset. Framed asymmetrically again, the soundtrack is triumphant and positive, the lighting soft and atmospheric, and the spectator seems asked to perceive something very different in these closing moments. An absence becomes a presence as the film offers not a vision not of Elwood walking off alone but a vision of Harvey and Elwood walking into the sunset together.

Moments like this are not rare; they appear throughout the film. There is an instance early on in the narrative, for example, when a hat left by Elwood is discovered with two rabbit-ear shaped holes cut into the rim, much to the befuddlement of the sanatorium workers. As the hat is lifted up, the spectator is encouraged to imagine a creature like Harvey wearing it, rather than simply seeing a hat with two holes in its rim. In another brief section, hospital orderly Mr. Wilson reads from an encyclopedia entry on pookas to try to understand Elwood's delusion, only to suddenly stumble over the words "how are you Mr. Wilson?" as if they

Figures 3.1–3.4. Elwood talks to empty screen space throughout *Harvey* (1950).

had appeared on the page by magic. Each moment like this encourages the spectator to at least entertain the notion of Harvey's existence, even if simply to enjoy a pleasure in the potential comedy or imaginative appeal contained in such an idea. Slowly, the film starts to build toward a dynamic in which the spectator is asked to reject the more obvious rational interpretation of what is taking place onscreen in favor of something impossible yet preferable. Not only that, but the spectator is encouraged to adopt a new way of looking at the events onscreen, one in which the empty screen space becomes something that signifies not an absence but a presence. By the end of the film, choosing to "see" Harvey onscreen as he walks off into the sunset with Elwood amounts to accepting a tacit deal offered by the film itself. The spectator sacrifices rationality in exchange for pleasure, and plausibility for frivolity and fun, allowing them not just to recognize intellectually that Elwood is better off with Harvey but to feel it experientially too. In the same way as the narrative makes it clear that Elwood's ability to see Harvey affords him a better life, the spectator is encouraged to also choose to see Harvey onscreen because it will make for a more pleasurable experience of watching the film.

The empty screen space used to denote the invisible rabbit within *Harvey* therefore functions throughout the film as a device somewhat akin to a literary technique Christine Brooke-Rose refers to as "under-determination," a strategy used in literary fantasy to achieve a sense of the fantastic through the withholding of key narrative information.[9] An example of such a technique would be a story such as Edgar Allan Poe's "The Fall of the House of Usher" (1839), a tale which withholds explanations as to how certain coincidences and events happen in the narrative in order to encourage readers to speculate toward supernatural explanations. A creaking house becomes haunted, a cold wind becomes a ghost, and a simple sentence like *something very strange happened last Wednesday* becomes license for a whole range of imaginative explanations as a result of the deliberate ambiguity contained within the description. *Harvey* operates in a similar manner, albeit through means that are specific to its status as a work of cinema. With *Harvey*, it is not the interpretation of language that is at stake, but the way in which phantasy is used by the spectator to inform their perception of individual moments onscreen. The spectator is asked to undergo a fundamental reversal of how they see the screen, moving from *not seeing* Harvey in the empty space to *seeing* Harvey in those very same or similar instances. In doing so, the film transforms from an otherwise nominally naturalistic (albeit heavily stylized) drama to an overt work of fantasy.

This shift from *not seeing* to *seeing* Harvey comes about through a recalibration of the spectator's introjective phantasies. In our daily lives, whether we are witnessing something mundane or something extraordinary, we are conditioned to contextualize the specific details of what we see, hear, smell, or touch in any particular moment against a set of imagined rules, principles, and conventions. These principles are not imagined in the same way we might imagine a unicorn or an invisible rabbit. They have a certain objective basis that distinguishes them from a pure act of imaginative speculation because they originate from perceiving certain external qualities in the world. Yet, at the same time, they are imagined in that they allow us to not only just see the world but perceive ideas about the world in certain sights and sounds that are, at least partially, the product of our own imaginations. A leaf falling from a tree may affirm to me the presence of gravity, but I do not see gravity when I perceive such an act occurring. Instead, I introject a quality from the world that allows me to then see the world for more than it actually is in any given moment. Likewise, a friend arriving late may confirm a belief that they are often tardy, but I can never see a tardy friend. I can only imagine one. Our introjected phantasies therefore help make the world seem more than it ever is at any one moment, making us feel safe and secure when the world matches up to our introjected phantasies, and surprising or shocking us when what we witness fails to match up to what we have imagined to be possible and not possible. This is because the ideas we bring to the world are never *in* the world but are always additional imaginative responses that help us to perceive it differently, embellishing what we see at any one moment through a process of introjection.

It is tempting to see cinema as operating in exactly the same way, working to either conform to our preexisting understanding of reality by allowing the introjected phantasies of the spectator to match with the images onscreen, or shocking them by showing them things that cannot be real. However, such a binary dualism does not actually make a great deal of sense if we consider some of the key factors that distinguish the process of watching cinema from seeing things occur in everyday life. Cinematic images, after all, have sensory qualities that are quite distinct from reality. They are flat, projected onto a screen, mediated through the presence of a camera reliant upon the basic optical trickery of projecting a certain frame rate, and filmed intentionally by someone to show to others. They are not natural, realistic, or directly comparable with everyday life. And, yet, as Robert T. Ederwein has previously argued, Hollywood cinema especially seems to encourage spectators somehow not to see cinema for the inherent illusion that it is, but as if those images possessed a physical reality that they clearly do not have.[10] Spectators are therefore much more like Elwood at the beginning of *Harvey* than the film's initial narrative dynamic seems to suggest. In the same way as Elwood's worldview seems to rely on him denying some rather obvious truths about the world, the spectator's approach to the raw sensory data cinema claims as an accurate representation of reality also requires a vast degree of denial and obfuscation. What is actually witnessed when we see Elwood speaking to thin air is a manipulation of light, color, and sound projected onto a screen. But what we see is a man talking to himself in the middle of a street, rather than an actor performing a role on a set, or even a flat image of an actor on a screen. The sense of distance achieved between Elwood's way of seeing the world onscreen and the spectator is therefore largely through an imagined construct. Because we are busy imagining that these images look and seem real, we are unable to imagine the possibility that Harvey the rabbit exists.

If there is no logical reason why we need to keep imagining that what we see when we watch cinema is real in order for us to obtain either pleasure or meaning from it, then this liberates both the way we might approach the screen and the external values we introject from it. In everyday life, the realization that what you are currently witnessing is, in fact, a temporary illusion is likely to cause far more distress than comfort. Knowing something is a hallucination blocks us from looking at reality as it actually is, prompting us into a rather traumatic encounter alluded to in psychoanalytic discussions of both psychosis and the uncanny in which we cannot trust our own senses.[11] Yet, because *Harvey* is a film—because it is not, nor has it ever been, an object whose images need to conform to the standards of three-dimensional reality—then the realization that what is happening onscreen does not have to conform with the standards of everyday life becomes an invitation to view it differently. The absence of truth onscreen becomes not an absence of meaning, but a recognition that there are more profound truths to be found in watching the screen's contents as if they are not real rather than watching them as if they are.

The experience the spectator is asked to undertake in *Harvey* is therefore not a shift from viewing the screen as reality to viewing it as a fantasy film but a shift from one kind of introjective phantasy activity to another. As Lia M. Hotchkiss argues, phantasies of introjection function within the act of film spectatorship to provide a bridge between "inside, outside and subject."[12] Just like their function in early life, they make the objective and the subjective one and the same by allowing us to take in external qualities perceived in the world as if we possessed them for ourselves, giving rise to the feeling we often get from watching films that our eyes are the camera and the screen is the world. *Harvey* seeks to shatter that central phantasy. Instead of wishing us to introject the qualities of externality and objectivity the screen offers us to make its images seem more like reality, the film instead allows spectators to take in qualities found elsewhere onscreen to imagine themselves into a point of view more in line with the film's protagonist, who sees things that nobody else can see. This might seem an unachievable task given that inhabiting Elwood's worldview requires such a state of denial about some of the basic truths about reality. And, yet, there are certain instances in our everyday lives when we are very willing to set aside our primary concern with seeing the world as an objective reality in favor of an alternative mode of perception that acknowledges that what we see is not necessarily what somebody else might see. During acts of creativity, for example, we do not imagine that the way we are currently seeing the world is the same as everybody else. Quite the contrary, we imagine that we are seeing the world in a way that makes us unique as individuals, and we relish that feeling of subjectivity as part of the thrill that comes from being creative. Creativity gives us license to temporarily displace the basic introjective phantasies governing our daily lives that seek to create a stable and ordered reality and construct an alternative phantasy that what we see is an expression of who we are.

In *Harvey*, the experience of the fantastic serves a similar function. Elwood provides the emotional and intellectual stimulation to engage in an act of introjective phantasy that rejects the need for the things witnessed to be perceived as they were reality, and encourages instead a relationship based on what Elwood's way of viewing can provide as a source of pleasure. An example of this dynamic can be witnessed in a key sequence within the film in which Elwood takes two staff members from the local sanatorium who have been appointed to look after him for the evening to his local bar. The people, Dr. Sanderson (Charles Drake) and Miss Kelly (Peggy Dow), seem to adopt a somewhat ambivalent relationship with Elwood's delusion that is neither hostile nor overly supportive. As health workers, they find it difficult to view Elwood's belief as anything more than a harmful delusion. Yet, they also like Elwood as a person and so find themselves drawn to his way of living despite the rational or logical problems it presents. The scene in question finds the three characters standing in the back alley of a bar engaging in conversation with one another, at which point Elwood launches into a somewhat reverent and poetic monologue in which he articulates the pleasure he feels when he gets to do what he loves the most: introduce people to his friend Harvey. As Elwood explains, he and Harvey like to hang around in bars because it gives them the opportunity to sit and speak with strangers, many of whom use the environment as a forum to unload their problems, concerns, and desires. Elwood introduces them to Harvey as a means of providing solace to their fears, and hope for their dreams. Because the notion of Harvey the invisible rabbit is "bigger" and "grander" than any idea they might be struggling with in their own lives, Elwood liberates them from any concern that their inner phantasy lives might be somehow blocking or preventing them from living successfully in reality, allowing Elwood and Harvey to "warm" themselves on these "golden moments" in which they get to watch people feel empowered to dream in their presence.

The speech is obviously key in articulating the film's central message that an essential part of the human experience lies in our ability to imagine, and that to deny someone their phantasies is to deny them their identity. Yet, its effect on Dr. Sanderson and Miss Kelly seems to highlight a perhaps more fundamental issue that is at stake in the film, one that speaks not just to the intellectual resolution offered by the film's narrative but a deeper emotional resolution as to how the spectator watches *Harvey* as a work of fantasy. Sanderson's and Kelly's function in the scene seems largely to operate as onscreen spectators to Elwood's magical musings (figs. 3.5 and 3.6). Sanderson stands while Kelly literally sits down to listen to him speak, and the camera cuts between the three characters all in a wide shot to a series of midrange shots and close-ups on Elwood's face and body. For perhaps the first time in the entire film, Elwood is given time and space onscreen to express how he feels without being confronted onscreen with the judgment of others who disagree with him (fig. 3.7). This, in turn, allows certain features of Elwood's worldview to be emphasized that might otherwise go unnoticed. The close-ups do not make his words clearer or his story more plausible. However, they do highlight the contented smile on his face as he speaks of Harvey, as well as a level of contentment and peace he finds in the world as he casually takes a seat on the ground and looks up to Sanderson and Kelly (fig. 3.8). The smiles on their faces echo his, as Elwood enacts the same dynamic in them that he describes in others. By talking about Harvey, he makes them feel better about the world itself, allowing them to see it with a smile on their face rather than through the concerned expressions that they exhibited but moments before.

What takes place in this exchange of glances is a dramatized process of introjection. Much in the same way that a child learns to look at the world differently by believing themselves to be in the presence of "good" and "bad" objects, here, Sanderson and Kelly are performing a relatively simple imaginative act that nevertheless completely alters their perception of what they see. They believe themselves to be seeing something good, and so choose to look at the world positively as a result. This exchange of glances therefore encourages a similarly admirable reaction from the spectator. As Elwood speaks of things that seem admirable and positive, despite not being real, the spectator is encouraged, like Sanderson and Kelly, to adopt a different mentality toward what they are seeing. Instead of dismissing Elwood's way of viewing the world, the scene encourages the spectator to take in the positive qualities they perceive in him and alter the way they view the world as a consequence. Each shot of Elwood looking at the world brings the spectator closer to him, both physically and emotionally, until eventually he is placed in a tight, lingering close-up that seems designed to let the spectator do what Sanderson and Kelly are doing: to imagine seeing the world through Elwood's eyes. What was once distanced becomes immediate and what was inaccessible becomes accessible, as the spectator takes in the qualities perceived onscreen to, in turn, change the way the screen is perceived.

The reversal of perspective *Harvey* offers spectators is therefore rooted in a pleasure in seeing that taps into certain ingrained pleasures within both the fantasy genre and the wider creative impulse more generally. Fantasy fiction is often described as a form of storytelling that has the capacity to remind us of the imaginative quality of our own senses. Eric S. Rabkin describes the genre as founded on the revelation of "perspective," a description that acknowledges the genre's historic function in challenging a worldview based on rationality alone and celebrating alternative worldviews based on the pleasures of the imagination.[13] However, while overwhelmingly this function of fantasy has been analyzed from the perspective of the genre's narrative and thematic considerations, *Harvey* also performs this function through the very relationship it achieves between the spectator's phantasies and their perception of the screen. In a key scene within the film, Elwood's sister Veta launches into a rather bombastic speech about the difference between a painting and a photograph, a speech that serves as a metaphor for the wider approach the film asks the spectator to take to its own fictional events. As Veta argues, the photograph shows only the "reality." A painting, however, "shows the dream behind it." Veta's argument sets up reality as a poorer version of a dream, something which focuses so heavily on an image's value as an objective representation that it denies the perceiver space to permit the

Figures 3.5–3.8. Elwood is given a moment to explain Harvey to Miss Kelly and Dr. Sanderson.

imagination to color and, ultimately, alter the world according to their own personality. It is somewhat ironic, then, that Veta makes this speech while standing behind a painting that she is unaware depicts Elwood and Harvey (fig. 3.9). The painting is the only visual representation of Harvey the rabbit within the entire film, and the way it is shown in the background of an otherwise photographed shot of Veta mirrors the very discrepancy between it and the reality she alludes to in her speech. If spectators wish to only focus on the photographic elements of the frame, they are required to look away from Harvey and Elwood and toward Veta. Alternatively, if they wish to focus on the painting, they must ignore the photographic elements in favor of an image that displays Elwood's own perception of world. One way of viewing forgoes a sense of reality; the other denies the spectator access to the sense of individuality, creativity, and play achieved in the image of the rabbit. One is a phantasy that insists on sight being reactive. The other allows sight itself to become an expressive force.

Figure 3.9. Veta explains the difference between "mechanical" photographs and paintings filled with dreams.

Harvey interrogates these ideas surrounding the role phantasy plays in individual perception overtly as part of the thematic interests of its narrative. However, what it ultimately encourages the spectator to participate in—to enjoy seeing, and to understand sight as an ultimately subjective process—becomes a crucial component of an experience that seems at the forefront of other more obvious examples of fantasy filmmaking produced during this era. When we think of the special effects–laden kind of fantasy cinema that would shortly come to dominate this era, we think of a filmmaking style dependent on producing a visceral rush in the act of seeing in its spectator. This is why the response to a film like *Harvey* is so important to understand. The film does not feature elements onscreen that possess some objective quality of wonder. Instead, the film rejects the dogmatic pursuit of objectivity as a way of perceiving film fiction. It asks instead for its meaning to be found through the introjective phantasy that sight is subjective, and to use that phantasy as a way of approaching the film-viewing experience to imaginatively mold and shape the nature of what is seen. Whether it be a belief in a particular ideology, religion, or ethical code, we all have our own six-foot, three-and-a-half-inch tall, giant, invisible rabbits that informs the way we see the world. *Harvey* allows us to befriend them once more.

The Fantastic and Idealization: The Wonder of *Mary Poppins*

Having theorized the importance introjective phantasy plays in the experience of an otherwise quasi-naturalistic fantasy film like *Harvey*, it is now time to consider how introjection functions as part of the feeling of wonder invited from some of the more effects-heavy productions typical of postclassical fantasy cinema. To do this, it seems almost necessary to turn to perhaps the most famous example of postclassical fantasy filmmaking, Disney's *Mary Poppins*. Both a commercial and critical success upon its release, *Mary Poppins* has remained a perennial favorite within the canon of Western cinema culture. Adjusted for inflation, the film is, at the time of writing, the twenty-seventh highest grossing film of all time at the US box office and holds the record for having received more Academy nominations and awards than any other production released by the Disney Studio to date.[14] Telling the story of the eponymous magical nanny's (Julie Andrews) adventures with the Banks family and known for its collection of famous song and dance numbers such as "Chim Chim

Cher-ee," "Step in Time," and "Let's Go Fly a Kite," *Mary Poppins* was celebrated at the time of its release not only for its achievement in blending elements of traditional photography with the latest advances in color processing, animation, and optical effects, but also for the way it used these "high-flying dreams and Technicolor fantasies" in order to function as a "musical fantasy."[15] These comments seem to capture an aspect of the film that, for many, allows *Mary Poppins* to remain such a vivid example of postclassical fantasy filmmaking. The film is as much an imaginative as it is a technical delight, entertaining audiences with its now famous images that seems to enhance the film's thematic treatment of ideas of creativity and individuality. It feels imaginative to simply watch *Mary Poppins*, almost as if the act of looking at its images could compare to the kite-flying, game-playing, and jolly holidays that the film presents onscreen as it creates an experience of wonder through a series of introjective phantasies forged in relation to what we see, and what we wish to bring to the screen.

In this desire to encourage spectators to adopt a certain attitude toward its narrative and special effects, *Mary Poppins* reveals itself, in fact, to be a very similar film to the far more austere and down-to-earth *Harvey*. Like *Harvey*, *Mary Poppins* tells the story of the intrusion of a magical character into a setting that is otherwise meant to represent reality. Like *Harvey*, these moments of intrusion are often played for laughs, the narrative pausing repeatedly to allow characters to rub their eyes, faint, or otherwise express their bewilderment and shock in what they are seeing. And, like *Harvey*, *Mary Poppins* has a narrative in which a supernatural being enacts a shift in perspective among the other characters who come into contact with it. These similarities are not purposeful, of course, but neither are they purely coincidental given the nature of what both narratives are interested in exploring. Rather than being solely interested in the power of magic to change the world physically, both *Harvey* and *Mary Poppins* seem equally invested in the idea that magic has the power to change the personalities and values of those who encounter it. They use their supernatural beings as catalysts for a wider change in attitude in the societies that encounter them, whether this be in the form of Elwood's relatives that come to embrace the positives in his way of seeing the world, or the Banks family who learn to live life differently thanks to the arrival of their magical nanny.

This shift in perspective is not just limited to one or a small number of characters in *Mary Poppins* either. Instead, it applies to every character in the film. Arriving from the clouds out of nowhere to look after the dysfunctional Banks family, Mary uses magic as a means of mending the broken bonds between families and coworkers, inspiring a change in behavior in others so that her presence is no longer needed. She teaches Jane (Karen Dotrice) and Michael (Matthew Garber) to channel their misspent youthful energies into acts of social consciousness by using her imaginative stories to make them see things "past the edge of their nose." She teaches George (David Tomlinson) and Winnifred (Glynis Johns) to appreciate the pleasure of being with others rather than focusing solely on their proper role and societal function. George learns to replace his obsession with order and regularity with a delight in nonsense and spontaneity and Winnifred, in perhaps the film's most problematic character arc, learns to be a more attentive mother by sacrificing her political ambitions, an act symbolized onscreen when her suffragette sash is used as a ribbon for her children's kite. For characters who have abandoned a sense of being fully in one moment, the sight of Mary's magic reminds them to see life as a realm full of imaginative possibility rather than a world of physical and social laws. Even Mr. Dawes Sr. (Dick Van Dyke), owner of the Fidelity Fiduciary Bank, learns to relax his stance on hard work and prudent investment once he develops a penchant for wordplay and puns. These changes to the film's characters rather than its space mean that, when Mary leaves behind Cherry Tree Lane, she leaves behind a world very different from the world into which she arrived. She has changed nothing physically, at least not permanently. What she has changed are the attitudes of the people she meets.

This presentation of magic not only contextualizes Mary's acts of impossibility within an overall narrative framework that seeks to highlight their usefulness to those characters around her. It also mediates the way in which the film's special effects and impossible scenarios are presented onscreen. Throughout *Mary Poppins*, characters constantly express disbelief and confusion, and offer rational explanations for the impossible situations they experience, making a virtue out of the fact that Mary's magic requires people to question the basic assumptions upon which they have based their entire understanding of reality. This presentation of magic can be traced back to elements in P. L. Travers's source novels, which likewise present Mary as a somewhat strange and ambiguous figure who is more often seen through the eyes of characters who do not understand her. However, the fact that this trait survives so prominently in Disney's adaptation is as much evidence of the creative and commercial strategy underpinning the film's production as it is a reflection of any strong desire to remain faithful to its literary original. Even hagiographic accounts of the film's production offered by the Disney Studio in films like *Saving Mr. Banks* (2013) have been forthcoming in the lack of concern displayed within the creative team in remaining faithful to Travers's original books. On the contrary, Travers's novels were seen as suitable for adaptation not because of the specific details of her narratives, but for the opportunity presented within those stories to create a visceral experience of wonder onscreen. Travers herself stated in numerous interviews that she preferred to align her novels to the Romantic traditions of wonder rather than to her contemporaries writing within the world of fantasy fiction, and scholars such as Nicole Didicher have identified Travers's recurrent interest in her characters' perception of magical events as one of the key strategies that helps her books achieve this goal.[16] Disney's *Mary Poppins* is designed to emulate that experience, adopting similar techniques to provoke a reaction from its spectator not unlike that of the characters experiencing Mary's magic.

Such a dynamic is cemented in the very first moments in which Mary appears. Disappointed that their father has not taken any of their suggestions to heart in search of a suitable new nanny for them, Jane and Michael sit forlorn in their nursery, looking out over the long line of candidates whose pristine appearances seem to confirm their worst fears about what kind of guardian they are about to be given. As they both peer down from the nursery window, a high-angle shot is employed to present the events that follow in a way that matches the position of the two characters in relation to what is taking place (fig. 3.10). As a gust of wind is seen to magically blow the rest of the applicants away, Mary descends from the clouds and arrives at the front door, the shots of the event constantly mediated both through the perspective of the children as the film crosscuts between them in the nursery looking on in disbelief and the event itself as it is occurring (fig. 3.11). This establishes a paradigm that will be continued throughout the rest of the film. In other set-pieces such as the "Spoonful of Sugar" sequence (figs. 3.12 and 3.13), Mary is continually presented through the eyes of others who witness her magic, allowing the filmmaking to exemplify the indecision, surprise, shock, and pleasure they might feel in relation to the magic that is conjured onscreen. The Banks family become, in effect, akin to Dr. Sanderson and Miss Kelly in Harvey—watching something "good" happen before their eyes and dramatizing the introjected emotion they are able to take from it—while Mary becomes analogous to Elwood or indeed Harvey the rabbit. She is the locus of the film's sense of the fantastic, and the source of both the narrative's and the spectator's fascination.

The strategies witnessed in Mary's opening moments onscreen are reminiscent of some of the strategies examined within psychoanalytic theories presented by Christian Metz and Laura Mulvey.[17] Somewhat akin to the traditional function of the fetishized female form in mainstream cinema, Mary exhumes a quality of looked-at-ness, becoming an object of fascination rather than a character with which the spectator is asked to align themselves with emotionally or intellectually. However, in contrast to the way in which such strategies are discussed within feminist theories of the gaze, the end result of these visual strategies is not to deny Mary a sense of agency at the expense of a controlling, powerful mastery of the image. Instead, the spectator's difficulty in identifying with Mary stems precisely from the abundance of agency she embodies. While Jane and Michael are presented as characters existing in a world of defined rules and regulations, Mary radiates an exotic and desirable quality through her powers to alter reality and do things that real characters cannot do. That distanced position between the spectator and Mary does not deny her a sense of power, as in the case of the objectified female form. If anything, it becomes the source of her power. While Jane and Michael function as effective stand-ins for the spectator because they are limited and restrained by reality, Mary is an object of fascination through the very lack of limitation she seems to embody. Her identity is tied to her ability to create wonder, both for the spectator and for the rest of the characters who encounter her, and this feeds into the way the film invites and encourages spectators to view the special effects she nominally creates onscreen within the context of the narrative.

The pleasure in watching a character like Mary, who seems to lack either the social or physical limitations that ground the rest of us to an interconnected, objective world, is rooted in some of the most fundamental anxieties individuals have in response to their own sense of identity. Born into the world without an understanding that *it is a world*, children first experience life by introjecting certain external qualities they perceive in surrounding people and objects to create a phantasy that the world is somehow synonymous with the self. Freud calls this phantasy the "omnipresence of thought."[18] As this phantasy is then shattered in later childhood development, its appeal does not subside despite its obvious unsustainability. Instead, the phantasy becomes the basis for our narcissistic tendencies in later life, often displayed in moments of compulsion or anxiety when our attention is drawn to our own behaviors and needs at the expense of thinking more objectively about the fundamentally small role we play within the broader context of the surrounding world. When

Figures 3.10–3.13. Mary's magic is almost always mediated through the astonished faces of the Banks children (*Mary Poppins*, 1964).

I wear the colors of Portsmouth Football Club (my soccer team) on match day, for example, I am constructing a narcissistic phantasy that the outfit I wear will somehow effect the performance of eleven professionals kicking a ball around on a pitch. That phantasy allows me to feel that I am somewhat in control of the events as they unfold before my eyes, and shields me from the fact that—in reality—it does not matter what color

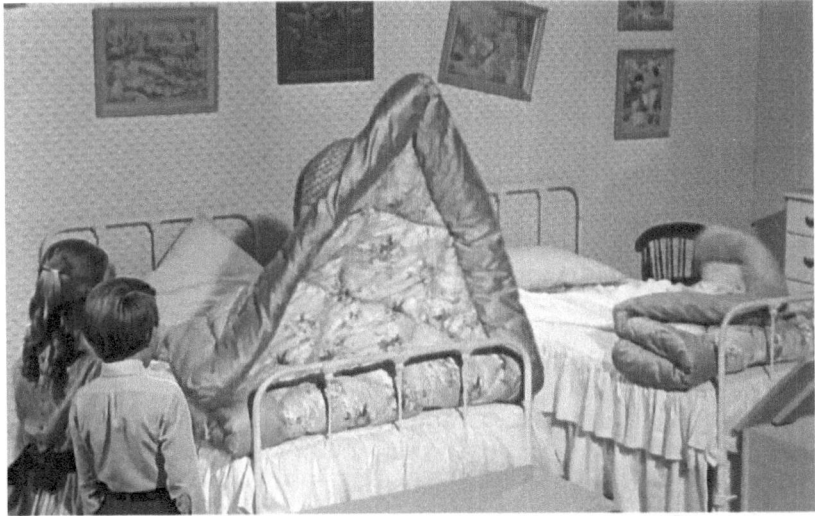

socks I choose to put on; that will not make my team play any better, or secure the likelihood of a win. I have learned this the hard way over years of supporting them. To take any comfort from such a phantasy, I must first abandon these more objective and, frankly, more rational ways of viewing the world and retreat back into a more egocentric but less nuanced understanding of the world fueled by my imagination.

As both Rosemary Jackson and Linda Hutcheon have previously argued, fantasy fiction is often able to offer a way of engaging with such narcissistic phantasies through the relationship it encourages with its characters and stories.[19] It encourages a way of thinking about narratives in which the central assertion that the world is what it is, regardless of what we would like it to be, becomes no longer true. The cause of the shattering of narcissistic thought in early life is no longer apparent, and fantasy fictions can instead embody visions of a world we would want instead, or a world molded in our own image. The same is true with a character like Mary Poppins. The reason she is such a profound object of visual spectacle and wonder is because she taps into these basic concerns relating to how we construct a sense of identity, and offers imaginary solutions to such problems. Like the ultimate narcissist, Mary constantly believes that her sheer will and determination is enough to fundamentally alter her surroundings, making the external properties of the world merely a reflection of her own desires. The only difference is that, unlike the narcissist, Mary is right. Her magic allows her to literally shape the world into whatever she wants it to be, offering a way of existing within the world that appeals to a basic narcissistic phantasy embedded within our very construction of identity. Unlike the imperfect but relatable characters who exist in the rest of the story, she is "practically perfect in every way," existing seemingly not to fulfill her own needs or desires but to help those who encounter her better understand their own.

Developing any kind of emotional or intellectual relationship with this kind of character therefore requires a rather complex form of introjection. Despite its usage in everyday parlance, narcissism is not simply the act of being obsessed with an aggrandized and inflated version of one's self. Instead, narcissism requires an individual to be able to phantasize multiple different visions of identity at the same time, and to use introjection as a means of processing and negotiating between these multiple ways of being that act of phantasy encompasses. If, for example, I become envious of a friend who earns a higher salary than me, then the narcissism involved in that reaction stems from my awareness of the difference between imagined visions of my own identity. In one phantasy, I imagine a version of who I am right now. In another, I imagine an *ideal* version of someone I would like to be. Both of these phantasies exist within my psyche and feed into my sense of identity. However, while I am able to identify strongly with one of these visions of my own identity as someone I feel I embody, I likewise feel partially separated from the ideal version of me that exists somewhere else, in an imagined space and time. As Klein argues, the idealized object "is much less integrated in the ego."[20] It is something we feel belongs to us (in the sense that it is unique to each individual) but it is not something that *is* us. Indeed, it is essential to the process of idealization that we recognize it as a phantasy. Without that feeling of separation between who we are and who we wish to be, I would cease to have the compulsion to look inward on myself in such a moment of anxiety and engage in a series of phantasies relating to my status as an individual. Narcissism therefore fuels a triad act of phantasy. It helps create an imagined concept of who someone is, an imagined concept of who someone would prefer to be, and a process of idealization by which someone imaginatively measures one vision of identity that they know is not real against another that they believe is.

Cinema is essentially a narcissistic medium. As a spectator, we are provided with what Jean-Louis Baudry describes as "the *mise-en-scène* of Plato's cave."[21] We are the center of the story world, the narrative is playing out for our benefit, and the camera seemingly exists to capture anything and everything we might need onscreen. This narcissistic way of viewing the screen is encouraged through a series of introjected phantasies that gives us a sense of an omniscient, ever-present, and controlling mastery over the image (as many feminist theorists have successfully gendered and attributed to patriarchal discourse). However, this does not happen in *Mary Poppins*. Instead of allowing the spectator to settle into a single, idealized mode of viewing that assumes the camera to be the eye and, in turn, the eye to be the source of all power, watching *Mary Poppins* essentially consists of looking at two very different kinds of images that, in turn, require two very different approaches. Throughout the majority of the film, we are presented with shots that encourage exactly the same relationship between the image and the spectator that Baudry and others have presented, allowing us to introject the external qualities perceived onscreen and construct a phantasy that we are looking at the Banks family go about their daily business. But other shots seem to look and behave very differently. When Mary conjures a magical moment onscreen, when she slides up a banister or makes toy soldiers independently walk across the floor, we are less ready and able to subsume them into a feeling that the camera belongs to us. Instead, such moments remind us that the screen is acting as a barrier between us and the pro-filmic event, that what we see is artificial and manipulated, and that the magic onscreen is not strictly ours but belongs to *Mary Poppins*, both the character and the film.

Such moments are where the feeling of the fantastic is located most intensely, and they require a process of idealization much in the same way that in life we idealize things we cannot hope to obtain or understand. They are not idealized in the sense that they present objectively ideal objects or scenarios (even if it often feels that way). Rather, they are idealized because we know what we are seeing is impossible and thus, try as we might, we are unable to introject them into that stable phantasy of ownership that most narrative cinema offers as part of its narcissistic appeal. Yet, contrary to what this statement seems to suggest, our inability to own the images imaginatively does not decrease our interest or fascination with them. It only increases it. Just like idealization in everyday life, our basic narcissistic tendencies encourage us not to simply give up on the images because we know they cannot possibly be real. Instead, our narcissism propels us to introject their positive qualities nonetheless due to the simple fact that we are seeing them. At a fundamental level, and despite our intellect informing us to the contrary, we cannot give up on ourselves and accept that we have been tricked into looking at things that are not real as if they are. Instead, we remain trapped within the hesitancy of the fantastic, going to greater and greater depths to take meaning from images we know are nothing more than illusions, and investing more of our imaginative selves in the screen as a result.

Such idealized images account for the richness of the experience that many associate with watching *Mary Poppins*, despite the fact that the film offers itself as nothing more than a fantasy that reveals its lack of reality proudly. Take, as an example, the "Feed the Birds" musical number. Beginning as a lullaby sung to Jane and Michael to prepare them for bed, the sequence starts by setting up the figure of Mary Poppins as a source of fascination. Utilizing similar techniques seen elsewhere within the film, shots of Mary singing are interspersed with shots of the children watching on and smiling widely, seeming to admire her voice and listening keenly to the song's lyrics. Spectators are encouraged to introject the qualities the characters display onscreen as a means of responding to and viewing the images, constructing an internal phantasy that they too are watching Mary from a similar position as the children. However, as soon as spectators are invited to start imagining that they are part of the scene, the visual register performs a dramatic shift that makes such a phantasy difficult to sustain. Suddenly, the film cuts from the nursery to an exaggerated, stylized vision of the steps of St. Paul's, telling the parabolic story of the bird woman selling bags of crumbs to the rich bankers passing by. The story displayed is strangely simplistic, possessing an almost Dickensian sense of the gothic that is used to both highlight the plight of the bird woman's poverty and to undercut any sense of realism through an exaggerated mise-en-scène. The images are distorted at the edge of the frame, giving them a blurry, oneiric quality; the color saturation is less pronounced than in the previous scene and the use of a fade edit between the images of the children to that of the cathedral creates a dreamlike quality to what is now seen that contrasts. While those aforementioned moments in the nursery seemed to claim to represent a moment in reality, here what is presented seems to be overtly belonging to a world of phantasy, a world owned and controlled by Mary Poppins.

The "Feed the Birds" sequence seems designed not just to make the spectator work harder to believe that what they see is real than other moments within the film set in the nursery or on Cherry Tree Lane, but to recognize that what they see does not belong to any kind of reality that they can hope to inhabit. These are Mary's images, Mary's world, bringing her song to life, and they do not exist for any other reason than to give a physical presentation to the lyrics she sings ("Early each day to the steps of St. Paul's / The little old bird woman comes") and the world she evokes while holding her snow globe. "Feed the Birds" distances us from the immediacy of being in the room with the children listening to their nanny sing. Yet, at the same time, it creates a perhaps more vivid sensation of being inside someone's phantasy. It is as if the camera has managed to photograph someone's dream, letting the spectator introject its hallucinogenic properties, providing access to a form of perception that is not available in everyday life and, yet, seeming to offer something far richer and more vivid than simply seeing as a result (fig. 3.14). The

Figure 3.14. The bird woman appears in a quasi-hallucinogenic manner.

images of the cathedral become a phantasy of a cathedral. The birds flying around her become not birds, but a phantasy of birds. And the bird woman becomes not a real woman but a spectacular phantasy of poverty who performs her suffering through song rather than living it. None of these images are ideal in the traditional usage of the word. But the way we are positioned to see it is idealized in that it lets us introject not only sights and sounds, but hopes and dreams, as if the camera had the power to enter into people's minds and emotions as well as just capture their faces and expressions. And, most significantly, those qualities do not make the images unworthy or alienating to our sympathies. On the contrary, the scene feels affecting because of the phantasy world Mary conjures before our very eyes.

By allowing Mary's magical images to take on this idealized quality within the narrative framework, *Mary Poppins* uses its display of special effects as a means of structuring the spectator's sense of wonder. Wonder is a pleasure in sights and ways of being that gesture beyond the typical and the everyday. It therefore requires an individual to be aware of who they are, what they are seeing, and to forge an imagined relationship between these two forces that makes sight itself take on a wondrous feeling or quality. Narcissistic phantasies restructure the sensory information we receive in relation to the world as an expression of a feeling. Rather than allowing the world to be objective and emotionless, they idealize whatever is seen in any particular moment so that it becomes a figure of curiosity, speculation, and enjoyment. *Mary Poppins* offers just such an experience through the relationship it encourages with its eponymous nanny, and the images she conjures onscreen. Her magic does not just offer spectators a vision of an idealized mode of being; she creates an experience of an idealized mode of seeing. In everyday life, we forgo or at the very least obfuscate many aspects of our sensory experience in order to focus on the world's role as a rational, objective entity. We look at how sights and sounds help us to understand the world logically rather than how they might make us feel, developing a way of seeing everyday life designed to support the process of rational, conscious thought. However, the experience *Mary Poppins*'s special effect seems to encourage from the spectator prioritizes an alternative mode of perception. Removing those objective restrictions and preexisting rules, the world onscreen becomes a realm of unknown laws and visceral experiences, allowing for a way of seeing that is closer to the kind of imaginative realm of early childhood phantasy than the restrictive, objective gaze of adulthood. Instead of focusing on order, rules, or reason, the images onscreen can be seen for their imaginative potential, for the way they address the emotional life of the individual rather than just the logical one.

This is particularly evident in arguably the film's most famous sequence, the moment in which the children, Mary, and Bert enjoy a "jolly holiday" in a cartoonish English countryside. Critical appreciations of this scene often emphasize the film's technical achievement in combining live-action footage and animation to create an illusion of interaction, with the scene held up as a key example of "mixed" media entertainment.[22] However, the sense of wonder achieved in this scene comes not from the spectator's perception of the two technologies as integrated, or mixed, together but from the very distinction between live-action and animation as sensory media. Unlike in "Feed the Birds" the film's ability to disturb the central introjected phantasy most Hollywood cinema relies on (that the camera is the eye) does not take place in relation to the entire image. Instead, merely parts of the image are disturbed within the spectator's perception of the screen. Graphic representations rendered through live-action photography (Mary, Burt, the Banks children) are presented to feel *real*, allowing the spectator to introject them as pro-filmic objects rather than as pictures. At the same time, other filmic objects rendered through cel animation (dancing penguins, Scottish-accented foxes, and painted backgrounds) look and feel *unreal* precisely because the process of introjection required from the spectator to imaginatively transform these images into the real-life objects they denote feels far more forced and overt. Contrasted with the photographic realism achieved elsewhere, the animation feels almost aggressively pictorial, challenging spectators to either reject the beauty of its construction due to its lack of sensory realism, or idealize that beauty as an aesthetic reaction that is somehow more important than the physical laws of reality that they know and understand.

As the characters arrive into the chalk painting, abstract colors fill the screen momentarily only to dissipate, revealing a grandiose landscape of green hills and pastoral country lanes. Accompanied by a score used to emphasize a feeling of delight in what is seen, the picturesque backdrop offers a deliberately stylized version of the objects they claim to represent in a way that highlights the artifice of the images by creating a particular set of introjected phantasies. Instead of experiencing such settings as one might do in real life, focusing on their intersubjective function, their geographical location, or indeed any other phantasy that might give the images a function or identity in an objective world, the spectator is instead encouraged to focus on their vitality and their beauty, and it is this focus on the capacity of sights and sounds to affect spectators over their capacity to be understood that gives these moments onscreen their spectacular quality. The song and dance number that accompanies the scene focuses particularly on this aspect. While nominally about the joy of having a "jolly holiday with Mary," the song focuses a lot of attention within its lyrics, its instrumentation, and accompanying dance number on a broader feeling of joy that comes from seeing the world in a certain way. Bert sings that "when Mary holds your hand / you feel so grand / your heart starts beating like a big brass band." His focus on emotion and color resonates with the painterly register the animation achieves, asking when the last time you have seen "the grass so green / or a bluer sky?" For Bert, like the spectator, the world's visual qualities are manifestations of an internal state of happiness, a feature that the scene then bears witness to as Mary and Bert skip down the country path. Expressed through dance, their movements are impossibly effortless in their synchronization and weightlessness, with characters sometimes even taking off from the ground as the scene's lighting changings from dull to bright light depending on what is being sung about in the song at any given moment. Such moments only have resonance if they are understood not as expressions of objectivity but subjective agency, literalizing as they do the emotions of the characters over the logic of the external world.

With all these qualities in mind, *Mary Poppins* is best described as a fantasy film that champions the subjective phantasies we need not just to make sense of life, but to enjoy life. George's character arc represents perhaps the most obvious demonstration of this aspect of the film's narrative considerations, presenting as it does the thematic notion that a life without fun and joy is no life whatsoever. But the narrative of George Banks is only one way this fantasy film created an experience that champions the role phantasy plays in creating our most fundamental impressions of the world. Instead, this is part of the film's broader function as both a wonder film conceived during the postclassical era and a fantasy musical that seeks to address and celebrate notions of impossibility within its narrative construction. The "Supercalifragilisticexpialidocious" musical number is perhaps the culmination of all of these features of the film (fig. 3.15). The eponymous phrase is, to paraphrase Mary's words, "a very good word to say when you do not know what to say." It does not make any sense, but the act of saying seems to alleviate the pressure to make sense. It allows you to speak without meaning, to say without discussing, and to exist without having to be defined by a set of laws, conventions, or regulatory practices. Watching Mary sing it over and

Figure 3.15. Live-action collides with cel animation.

over again while the rest of the characters join in allows us to construct a phantasy in which words are not a limitation of subjective expression. Instead, subjective expression is an innate right within all of us, as long as we are living, breathing individuals capable of seeing the world not just as a reality but as our subjective and idealized phantasy. As we move on to our final case study of this era, it will be interesting to see what other phantasies might be conjured for the spectator through a process of introjection, and what other worlds they are asked to internalize as a source of wonder.

The Fantastic and Internalization: Metamorphosis in *The Golden Voyage of Sinbad*

If the pleasure in watching *Mary Poppins* resides in a relationship between phantasy and identity, then the appeal of a film like *The Golden Voyage of Sinbad* emerges out of a similar relationship between phantasy and the cinema. A nominal sequel to *The Seventh Voyage of Sinbad* (1958)—though with a production gap of fifteen years between them—the film is neither the most critically acclaimed nor the most commercially successful of the films produced by the famous partnership of stop-motion animator and special effects pioneer Ray Harryhausen and producer Charles H. Schneer. That accolade is typically reserved for their earlier work *Jason and the Argonauts* (1963). However, if *The Golden Voyage of Sinbad* cannot claim to be the best example of Harryhausen's oeuvre, it does merit consideration as his most typical film, for better and for worse. Opening to largely apathetic reviews at the time of its release, *The Golden Voyage of Sinbad* was widely criticized for its bland characterization and perfunctory plotting. However, as Philip Strick argued in *Monthly Film Bulletin*, critics forgave these features because "what matters, of course, is the contribution of the great Ray Harryhausen, and here the only complaint is likely to be that his creations are too often swept from the screen by petulant little humans."[23] The effects were amazing enough to justify the price of entry, a judgment that seems indicative of a wider response found across Harryhausen's body of work. The film is therefore worth focusing on as a representative example of the vivid power of Harryhausen's effects to produce an experience of wonder within the overall context of postclassical fantasy filmmaking.

The Golden Voyage of Sinbad tells the story of the struggle between the legendary sailor Sinbad (John Phillip Law) and the evil wizard Koura (Tom Baker), both of whom embark on a journey to the lost island of Lemuria in search of the fountain of youth. Sinbad wants to find the fountain because he has been made to believe that its magical powers will help bring peace and stability to the land of Marabia, the ruler of which he has recently befriended. Koura, however, wants to use those same powers to conquer Marabia, leading to a contest between the two that involves a battle against numerous magical spells and monsters, all of which are rendered onscreen through Harryhausen's innovative process of blending live-action with stop-motion animation that he referred to as "Dynamation." Through a distribution agreement with Columbia Pictures, Schneer and Harryhausen produced a series of films throughout the postclassical period designed to showcase this Dynamation process to audiences, creating iconic sequences such as the giant crab attack in *Mysterious Island* (1961) and the climactic battle with the skeleton army in *Jason and the Argonauts*, both of which required Harryhausen to push the boundaries of rear projection and double exposure technologies to create an experience of animated creatures interacting with real-life actors onscreen. Such sequences are abundant within *The Golden Voyage of Sinbad*, as the battle between the eponymous hero and Koura plays out largely through a series of episodic action-sequences with an emphasis placed not on complex plotting or character but, to paraphrase Joshua David

Bellin, in achieving "the dreamlike feel" that Harryhausen's stop-motion creations rested their popular and critical reputation on generating.[24]

This focus on Harryhausen's monsters at the expense of his human characters makes the film's status as a work of fantasy somewhat difficult to articulate. In telling its central story, *The Golden Voyage of Sinbad* trades on an orientalist iconography of faraway lands and enchanted kingdoms emblematic of what David Butler describes as the "Arabian nights" subgenre of fantasy cinema.[25] The Arabian nights fantasy film has its beginnings in the imperialist origins of cinema reflected in films such as Georges Méliès's *The Palace of the Arabian Nights* (1905), as well as early US studio features including *Ali Baba and the Forty Thieves* (1918) and *The Thief of Bagdad* (1924). The cycle of fantasy filmmaking displays a recurrent fascination with an Anglo-Eurocentric vision of Asia in which the nuances of different cultures and nations are submerged together into an exoticized, othered world of racial stereotypes, all of which are on display in *The Golden Voyage of Sinbad*. Yet, alongside these problematic elements, the film's more fundamental focus seems to be not on a phantasy of race, but a phantasy of technology and physicality. Echoing strategies used in *Mary Poppins*, the film aligns the spectator's perception of Harryhausen's special effects with the characters experiencing it within the context of the fiction. This means that sequences such as Sinbad's encounter with Koura's army of "homunculi" (winged, batlike creatures that the wizard is able to summon to do his bidding) consistently intersperse shots of the live-action actors looking bewildered and shocked by the appearance of the creatures with the shots of the creatures themselves, a device that directs the spectator's attention toward the sheer act of physical impossibility Harryhausen's creatures represent. In this sense, although borrowing from an iconography and lexicon associated with the "Arabian nights" fantasy, the film's sense of impossibility is rooted far more fundamentally to the sheer physical rupture in physics that the film achieves by having Harryhausen's animated creatures come to life and interact with the characters onscreen. The world of Sinbad is normalized in comparison with the monsters he encounters, creating a fantasy film that, for better and for worse, is less invested in presenting a xenophobic view of an othered "orient" than it is in the imaginative appeal of watching creatures come to life onscreen.

The introjected phantasies that the film encourages through these displays of impossible creatures moving and interacting onscreen are rooted in some of the most deep-seated pleasures associated with fantasy storytelling. As Marina Warner argues, ideas of transformation and metamorphosis lie at the heart not only of modern fantasy literature but of many classical myths and religious stories that serve as antecedents to the genre.[26] The act of phantasizing is, in essence, the ability to imagine a world without static or fixed states, something the fantasy genre attempts to emulate and yet struggles to sustain given that it almost inevitably creates new structures and laws to replace the old ones it transgresses as part of its storytelling process. Metamorphic imagery, however, allows the unbound physics of phantasy to be expressed without the seemingly inevitable stabilization that is created by a narrative context. It creates a scenario, however temporary, wherein fixed matter and identity becomes fluid and changeable, creating a dynamic that not only offers up offers up a vision of the world that is fantastic but, in the words of Jean-Paul Sartre, has the effect of allowing the individuals who experience them to "becom[e] fantastic."[27] Metamorphosis serves as an invitation for the spectator to enter into an experience with the world's objects and persons in which the logic of reality gives way to the logic of phantasy, providing an imaginative release through the material approach to the world it encourages.

These metamorphic tendencies are embedded within the visual spectacle offered by *The Golden Voyage of Sinbad*. The film is not only metamorphic on a technical level, incorporating stop-motion animation into live-action footage so as to make objects come to life onscreen, but through a narrative that constantly frames the encounter between Sinbad and Harryhausen's impossible creatures as a clash of weight, shape, and materiality. In this way, the relationship between narrative and spectacle is far more intertwined than it might otherwise appear. Rather than existing in transcendence of the story being told, the encounters between characters and Harryhausen's creatures are aided in their imaginative appeal to the spectator by being mediated by what they represent in terms of the story. The antagonism between Sinbad and Koura only works on a dramatic level because of the contrasting relationships the two characters have to the external world. Sinbad's status as a heroic character is located primarily in his bravery and physical strength. He is able to lift heavier things, fight more skillfully, and otherwise adapt better to the physical restrictions and problems posed by his environment, a feature that makes him an effective hero in bringing resolution and stability in a narrative in which most of the challenges he faces are physical. Koura, in contrast, does not seek to negotiate with the physical world. He seeks to transcend it. His magic gives him the ability to avoid physical limitation altogether, bringing to life a series of creatures that serve as manifestations of his own agency. The film therefore aligns its presentation of Dynamation to Koura's magic, assigning him ownership over many of the special effects much in the same way as in *Mary Poppins*.

This alliance between Koura and the film's Dynamation might strike some as somewhat anachronistic. Given how self-conscious Harryhausen and Schneer were of the fact that the ultimate appeal of their movies was in their display of stop-motion, one might be forgiven for thinking that the filmmakers would be tempted to valorize the metamorphic creatures much in the same way that the magic of *Mary Poppins* is idealized throughout Disney's fantasy musical. But contrary to these assumptions, it is in fact that villainous wizard Koura who functions most closely as an onscreen doppelganger for Harryhausen, as opposed to Sinbad or any other force for good within the story. This at least serves the function of bestowing Harryhausen the status of a wizard, albeit an evil wizard, and assigns his animation a magical quality onscreen. But, beyond this correlation between animation and magic, presenting the film's Dynamation as a threat to Sinbad's reality also serves to allow the film's presentation of metamorphic imagery to offer a more medium-specific reflection on cinema's capacity as a representational system. It is not just Koura and Sinbad who are pitted against each other in *The Golden Voyage of Sinbad*; animation and live-action are also framed as antagonist and contrasting foes. When they appear in the same frame together, they do not do so harmoniously or symbiotically. Instead, they represent two different forces, with two different agendas, fighting for supremacy within the story, a dynamic that effects both what the animation represents onscreen and the kind of imaginative response it entails from the spectator.

Take, for instance, a sequence that takes place approximately one-third of the way through *The Golden Voyage of Sinbad* in which the wizard Koura uses his magical powers to bring to life the figurehead of Sinbad's ship. The moment in question begins with a series of establishing shots taken from the front of Sinbad's vessel, wherein the static figurehead carving is placed in the central foreground of the shot. The object is therefore introduced to the spectator as part of a standard continuity filmmaking convention used to establish the pro-filmic event that the rest of the scene will capture through a series of mid-shots and close-ups. That sense of the pro-filmic is crucial for a number of reasons. Not only does it allow the spectator to establish coherent, spatial relationships between one shot and the next. It also allows the film to present the feeling that something has been captured by the camera, giving the scene a feeling of partial realism. Even if the setting is not believable as a representation of reality given its stylized and exotic nature, it is at least believable as a moment *that was once filmed*. The figurehead becomes a key focal point in establishing both of these impressions. As the character of Haroun (Kurt Christian) wanders into the frame and drunkenly staggers against the wooden sculpture, the cut from wide shot to close-up is oriented through the physical presence of the large object, giving a sense that, at the very least, an actor once touched a prop on a set (fig. 3.16).

As the creature then begins to move, that impression of a pro-filmic reality existing independently of the camera is shattered by an experience of the fantastic (fig. 3.17). Haroun reacts in shock and disbelief, stumbling backward before running to his fellow crew members shouting, "It's alive! It's moving!" The figurehead's movements become impossible within the context of the story established thus far while also undermining the spectator's ability to imagine a cohesive event onscreen. What was once an object on a photographed set becomes a creature whose sheer act of movement highlights its inability to have shared the same space as the human actors, creating a sense of impossibility that is rooted as much to the physics of the film's construction as it is to anything taking place within the narrative. The kind of phantasies the spectator is encouraged to introject become unstable and ill-defined, with the photographic realism of the human actors contrasting with the metamorphic sensibility of the animated creature. Like mixing oil and water together, the very dynamic of the sequence seems to come from the way these two irreconcilable types of images are brought together into the same frame, as if they were one and the same, despite the obvious differences that permeate between the creature and the human characters.

The experience of hesitation generated in such a sequence can therefore be traced to many of the long-standing assumptions surrounding the distinction between animation and live-action as different media that exist to this day. Thanks in part to the filmmaking style promoted by Hollywood cinema and in part to arguments advanced by classical film theorists such as André Bazin as to the indexical quality of celluloid to preserve or capture space and time onscreen, ideas which have seeped into many strata of film culture, live-action photography (whether digital or analogue) retains to this day certain connotations with naturalism and realism.[28] Animation (cel, digital, or stop-motion), by contrast, has an equally long-standing cultural association with fantasy storytelling.[29] Rooted in the medium's lack of physical restraint, animated imagery has been theorized as exhuming a quality once described by Sergei Eisenstein as "plasmaticness" and by Paul Wells as "metamorphosis."[30] It offers film-

Figure 3.16. The presence of a pro-filmic, photographed ship's mast is highlighted (*The Golden Voyage of Sinbad*, 1974).

Figure 3.17. The previously photographed ship's mast becomes animated.

makers and audiences a liberation from the physicality of everyday life, creating opportunity to make creatures come to life that do not exist, as well as for objects to be molded, shaped, and to transform into one another effortlessly onscreen.

This contrast made between animation and live-action is not simply of a cultural or even ontological distinction. It is also a means of separating each medium according to the way each is approached through phantasy. In order for a person to forge a subjective judgment as to the nature of any external object in the world, they must first measure that object up against an imagined concept of how it should operate in the abstract. The strength and function of an individual can opener, for example, can only be measured against an internal understanding of what a can opener is supposed to do. A person creates an internal phantasy of a can opener and judges a real object in response to the phantasy. The process, which, in Klein's psychoanalysis of phantasy, is referred to as the introjection of an "internal object," begins in the early stages of object relations and persists throughout life as imagined concepts constructed within the psyche become effective representations of some objective concept or entity. Whether this be the notion of a can opener or the idea of a mother, an individual is able to phantasize internalized versions of the objects and persons they encounter in life by introjecting the qualities they perceive in the world, a process that not only alters their subjective understanding of what such ideas or notions might be but how they are encountered in objective life.

Both cinema and animation operate as two examples of such internal objects. When theorists such as Bazin ask large, seemingly unanswerable questions like *what is cinema?*, they often acknowledge that their object of consideration is not merely the material reality of a particular apparatus but an imaginary idea appropriated by spectators as they adopt a phantasized mode of viewing. Likewise, when spectators go to see a film, they are implicitly mediating that experience against a set of imagined characteristics that has been introjected through their previous encounters. Cinema becomes understood for the imagined totality of what it might be as much as what it actually is in any given moment, an idea which emerges out of an internal object constructed through the different encounters the spectator has had with the medium. The same is also true of animation. Perceived as sharing the same "formlessness" that Winnicott associated with both play and with the dream environment,[31] animation seems to share an affinity with phantasy because it allows objects to exhibit the same metamorphic logic of the imagination. Animators can use the technology to render things from their imagination that have no physical existence into objective reality, and audiences can find in the technology a way of approaching the world wherein fixed forms are not secure but instead are constantly adaptable. Yet, this approach to animation is as much a result of a process of phantasy as it is from anything fixed or determined about the technology itself. After all, to assign the medium of animation any firm set of principles or traits is as much a subjective act of self-expression as it is a reflection of the objective status of the object itself.

By understanding the status of both live-action cinema and animation as imagined, internal objects, we might begin to pinpoint the source of wonder that is on display in a film like *The Golden Voyage of Sinbad*. In his theory of cinematic spectacle, Steve Neale argues that what separates the scopic register of spectacle from other cinematic moments is its ability to communicate to the spectator the "visibility of the visible."[32] Informed by psychoanalytic thinking, Neale locates the pleasure of spectacle in a self-conscious appreciation of the act of sight, one that filmmaking is able to provoke through a variety of different methods. In *The Golden Voyage of Sinbad*, this sense of self-conscious distance or alienation from the immediacy of sight as an everyday, sensory phenomenon is achieved through a recalibration of the relationship between the spectator and the internal object of cinema. The experience of the fantastic achieved through the Dynamation process means that, during certain moments throughout the film, the spectator is unable to fully settle on a stable introjected phantasy of the medium of cinema through which the narrative can be experienced. The internal object of cinema is, in effect, split between two different concepts. Parts of the film seem to reflect a phantasy of preservation and transparency, one wherein the internal object of cinema functions as a device that records space and time without effecting it. Other parts of the film offer the spectator an alternative phantasy of changeability and performativity, one in which the cinema is able to bring into being objects and persons that can otherwise never exist through the mediating presence of a camera. The film proceeds to ask the spectator to juggle these two internal objects simultaneously so as to invest different moments with different sensibilities, metamorphosing not only the objects onscreen but the object of cinema itself. In such moments, cinema cannot be distilled into a series of coherent principles or values, and that incoherence encourages the spectator to direct a degree of imaginative activity at the screen as they begin to wonder about the nature of what they are seeing.

In Kleinian theory, the sense of splitting that *The Golden Voyage of Sinbad* achieves is part and parcel of early object relations, emerging "as a consequence of conflict in the ego engendered by the polarity of the two instincts."[33] Rather than accept the contradictions that are inherent not only in our interactions with other people (people can be both reasonable and spiteful, parents can be enabling and restrictive), children learn to split their phantasized internal objects into separate components, introjecting some aspects while holding others at a distance. The best example of this appears in the way we internalize a notion of identity. In order to construct a stable phantasy of who we are as an object, certain internal objects are phantasized as belonging to the self (in my case, for example, the notion of being a university lecturer, or being the author of a book), while others are held at a distance to be introjected either as instinctual urges (hunger, lust) or societal expectations (politeness, for example, or the necessity to tip at the end of a meal). The way we think about own contradictory impulses and thoughts is to split ourselves into different internal components, negotiating between the three competing Freudian notions of the id, the ego, and the superego in order to establish a stable phantasy of who we are. With *The Golden Voyage of Sinbad*, a similar contradictory view of the film as both a live-action and animated object allows for a similar process of splitting. Rather than accept the inherent contradiction that the film does not have a cohesive identity at a material, ontological level, the spectator engaging with the Dynamation process creates an experience of hesitation in which the object of cinema becomes an impossible object, increasing rather than decreasing our fascination with it in the process.

The splitting effect is witnessed most profoundly in the film's climatic sequence, wherein Sinbad and Koura face each other off in a final showdown that involves a battle between two of Harryhausen's stop-motion creatures. As both hero and villain attempt to access the coveted fountain of youth, the film culminates in a contest between two of Harryhausen's monsters: a "guardian of evil," in the form of a centaur controlled by the magic of Koura, and a "guardian of good," in the form of a griffin, who exists to protect the site from intrusion. The two creatures function as surrogate stand-ins for the two human characters, a dynamic reinforced by the staging of the encounter itself. Sinbad encounters Koura alone, drinking from the enchanted waters, and proceeds to draw his sword to fight the evil wizard. Koura, sensing that he will be unable to match Sinbad physically, performs a theatrical lamentation to the gods to rid him "forever of this enemy," a spell that seems to awaken an unseen power as soon as it ends. The sounds of heavy footsteps are heard, and a centaur is seen entering from the tunnel at the far side of the set. Koura flees to the extremity of the room while Sinbad attempts to fight the creature. However, very soon, another sound is heard from the other side of the room and, out from this tunnel, emerges the griffin. What follows then is an action sequence in which two animated creatures battle on a live-action set, the human characters pushed to the extremities of the setting as they stand with their backs against the walls, watching helplessly as the fight takes place.

Beyond the obvious technical advantages of removing human actors from this final battle sequence, the decision to stage this final battle between two animated creatures seems to be a logical extension of a dynamic established within the narrative thus far. The scene is a visual manifestation of the desire expressed by a number of reviewers at the time of the film's release to do away with the necessity of the perfunctory live-action story in favor of prioritizing the film's spectacular animated creatures, a wish the film grants in this moment. In previous scenes, live-action characters would be seen to interact with the animated creatures both by sharing the frame through a number of wide shots, or through the use of editing techniques that stitch together movements of the actors and creatures to give the illusion they are sharing the same space. In this sequence, both of these techniques are still used. Wide shots of the two creatures battling one another give the illusion of them fighting within a photographed film set, the water in the background adding a particular element of detail to remind the spectator of the pro-filmic nature of what is seen, while shots of Sinbad and Koura watching the battle are interspersed continuously to give the sense that they are watching the events unfold and sharing the same screen space. Sinbad and Koura flee to the extremities of the room, and hero and villain alike become onscreen spectators, watching the events unfold as we watch characters watching the events unfold (fig. 3.18). Rather than the filmmaking following the movement of the main characters, the humans give way to the animation, creating the effect of a sequence that somehow feels distanced from the rest of the object of the film. It is dis-

Figure 3.18. The climactic battle.

tanced technically, rendered largely through animation, while most of the film is rendered through live-action. It is distanced emotionally, the source of identification in the scene is not on the monsters but on the characters they seem to represent, and it is distanced spatially, happening away from the human actors. The sequence operates self-consciously as an exception, one that the spectator is encouraged not to normalize as part of a coherent film but spectacularized as something in and of itself. If Sinbad and Koura personify the two different cinematic objects at play in *The Golden Voyage of Sinbad* at that level of narrative, then their positioning in this sequence should clarify the kind of cinematic phantasy the film is offering. The film disturbs the object of cinema to reveal the level of phantasy attached to such an object, requiring the spectator to hold their internal understanding of the medium as something that can be self-consciously scrutinized rather than something that simply exists a priori.

Many films are supposedly "about" cinema, almost to the point where that shorthand has become a cliché that obscures far more than it reveals. *The Golden Voyage of Sinbad* is not about cinema. However, it does rely on challenging a certain imagined belief about cinema as a cohesive object and seeks to create a sense of spectacle and wonder by challenging the spectator to rethink and reorient themselves in relation to that imagined object. On the one hand, the spectator must occupy a viewing position that recognizes that the images onscreen cannot exist in everyday reality, a process vital if they are to avoid the element of fear such images might evoke were they to fall within the realm of the uncanny. On the other hand, the spectator must also create an alternative viewing position through a series of introjective phantasies in which the events are witnessed as really occurring due to the fact that they are present through a series of objective sensory stimuli, making them more than a hallucination or dream. It is through the synergy of both these viewing experiences that this film functions as both a narrative concerned with, and an experience that embodies, qualities of metamorphosis that allow it to provoke phantasies of introjection. It is the ability of the film to position the spectator to engage with the film fiction through such phantasy activity that creates the experience of the fantastic.

Conclusion:
Introjecting Wonder and the Wonder of Introjection

I have labeled the era of postclassical fantasy filmmaking as the era of the wonder film, but wonder is by no means unique to an arbitrary historical epoch demarcated within the ever-evolving history of Hollywood film production. Wonder did not begin with the 1948 Paramount Studios decree and it certainly did not end with the release of arguably the world's first blockbuster, *Jaws* (1975). Instead, it is a key part of fantasy filmmaking as much as it is a key part of Hollywood filmmaking more broadly, stretching back to the early days of cinema through to early studio efforts, such as the wonder films shaped by stop-motion pioneer Willis O'Brien such as *The Lost World* (1924) and *King Kong* (1933). O'Brien and his form of wonder cinema would serve as a key inspiration and mentor figure for Ray Harryhausen, who would in turn inspire filmmakers like Steven Spielberg or Joe Dante. Nor is wonder within the fantasy genre located exclusively to moments in film history where special effects are prioritized. This is why *Harvey* is such an important film to highlight, as it serves as a representative example of a long heritage of fantasy filmmaking, one that is perhaps quieter and less assertive than its more spectacular cousins, but one which nevertheless relies upon an extremely imaginative sensory experience by offering spectators an opportunity to look at mundane, urban settings in new ways.

The story of wonder in fantasy cinema is therefore bigger and grander than anything that can be told in a few decades. However, postclassical Hollywood is a useful period to examine the wider opportunities made available to the spectator for experiencing wonder, not simply because it was an era in which the film industry sought to partner innovative special effects practitioners and independent producers working both inside and outside the studio environment to create a unique mode of entertainment within a competitive media landscape. In blending the kind of imaginative storytelling practice exemplified in films like *Harvey* with the special effects–driven logic of films demanded by productions like *Mary Poppins* and *The Golden Voyage of Sinbad*, postclassical Hollywood essentially created two key strategies in offering spectators a narrativized experience of wonder that would prove highly influential on future fantasy filmmakers. First, their use of fantasy storytelling techniques provoked a series of introjected phantasies that idealized the display of special effects onscreen, a technique I examined in relation to *Mary Poppins*, and replicated in a wave of films made in its immediate aftermath like *Bedknobs and Broomsticks* (1971) or, further down the line, *Willy Wonka and the Chocolate Factory* (1971) and *Edward Scissorhands* (1990). Each of these beloved fantasy classics locates its presentation of magic onscreen to the magic of a central and idealized character, allowing Hollywood fantasy films to align the display of special effects to the spectator's wider practice of forging imaginative relationships with characters and narrative scenarios, fueling the experience of wonder in Hollywood fantasy fiction for decades to come. Judging by the recent release of *Mary Poppins Returns* (2018), it is a process that shows no signs of stopping.

Second, if Hollywood did not idealize its characters through the experience of wonder it offered, it often idealized itself. As I discussed in relation to *The Golden Voyage of Sinbad*, special effects–driven fantasy films became opportunities for filmmakers to show off technical advances while lending it a creative, imaginative sensibility, creating films that ignite a series of introjected phantasies about the nature of what cinema can be both as an apparatus and as an experience. Perhaps in a self-conscious awareness of the role effects have played in the shaping of popular attitudes toward the medium of cinema, future advances in special effects would continue to return to narratives in which notions of metamorphosis were writ large into the diegesis onscreen. Films like *Who Framed Roger Rabbit?* (1988), *Jumanji* (1995), or *Avatar* (2009) brought fantasy storytelling devices to bear on acts of technological display, tying the experience of the fantastic to an interrogation of the phantasy of cinema itself as an object that new technologies like CGI or digital 3D might disrupt. The magic displayed in cinema became a magic of cinema, as Hollywood mediated the public's phantasies of its own product through films that ostensibly wondered about the nature of the object onscreen. In doing so, they would maintain a widespread fascination with big screen, auditorium-based entertainment as screen culture itself became more proliferate and ubiquitous, a strategy the Hollywood film industry seems to be pursuing relentlessly as fantasy cinema continues within the contemporary media landscape.

The experience of wonder straddles a line between intellect and instinct, making it as much a product of the imagination as any other act of speculation that helps to make sense of our lives without the evidence within the physical world. Its experience within the context of fantasy cinema is therefore a by-product of the fantastic's ability to provoke, reorientate, and realign the fundamentals of our way of approaching the world, allowing us to both internalize and idealize the external properties perceived on the screen as part of our imaginative engagement with impossible fiction. Postclassical fantasy films demonstrate the affective potential wonder can have when utilized as part of a narrative framework that allows events onscreen to be seen not as representations of a world but as idyllic visions of a better world that, in turn, offers a better way of perceiving. It is no surprise, then, that Hollywood's fantasy films repeatedly return to these kinds of narratives. Getting spectators to want to look at special effects seems an obvious by-product of the wonder film. Yet, what that actually entails interrogates the very nature of what it is to finding meaning in sensory perception. As the era of the blockbuster dawned and the paradigms present in postclassical Hollywood intensified and solidified into a new filmmaking regime, fantasy cinema would be reborn out of the imaginative precedent established during this era.

4

High Fantasy Blockbusters

Alternative Worlds and Phantasies of Projection, 1976–1991

THE 1980S REPRESENTS ARGUABLY the most dynamic period in the history of the Hollywood fantasy genre, an achievement helped in no small part by the arrival of the blockbuster as the dominant form of large-scale commercial filmmaking. By the mid-1970s, Hollywood studios had experimented with a number of different commercial strategies to address the steady decline in box office revenue that had been taking place since the mid-twentieth century. Creative solutions ranged from the wonder films produced during the 1950s and 1960s (which were intermittently successful but necessarily costly and therefore risky endeavors) to the brief foray into director-driven productions of the early 1970s, during which time works such as *The Godfather* (1972), *Badlands* (1973), and *Mean Streets* (1973) became box office hits. While the appeal of these arthouse-inflected dramas among mainstream audiences was to be relatively short-lived, the rise in director-controlled productions saw the emergence of a number of creative voices whose commercial and artistic aspirations altered the landscape of the Hollywood film industry forever as the enormous success of Steven Spielberg's *Jaws* (1975) and George Lucas's *Star Wars* (1977) established a rough template for a new production mode among the major Hollywood studios known as the blockbuster.

Although essentially an evolved and updated version of the already existing wonder film, the arrival of the blockbuster was a crucial turning point in the history of fantasy cinema, and, more broadly, the Hollywood film industry. From a production standpoint, the blockbuster represented the final break from any remaining traces of the assembly line–esque methods that dominated the classical era toward a package-unit system of production. As J. D. Connor has previously argued, the blockbuster epitomized the final shift toward a more singular and individualized Hollywood production culture, one that placed greater emphasis on the success or failure of "event" movies within a studio's commercial strategy and a process that then allowed the practice of filmmaking itself to be more easily subsumed within a wider multimedia strategy that reflected the makeup of Hollywood's new owners.[1] Famous names like MGM and Paramount were sold off to large multimedia corporations who sought to target consumers across a broader range of media platforms, and the blockbuster became a crucial strategy that allowed film production to galvanize a collection of cross-promotional strategies aimed at a target audience of late baby boomers and early generation Xers with disposable income and leisure time to match their relative youth. Old Hollywood, the one that spoke across generations and filled the seats of theaters each week with its latest, equally worthwhile release, was gone. New Hollywood—blockbuster Hollywood—was what remained in its stead.

In search of suitable content for this new blockbuster format, producers cast their eyes to what Thomas Schatz argues to be an "increasingly 'fantastic' " set of narrative patterns that had emerged within US popular culture during the mid-twentieth century.[2] In particular, producers gravitated toward a style of fantasy literature that had become increasingly popular among a youthful subculture of readers thanks to the efforts made by publishing firms such as Ballantine Books during the 1960s and 1970s to cash in on what Edward James describes as a relative "fantasy boom."[3] The phenomenal success of novels like C. S. Lewis's *The Lion, the Witch and the Wardrobe* (1950) and J. R. R. Tolkien's *The Lord of the Rings* (1954) created a literary and publishing revolution that saw the rapid expansion in production of a subgenre described by literary scholars as "high" or "heroic" fantasy.[4] Epitomized by a number of narrative features including the presentation of a vast, alternative world; the use of folkloric creatures such as elves, goblins, and trolls; and a mythic question narrative in which a lowly hero must journey across a magical land to retrieve a magical talisman or save the prophesized princess, this new style of popular storytelling set the standard for what constituted fantasy fiction within the wider public consciousness. By the beginning of the 1980s, a vast subculture of fantasy fans were showing their appetite for this strand of high fantasy fiction not just by purchasing the latest paperback edition, but by engaging in table-top role-playing games such as Dungeons and Dragons (1974), emerging video-game platforms such as the *Ultima* series (1981–), and attending fan conventions that were attracting increasing visibility within the media as fascinating epicenters displaying a new form of youth popular culture that threatened to infiltrate society at large.

During the early 1980s, Hollywood aimed to capitalize on the popularity of high fantasy fiction within the newly emerging blockbuster form, creating a series of largely midrange efforts that drew either loose inspiration from, or adapted directly, the kind of literary sources that had been popularized in other media outlets over the past few decades. Studios embarked on ambitious retellings of Arthurian legends (*Excalibur*, 1982), adapted popular high fantasy novels such as *The Lord of the Rings* (1978) and *The Black Cauldron* (1985, adapted from Lloyd Alexander's *Chronicles of Prydain* series, 1964–1968), and produced original screenplays indebted to the conventions of this new model of heroic fantasy (*Wizards*, 1977; *Willow*, 1988). Major studios signed distribution deals to package and sell films like *The Beastmaster* (1982), fledgling production companies tried to compete against the larger industry players with works like *The Sword and the Sorcerer* (1982), and coproductions between US and UK studios created films like *The Dark Crystal* (1982) and *Krull* (1983). Filmmakers working across the spectrum of Hollywood's commercial activity pushed the narrative depths of fantasy cinema by telling complex mythologies set in strange, alternative worlds, challenging Hollywood's technical arsenal to render such worlds onscreen through the innovations in both practical and visual effects taking place during this era. In doing, so they created a number of fondly remembered cult classics of the fantasy genre that live on in the memories of fans to this day.

Creating these high fantasy blockbusters required producers to concentrate their efforts on producing a different kind of story that achieved a very different kind of cinematic spectacle than that which had been offered in previous cycles of the genre. In his analysis of the relationship between spectacle and narrative, Geoff King describes the experience of the blockbuster as an encounter with a "frontier" realm onscreen.[5] Incorporating elements of both an imperialistic logic of expansion into a unknown and exotic other and a particularly Anglo-American cultural fascination with landscape as an unknown and precivilized entity, the frontier narrative and its associated imagery played a key role in shaping not only the kind of stories told by blockbusters but the function of spectacle within said narratives. Blockbuster narratives often involve characters journeying into unfamiliar territories that they must overcome through physical force (whether this be in the form of action-adventures with fantasy elements like the *Indiana Jones* series, 1981–1989, 2008, or sci-fi films like *Empire Strikes Back*, 1981) while spectacle becomes a device used to evoke a feeling of excitement at being exposed to these unknown and unfamiliar landscapes. Postclassical fantasy cinema had alluded to this kind of spectacular storytelling on occasion in its varied production cycles. Ray Harryhausen's adaptations of ancient Greek mythology and Arabian nights folklore were, for example, not devoid of the pleasures that blockbuster films seem to provide spectators, and it is therefore not surprising to see him end his feature film career during this era with the MGM-backed *Clash of the Titans* (1981). However, within this new production era, what had been just one aspect of the multifaceted appeal of the wonder film became the fantasy genre's key virtue. High fantasy is, after all, perhaps the most extreme manifestation of the blockbuster's ideal of an encounter with a spectacular frontier. While other film genres would suggest at or hint toward an experience beyond reality through the extreme scenarios that typically populated the blockbuster narrative, high fantasy cinema was able to tell stories that were not only set in an unfamiliar world but an entirely different world, offering spectators what John Clute describes as the genre's "experience of alterity."[6] By locating the source of the fantastic to a world (as opposed to a single being, creature, or event), the high fantasy blockbuster offers a frontier encounter like no other, allowing spectators attracted to the idea of leaving reality behind altogether access to the kind of stories they had grown up with in cheap paperbacks and pulp magazines, told through the increasingly familiar vocabulary of the spectacular blockbuster.

To understand the imaginative appeal the alternative world offers spectators within the high fantasy blockbuster, it is important to recognize the experience of the fantastic it relies on generating. Contrary to their seemingly hyperbolic and transcendent status from reality, alternative worlds rely upon an act of imagination that is actually invested in the same meaning-making processes that allow us to make sense of reality. Just as in everyday life, they require us to generate a set of imagined rules, conventions, and principles that govern the possibilities of their diegesis and to use these rules as means of assessing the significance and value of the narrative events. The only difference is that, while in everyday life, we already have a preestablished set of rules against which our daily lives are measured, the alternative world requires us to start again from scratch. This means that the function of phantasy takes on a role not unlike its function in the way the child approaches a concept of reality for the first time. Like the spectator of a blockbuster, the child is placed in a position wherein they are able to recognize that the places and people they experience need to fit together according to some sort of coherent or logical pattern, leaving them to speculate imaginatively as to what these rules might be in order to begin to make sense of their experience.

Within psychoanalytic theory, such an activity of imaginative speculation is often labeled as a specific kind of phantasy activity known as projection.[7] An alternative to the idea of introjective phantasy considered in the previous chapter, projective phantasy is not an inward-looking process aimed at understanding the relationship between the self and the sensory experience of the surrounding world but an outward-looking one. It is an imaginative act of imposition, one that pushes the thoughts and emotions onto the world without recourse to what the world is actually like, whether this be in the form of a daydream taking ascendancy over the more immediate sensory sensations taking place in any one moment or a more conscious and intentional imaginative act like pretending that a lifeless object like a puppet possesses a life and spirit of its own. Neither projection nor introjection can exist in total isolation of one another; the internal is fed by the external and vice versa. However, the specific act of projecting phantasies onto the world allows us to express our thoughts and feelings with little to no recourse to the objective values of the world itself, fulfilling an important emotional and intellectual function by providing an imagined sense of distance and perspective that we use in order to understand not only who we are in the world but what we are in transcendence of the world.

Projective phantasy manifests in the early dynamics that shape of our first interactions with the world. When first born, children are required to start making meaning out of the complex situation they find themselves in without knowing there is either such a thing as a world or that they are a person within that world. The child therefore has a great deal of catching up to do. First, they must recognize that they exist. Then, they must recognize that there is a surrounding world in which they exist. In order to meet this challenge, the child has little option other than to start to test the groundwork for understanding both the world and the self through a series of imaginative exercises. Without knowing anything about who they are or what external forces they encounter, and without the intellectual capacity to experience the world through conscious thoughts, the child begins to place onto the world a set of imagined values without knowing if they are real or not (without even knowing there is such a thing *as* real), using their imagination as the only means of finding answers to the knowledge they do not even realize they do not have. This process, referred to by Klein as "phantasy-building," precedes but assists the later development of conscious reasoning.[8] The phantasies that the child projects on the world become evidence for its existence and provide us with a way of experiencing external objects as manifestations of our inner life.

Projection is therefore not only a necessary activity to understand the world; it is also an essential imaginative activity if we are to understand our response to that world. Imagining the world in defiance and transcendence of its objective characters—indeed, giving it objective characteristics we know it does not have—is a key way we process our emotions and respond to the world's difficulties and pleasures. Whether this be imagining a world in which we get to throttle those who anger us without consequence or a world in which we can eat as much cake as we want without gaining weight, projection allows us to understand what we want and where we are emotionally in relation to the world around us. We are therefore both liberated and cursed by our ability to form such phantasies of projection. The fact that a world is first created by our imaginations rather than understood rationally lies at the root of a lot of the supposed tensions and anxieties we feel between our logical and imaginative selves. Not only does the material conditions of the world often deny us the things we want the most but, in later life, the social dynamics in which we live often insist that we forgo these early projective phantasies in favor of the more rational principles that we come to adopt as we embrace the world's paradoxes, complications, and nuances. Yet, no matter how concretely the world tells us to forget our dreams, a very deep and essential part of us cannot let go of the fact that the world once represented a site of imaginative speculation rather than a site of adherence and adaptation. Projection allow us to use that primal way of experiencing the world as a fundamental way of processing, understanding, and experiencing the people and places that surround us.

In this chapter, I wish to demonstrate how these same desires, pleasures, and anxieties embedded within the process of projection lie at the heart of the imaginative experience of the fantastic generated by Hollywood's cycle of high fantasy blockbuster cinema. Encouraging the spectator to utilize their encounter with impossible worlds as an opportunity to jettison the typical experience of the world that dominates everyday life, these high fantasy films offer an entirely different way of using phantasy rooted in the creative, projective development of early childhood. By creating an experience wherein an alternative world can be constructed purely out of the spectator's phantasies, the fantasy blockbuster achieves a dynamic that seems to take us back to a place similar to the child's early experiences of the world as a site for projection. Once projective phantasy becomes a dominant strategy for appreciating and experiencing these films, this then unlocks a whole manner of internal impulses that might otherwise be unavailable to the spectator when required to relate to fiction through the same psychological techniques we have developed to understand reality. Examining *Conan the Barbarian* (1981) alongside two other high fantasy blockbusters in the form of *The NeverEnding Story* (1984) and *Hook* (1991), I will consider how the experience of the fantastic allows the spectator to experience pleasures rooted in projection, namely, how each reside in phantasies of power, desire, and freedom that are rooted in an imaginative release from objective concerns. This will then allow a better understanding and, hopefully, appreciation of the awesome imaginative potential these film offer to the audiences that engage with them.

The Fantastic and Alternative Worlds: Projecting Power in *Conan the Barbarian*

The release of *Conan the Barbarian* in May 1982 marked a significant moment in the evolution of the Hollywood fantasy genre. A partnership between Universal Studios and independent producers Edward R. Pressman and Dino De Laurentiis, the film was greenlit by financiers as a calculated response to the success of films like *Star Wars*, replacing the space opera's spaceships with dragons and its lightsabers with actual swords. Adapted from Robert E. Howard's series of novellas and rated "R" upon its initial release for its strong violence and nudity, the film was arguably the first high-profile attempt made by studios to produce a work that would appeal to an audience demographic raised on a diet of pulp comics and high fantasy novels. This strategy paid off with dividends as the film went on to gross over ten times its original budget and spawn both a direct sequel, *Conan the Destroyer* (1984), and a spin-off film *Red Sonja* (1985). The film's commercial success was matched by its acclaim among its target demographic. At the time, Paul Sammon described *Conan the Barbarian* in his review in *Cinefantastique* as "one of the finest fantasy films ever," while fantasy historian Alec Worley has since labeled the film as a "benchmark for heroic fantasy."[9] *Conan the Barbarian* visualized onscreen an alternative secondary world with a level of consistency and complexity unrivaled by the fantasy cinema that had come before it, paving the way for the wave of blockbusters that would shortly follow. This makes it a vital case study for analyzing the type of experience that the high fantasy film offers.

Ostensibly, *Conan the Barbarian* tells the story of the adventures of its eponymous hero, a warrior raised among the fictitious Cimmerian people. At the beginning of the film, Conan's (Arnold Schwarzenegger) tribe are mercilessly slaughtered by the forces of the evil wizard Thulsa Doom (James Earl Jones), leaving Conan as the sole survivor of the massacre. Conan proceeds to wander the earth alone, moving from one location to the next, getting involved in various adventures before eventually embarking on a mission to defeat Doom and his evil cult of followers. The film is therefore loosely structured around a revenge narrative that pits the hero Conan against the villain Doom, the vanquishing of the latter providing the story with its climax. However, limiting Conan to less than twenty-five lines of dialogue, the vast majority of the film's running time is composed of a series of loosely connected episodes that fit together to form a kind of travelogue across the fictional world in which the story takes place. Conan travels from the alpine setting of his nomadic village in which he is first brought up, which seems loosely inspired by a mixture of Native American and Viking heritage, to the Wheel of Pain he must work on as he is enslaved by bandits and dragged across a dry, desert landscape, through distant cities that share architectural styles with Western European, Middle Eastern, and East Asian ancient empires, and to the volcanic, ash-covered setting of Doom's own Mountain of Power. The contrasting typography in each of these settings gives the spectator a sense of a vast realm of action, while the obscure references to a fabricated mythology, history, and civilization that proliferate the film's dialogue allude toward a feeling of a lived-in space full of customs and conventions that need to be understood if the story is to be fully unpacked.

To emphasize the presence of this imagined, secondary world, *Conan the Barbarian* relies on two techniques. The first is lifted from its literary source, employing a style of narration that, within studies of fantasy literature, is often referred to as a rhetoric of immersion. Coined by Farah Mendelsohn, immersive fantasy fiction seeks to communicate a sense of magic to the reader through what she refers to as an "irony of mimesis."[10] The story is told in such a way so as to present its impossible situations as if they were everyday occurrences, leaving it up to the reader to recognize that gap between the world in which the narrative takes place and reality. *Conan the Barbarian* adopts a similar technique. Without pausing to explain itself to the uninitiated, the film partially normalizes the magical events within the context of the world in which they are taking place, leaving spectators to discover the rules of that fictional landscape through a process of deduction and inference. This provides the necessary intellectual stimulus for the spectator to start to build a coherent picture of an alternative world that binds the various circumstances displayed together, watching the narrative unfold in a way that is not unlike the satisfaction of finding your way along a map or solving a puzzle. This intellectual impetus toward problem-solving is then matched with an equally strong emotional appeal that the film aims to generate through its use of visual spectacle. Drawing on the frontier imagery associated with the blockbuster, the film locates the source of its visual pleasure onscreen to the display of new territories and new settings shot through a combination of different filmmaking strategies—including the frequent use of slow-panning and wide-angle shots—designed to show off the elaborate locations, set designs, costumes, and optical tricks required to render this alternative world onscreen (fig. 4.1). Used most frequently as Conan enters each new location, this evocation of visual spectacle seems designed to generate the crucial feeling of excitement from the

Figure 4.1. Conan traverses various spectacular frontiers (*Conan the Barbarian*, 1982).

spectator at being in the alternative world, the film's action pausing to revel in and marvel at the world that both surrounds the narrative action and exists in excess of it.

As explored in the previous chapter, spectacle is often genre-specific, with different kinds of narratives offering different kinds of spectacular experiences depending on the way moments of intended visual pleasure interact with—and help to punctuate—the storytelling. In the case of *Conan the Barbarian*, the filmmaking techniques employed are partially reminiscent of the impossible sense of space offered by a film like *The Wizard of Oz* (1939). Yet, the focus on scale within *Conan the Barbarian*'s presentation of frontier imagery, highlighted by its frequent use of wide lenses to capture a large-scale pro-filmic event, makes the film's spectacle equally reminiscent of a technique identified by Tom Brown within the historical epic as the "spectacular vista."[11] To explain the spectacular vista, Brown highlights a memorable moment in *Gone with the Wind* (1939) where a close-up of Scarlett O'Hara (Vivien Leigh) slowly pans out to reveal a wide shot of the vast, uniformed row of casualties caused during the siege of Atlanta. For Brown, the experience of spectacle in this moment is twofold in that it gives a sense of the vastness of the action, both in terms of narrative consequence and in terms of the nature of the pro-filmic event, while also placing the character in dialogue with the surrounding space in a manner that "vivifies or actualizes the sense of a character's relationship to the world constructed around them."[12] Likewise, in *Conan the Barbarian*, spectacular vistas are used to help punctuate a relationship between character and world that feeds into both the narrative causality and blockbuster logic of the unfolding spectacle. It is the desire to see more of Conan's world that generates the "moment-by-moment anticipation" that David Bordwell earmarks as a key feature of the intensified style of filmmaking associated with blockbuster.[13] The use of spectacle pulls the spectator away from a pure process of *narrativization* (ordering the events into a logical sequence of causality) and instead into a process of *diegiesization* (combining individual moments onscreen into a picture of a coherent story world of topologic and topographic relationships), and it is this relationship that most clearly defines the nature of the experience of the fantastic the spectator is asked to undergo as they respond to the impossible features of what is displayed onscreen.

On one level, the efforts made within *Conan the Barbarian* to orient the spectator into a story world that exists independently of the narrative achieves a sensation that is by no means unique to either to the film or to the genre in which it operates. As V. F. Perkins has famously argued, part of film's unique system of communication as a narrative system is that it does not just present spectators with a story within a world but a world itself onscreen.[14] However, factoring in the role of the fantastic within such a process begins to highlight the fundamentally different approach the spectator is asked to take in relation to a film like *Conan the Barbarian* compared to the typical attempts at world-building within cinema at large. In the vast majority of Hollywood films, the role the imagination plays in the process of maintaining the presence of a world onscreen matches closely with the same way world-building operates in everyday life though an experience of projective phantasy. Most film fictions presume that the spectator already possesses knowledge of a set of imagined values and qualities about what the world is, and cinematic narratives either affirm those values or tweak them subtly according to the demands of their respective fictions. When we see, for example, a close-up of a character, or a single shot of a location, we do not imagine that the bodies or settings we see merely stop at the end of the frame. Instead, we use phantasy to fill in the gaps, a process McGowan refers to as the repressed "excess" of psychic engagement.[15] When applied to a fictional world, these projected phantasies allow us to take a story like *Citizen Kane* (1941) and match its individual moments as closely as possible to our previous understanding of reality. We may recognize, for example, that, in this filmed world, there is no film director called Orson Welles, while there is a fictional media mogul called Charles Foster Kane (Orson Welles). However, we can imagine that its geography, terrain, and history remain largely the same as our own; that Paris is still, presumably, the capital city of France; Los Angeles is still in California; and the dollar is still the currency of the United States, even if some or all of these things are not mentioned explicitly within the context of the story.

The same is also true of many fantasy films produced prior to the arrival of high fantasy as both a literary and cinematic phenomenon. Despite its magical and indeed heavily stylized elements, the world of Cherry Tree Lane in *Mary Poppins* shares far more in common with our own world than it might appear. St. Paul's is still a cathedral situated near London's financial district and George Banks still needs to go to work to earn money in a capitalistic system of economy. Even fantasy films like *The Wizard of Oz* that present alternative worlds do so by contextualizing them against a reality that seems far more like our own and, as such, encourage the spectator to imagine new settings and sights in partial dialogue with a preexisting worldview that requires a process of projection to affirm existing rules and principles within our world. But *Conan the Barbarian* does not operate like this. Instead of witnessing impossible ruptures from the norm, the spectator is asked to recognize that the world onscreen is impossible from its outset and to therefore use their imagination not to maintain the existence of a preexisting structure, but to create a new structure altogether out of the projected phantasies that the details of the film world will support. Projective phantasy becomes an imaginative device that does not support or maintain the existence of a world but that helps to build a new world out of the departure from the norm offered by the film's sense of the fantastic.

The opening scene of *Conan the Barbarian* is indicative of the kind of experience that the overall film affords its spectator. Opening on a blank screen, a grand, unseen narrator begins to tell the story of Conan through a voiceover with little thought or apology for those unfamiliar with Howard's original tale, stating:

> Between the time when the oceans drank Atlantis and the rise of the sons of Aryas, there was an age undreamed of. And, unto this, Conan, destined to wear the jeweled crown of Aquilonia upon a troubled brow. It is I, his chronicler, who alone can tell thee of his saga. Let me tell you of the days of high adventure!

This opening monologue, containing semi-obscure references to classical mythology before listing a series of names and titles that possess no meaning within the context of everyday life, foregrounds the narrative strategies that will be utilized within the rest of the film. The strangeness of the information evokes the distance between Conan's world and reality, while the featureless, black screen it accompanies evokes the unknowability of what is about to follow, as the film promises a world without set rules or boundaries. This sense of not knowing generates a feeling of the fantastic, as the spectator is asked to respond to a feeling of hesitancy caused by a rupture in the known laws and conventions that govern reality. Like a young infant encountering the world for the first time, the spectator is faced with the knowledge that they will be unable to place the sensory information into any preestablished context and so instead experience it purely on a moment-by-moment basis.

In psychoanalytic theory, Klein refers to this sensibility that the spectator is placed in in the film's opening moments as the "paranoid-schizoid" stage of early infancy.[16] Because the child has no preestablished phantasies about the world, they use projection to assign the objective space meaning by giving it imagined qualities that originate from the internal state of the psyche. That which is felt becomes part of that which is known about the world, making the relationship between individual and world dependent on the emotions of the beholder. The opening moments of *Conan the Barbarian* require the spectator to do the same thing. As they are greeted with a series of close-up shots of fire and metal, and the editing patterns utilize a series of graphic mismatches to continually disorient and confuse the spatial-temporal patterns on display (fig. 4.2). In order to assign meaning to such images, the spectator is required to use phantasy to assign the images certain qualities and values. If the spectator is confused, the images become confusing. If the spectator is excited, the images become exciting, and it is this influx of different meanings created through the subject's ability to project their inner experiences onto the images themselves that makes the scene spectacular.

In these vital early stages of the film, then, the spectator must battle with the scene imaginatively in the same way the child must battle with the world. The film's editing style is used to visceral effect as the film announces its journey into an unknown world as a source of spectacle, encouraging the spectator to see the lack of context as an opportunity to be as creative as they like with the events presented onscreen. The projective phantasies they create are no longer based on

Figure 4.2. The title card of *Conan the Barbarian*.

a purely moment-by-moment encounter, but rather merge together with the external qualities perceived onscreen as the spectator is positioned in a manner akin to Klein's notion of the child's "depressive" phase of development.[17] Rather than being ignorant that the world has objective qualities, the child becomes aware of the objectivity of the world as an absence. However, the only thing the child knows about the world is that he or she *does not know*. As Winnicott argues, it is the emotional desire to overcome that experience of seeing the world as an absence of knowledge that means that the "imagination is apt to fill in details on a fantastic basis."[18] A similar process is replicated in *Conan the Barbarian*. As the editing patterns then settle down, the title sequence introduces more images from the fictional world onscreen by utilizing the motif of metalwork to provide a series of graphic matches between different shots of locations and scenery. Contrasting shots of snow, arid landscapes, and vast mountain ranges, the world presented onscreen begins to develop a sense of spatial and logical consistency as the spectator places these images in dialogue with one another to establish a sense of the vast and sprawling nature of this world. Initially positioning the spectator to acknowledge their own lack of knowledge of reality, the film relies on them utilizing projective phantasies to slowly shape a coherent understanding of the alternative reality out of the images onscreen that the film continually challenges, embellishes, and alters.

The pleasure *Conan the Barbarian* offers spectators through phantasy, then, is partially one of liberation and partially one of affirmation. By removing any sense that the fiction can be better understood by matching it against the corresponding rules of reality, even as means of contrast, the film allows spectators to process the information onscreen in a way that is largely inaccessible in everyday life. The film removes the anxiety about getting things wrong about the world that pervades over our day-to-day existence, as we constantly try to make judgments based on how a particular situation matches up to a preexisting standard of how life is supposed to work. As spectators are freed to project phantasies onto the world of *Conan the Barbarian* without recourse to the reality they are leaving behind, they are also emboldened by the fiction that their assumptions about where one location sits in relation to another matter. Their phantasies, whatever they are, shape their experience of watching the film, and do so without them feeling a responsibility or duty to get things right or match their vision of the alternative world with another's. Whatever they say goes, because they make the rules in this world, giving them a feeling of imaginative mastery that is so often denied to them in life.

This aspect of the spectator's experience of the fantastic within the film seeps into the construction of the narrative of *Conan the Barbarian* in challenging and often controversial ways. Leaving behind reality in favor of something else altogether seems to afford filmmakers the same license as it does to spectators, allowing them to tell stories that might otherwise be deemed problematic within a world governed by existing societal rules and expectations. In particular, the film was criticized at the time of its release by a number of critics as a politically regressive film containing an almost fascist-like celebration of the power of the individual. Roger Ebert, for example, stated in his review of the film that the climactic sequence in which the white, muscular Conan defeats Doom (played by African American actor James Earl Jones) resembles a scene "that Leni Riefenstahl could have directed . . . and that Goebbels might have applauded."[19] Beginning with a quotation from Friedrich Nietzsche and valorizing Conan's white muscular body throughout, the film appears to promote a quasi-fascistic triumph of the individual against the masses. However, in order for any ideology to be believed, it must be perceived by the beholder to offer a coherent and viable way of living within reality. *Conan the Barbarian*, however, offers a way of engaging with its subject matter that eschews the need for such intellectual engagement, investing its time and energy instead to entertain the spectator through the display of a fictional world rather than offering its world as a credible solution to reality's problems.

Take, for example, a moment toward the end of the film where Conan and his small group of allies stage a conflict against a vast horde of Doom's army. Mounting a small resistance against the horseback warriors by setting up a series of battlements against a nearby hilltop, Conan watches as the army gallops toward him, ready for battle. At this moment, Conan looks to the heavens, offering a rare prayer to the god Crom, whom he references throughout the narrative but, as he also states, "seldom prays to." As established early on in the film, Crom represents a god of strength, a titan raised by giants who searches for the so-called "riddle of steel." This riddle of steel becomes a thematic motif running throughout the film's episodic narration, which climaxes in this exchange. The prayer Conan says aloud in these moments goes as follows:

> Crom, I have never prayed to you before. I have no tongue for it. No one, not even you, will remember if we were good men or bad. Why we fought, or why we died. No, all that matters is that two stood against many. That's what's important. Valor pleases you Crom, so grant me one request. Grant me revenge. And if you do not listen, then to hell with you!

Conan's somewhat fascistic words seem to celebrate individual strength over morality, an idea which finds supporting evidence in the scene that follows. His words are accompanied onscreen by shots of the army galloping toward him, Conan's voice dominating over the shots of an anonymous soldiers, and the action sequence that follows seems to ask the spectator to derive pleasure from the spectacle of a small number of skilled warriors defeating a faceless army, something that would become a mainstay of the heroic fantasy subgenre in films like *Willow* or, later on, *The Lord of the Rings* (2001–2003). The temptation to read the scene as a right-wing celebration of the might of individualism is apparent throughout. Yet, as Conan continues his speech, what at first seems a rather eloquent, if disturbing, celebration of the power of the individual quickly descends into something else altogether. Conan makes an appeal to God for strength only to announce himself stronger than God, the contradiction of such a statement seemingly not necessarily lost on the filmmakers. Conan speaks his words forcefully, declaring the oxymoron proudly as he dismisses the gods almost as a badge of honor, and the moment becomes rather parodic in its operatic exaggeration and hyperbolic gesturing. The sequence does not seem designed to evoke credibility from the spectator. Instead, it is the overriding falseness of the moment that is important to its sense of affirming power. By giving spectators the creative license to make things that *should* matter *not* matter (and vice versa, to make things that *do not* matter seem important), the film provides them with the opportunity to project phantasies onto things simply for the sake of it rather than because it has an existing meaning or purpose. This does not mean that considering the spectator's experience of the fantastic within this action sequence excuses the scene's ideology. It does mean, however, that any ideological effect such a scene is able to generate is mediated partially through the projective phantasies that the film is reliant upon creating, phantasies which serve to continually differentiate the rules of this world onscreen and the rules of our own. If Conan is a fascist, he is also an impossible fascist. He needs to be if we are to enjoy him operating in a fantasy world.

If *Conan the Barbarian* promotes individualism, it does so in an emotional as well as intellectual sense. Through the imaginative experience it generates, it encourages the spectator to reject preexisting ideas and rules rather than to follow said rules, generating an experience of the fantastic that allows for the expression of certain kinds of phantasies that are deemed either irrelevant or impermissible in everyday life. This has the potential to be both regressive and progressive politically. To reject the world of others in favor of celebrating the world of the imagination is to create a new world without others and, therefore, without responsibility. Yet, fantasy fictions' ability to imagine a world better than reality itself has seen theorists such as Theodor Adorno, Fredric Jameson, and Rosemary Jackson declare the genre as a potentially politically subversive mode of storytelling.[20] Just as Conan dominates his surrounding world physically, so too phantasies of projection allow spectators to construct a vision of the reality onscreen that is not dependent on a set of pre-existing laws and principles but the laws and principles they choose to give it. The film is about hopes, dreams, and phantasies of power, for better and for worse. The wider potential of the fantasy blockbuster to confront similar issues through the experience of the fantastic it creates will be analyzed in the proceeding sections of this chapter, as different fantasy films that position the spectator to engage in this experience offer different means of expressing these repressed components of the self through projective phantasy.

The Fantastic and Desire: Projecting the Unconscious in *The NeverEnding Story*

The pleasure in *Conan the Barbarian* resides in an imagined projection of power. The film gives the spectator the confidence to make a world in their own image, affirming their individuality through an empowering celebration of phantasy forged without recourse to an objective, fixed, or determined world. *The NeverEnding Story*, another prime example of the popularity of high fantasy within the first age of the blockbuster, offers a comparable but contrasting pleasure based upon the projection of desire. Unlike *Conan the Barbarian*, the narrative does not simply seek to place spectators in an alternative world without concession or acknowledgment of the reality it leaves behind. Rather, *The NeverEnding Story* tells two stories simultaneously, one set in reality and the other set in the fictional world of Fantasia. This particular dynamic is not particularly noteworthy as a feature on its own. There are plenty of 1980s fantasy films that feel the need to return to reality on some occasions, not least the now-beloved *The Princess Bride* (1987), which tells its high fantasy narrative through a framing device involving a sick young boy being read a storybook by his grandfather. But *The NeverEnding Story* seems to do something more than simply wrap or frame its high fantasy narrative within a story set in our own world. Instead, the film seems to use its balance between reality and high fantasy to celebrate the value of the latter in engaging with the former. It is a film about the value of imagining whatever you want, not because such phantasies might come true, but because it is sometimes pleasurable, perhaps even necessary, simply to desire.

Directed by Wolfgang Petersen as a follow-up to his acclaimed art house success *Das Boot* (1981) and based on the best-selling fantasy novel by Michael Ende, *The NeverEnding Story* began its life as an exclusively West German production. Shot almost entirely in Bavaria (aside from a few location shoots filmed in Canada), the film was initially conceived as a solo effort by the production company Constantin Film before an eventual international distribution agreement with Warner Bros. saw the film repackaged and sold as a typical example of Hollywood filmmaking, reportedly given over to Steven Spielberg to reedit in preparation for a US release.[21] Given these interferences, it is not surprising to find that the film was received much in the same way as other Hollywood blockbusters of its era, reviewed favorably as a "extravagantly mounted fairy-tale" (*Box Office*) that offered audiences a "marvelously realized flight of pure fantasy" (*Variety*) as it opened to a generally positive but hardly enthusiastic set of opening numbers at the box office.[22] Yet, the film's popularity would prove durable enough with audiences thanks to a strong performance in the 1980s rental charts to spawn two sequels (*The NeverEnding Story II: The Next Chapter*, 1990; *The NeverEnding Story III: Escape from Fantasia*, 1994) and associated television series (*The NeverEnding Story*, 1995; *Tales from The NeverEnding Story*, 2001). *The NeverEnding Story* has thus become established among a generation of fantasy fans as a prime example of the kind of genre cinema popularized by Hollywood during this era, offering an enduring example of an alternative world that has successfully triggered the imaginations of countless audience members since its initial release over twenty-five years ago.

While it is not possible to say with any certainty why the film has become such a fondly remembered example of fantasy cinema, one of the things that does separate *The NeverEnding Story* from other blockbusters of this era is the manner in which the film's high fantasy narrative is mediated through a plot set in a world that is ostensibly our own. The film begins by following a young boy named Bastian (Barret Oliver) who, struggling to deal with the death of his mother, decides one day to skip his lessons and hide in the school attic in order to read a strange book he has obtained from a local bookstore. As Bastian begins to read the eponymous novel, the film visualizes the high fantasy narrative that he experiences, allowing this story within a story to take up the vast majority of the film's running time. Bastian's role within the film therefore seems, at least at first, to be similar to the way that characters were typically utilized within the postclassical wonder film, providing little more than an intended guide onscreen for the spectator toward a dramatic encounter with the spectacular frontier realm of Fantasia through his often visceral responses to the story's action sequences (fig. 4.3). However, as the narrative progresses, the divide between the worlds of reality and high fantasy the story demarcates begins to become rather more complicated.

When Bastian first comes across the book *The NeverEnding Story*, he is told by the bookshop's owner Mr. Coreander (Thomas Hill) that it is "not safe." Without saying directly why, Coreander alludes to the book's potential dangers by stating that, unlike the process of imagining yourself to be Captain Nemo, trapped inside the *Nautilus* submarine in Jules Verne's *20,000 Leagues Under the Sea* (1870), this particular story will not let Bastian "be a little boy again" after he is finished with it. Attracted by this idea partially as a means of escaping his grief and par-

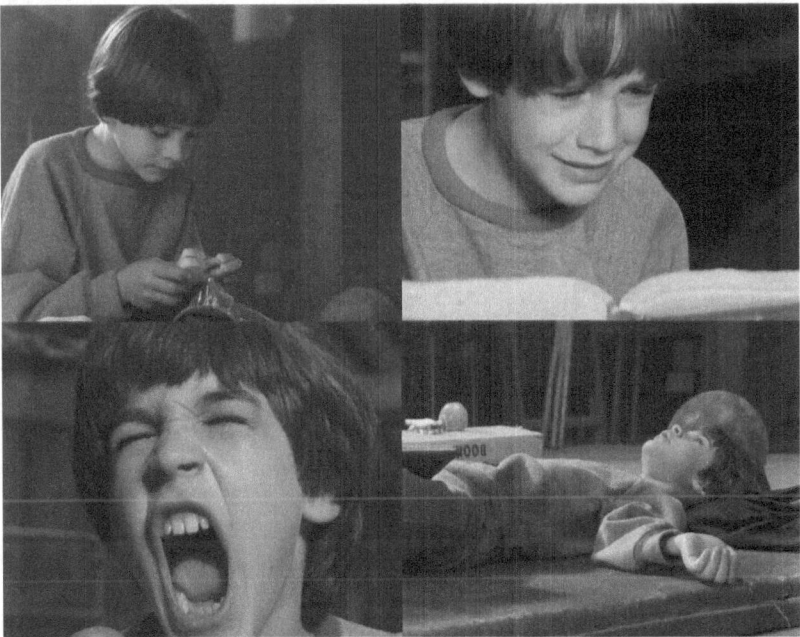

Figure 4.3. Bastian reacts viscerally to the events taking place within the book of *The NeverEnding Story* (1984).

tially to avoid the more immediate threats of a math test and the bullies he faces in school, Bastian takes the book anyway and quickly becomes engrossed in the high fantasy tale contained within it. As such, a sense of a felt loss of reality, self-conscious and deliberate on the part of both the protagonist and the filmmakers off screen, becomes more and more apparent. This is not a story about a boy lost in a fantasy land trying to get home. This is a story about the desire to leave reality behind, both intellectually and emotionally, and the consequences that entails.

In the high fantasy story that unfolds, a young warrior named Atreyu (Noah Hathaway) is charged with the task of saving the magical land of Fantasia where he lives by preventing the spread of a strange and dangerous force called the Nothing. The Nothing is destroying Fantasia piece by piece, emptying the magical lands of its realms and inhabitants and mysteriously causing its childlike empress (Tami Stronach) to fall ill. Atreyu must therefore journey to the farthest reaches of Fantasia to find a cure for the empress and stop the Nothing, a task which he seems somewhat ill-equipped for given that, like Bastian, he is just a boy. The relationship between Bastian and Atreyu does not stop with the similarity of their ages either. From the first time Atreyu appears onscreen, the film makes it clear just how much of himself Bastian invests in the novel's protagonist. The very mention of his name, coupled with the information that he is a member of a tribe of plainspeople "who hunt the purple buffalo," is enough for Bastian to reach for his backpack and, looking fondly at the Native American scene embroidered on the back, repeat Atreyu's name out loud as if he were proudly naming a child or knighting one of his royal subjects. Bastian is more than simply reacting to the drama; he is projecting onto the drama aspects of his own life, shaping the figure of Atreyu to give him a life and vitality beyond the information he is provided on the page. Atreyu becomes, in effect, part-Bastian, the high fantasy setting partially mediated through the real-life imagination of a young boy.

The sense that Fantasia is a by-product of Bastian's imagination enables the story to push beyond the merely reactive relationship between reader and story it might otherwise establish, creating a more interactive relationship between phantasy and phantasizer that the narrative exploits for dramatic potential. Fantasia becomes coded as Bastian's world, its creatures and lands filtered through his imagination. As the narrative progresses, the implicit authority Bastian has over these images becomes ever more explicit. Characters in Fantasia seem to be able to react to Bastian's thoughts and emotions, as if they were aware of his omnipresence, while Bastian's relationship to the narrative seems to be so intense as to suggest more than a relationship between reader and story. As the high fantasy story becomes focused on Atreyu's search for a human child who lives beyond the boundaries of Fantasia, Bastian, in turn, becomes more and more invested in the world he imagines, to the point that he feels the need to ration his food, to mourn lost friends within the story, and even to scream in terror as he witnesses the events taking place on the page. As these little moments recur, the films starts to call into question whether the fictional world contained within *The NeverEnding Story* really is "just a story," as Bastian repeats to himself throughout the film, or else is somehow "real," an ambiguity that the narrative sustains up until the film's climax. As Atreyu finds himself in the last remaining location in Fantasia yet to be swallowed up by the Nothing, he comes into contact with the dying childlike empress. She informs him that the only way to stop the Nothing is for the human child he has been searching for to give her a new name, something which the young warrior has made possible by allowing someone to read along with his journey. Seeing his name appear in the very book he is reading, Bastian becomes incredulous, refusing to believe that his presence has any ability to impact the tale he is reading, leading to the increasingly desperate empress to shout, "Bastian! Why wouldn't you call my name Bastian?" Eventually, Bastian succumbs, shouting a new name for the empress and saving Fantasia from the Nothing in the process.

In telling its story of Bastian's journey from passive reader to active savior of the land of Fantasia, *The NeverEnding Story* not only dramatizes an intended reaction it aims to elicit from its spectator through the display of its high fantasy narrative. It also provides a self-reflexive commentary on the value of such a process. We have seen examples of previous fantasy films where protagonists from our own world interact with spaces that are deemed alternative from reality. Alice (*Alice in Wonderland*, 1933) and Dorothy (*The Wizard of Oz*) are perhaps the two prime examples, as well as George (*It's a Wonderful Life*, 1946), Sinbad (*The Golden Voyage of Sinbad*, 1973), and, to an extent, the Banks children (*Mary Poppins*, 1964), each of whom enter into spaces that they recognize as operating according to different rules from their own realities. However, what separates Bastian from these examples is that, at least for the vast majority of the film's running time, he is unable to physically interact with his imagined world, nor is it physical interaction that the inhabitants of Fantasia need from him. To save Fantasia, Bastian does not need to defeat a monster or go on a journey; that is Atreyu's role. Instead, all Bastian needs to do is to accept and celebrate the fact that he is imagining these events into being. The narrative makes this abundantly clear when it performs its plot twist, revealing to Bastian and to the audience that what is "not safe" about *The NeverEnding Story* is that the alternative world of Fantasia represents the realm of human phantasy. It depends on humans like Bastian to invest enough emotionally into its otherwise unreal setting to give it life. Without that desire to project phantasies onto the world, Fantasia will fade away into nothing and reality will be left without dreams. This narrative revelation is therefore somewhat complex. Unlike previous magical lands analyzed, Fantasia is not a place that can be reached geographically, even within the context of the fiction. Instead, it is a place that needs to be reached for emotionally, making it an effective metaphor for the capacity of human imagination to transcend a concern with the material practicalities of life and find value in things that are not physically "real." It is therefore imperative that Bastian not only keeps reading the eponymous novel but, perhaps more importantly, keeps *wanting* to read. It is his desire for the explicit phantasy that Fantasia represents that is ultimately celebrated within the film's climax.

This feature of Bastian as a desiring protagonist reveals the distinct nature through which *The NeverEnding Story* operates as a high fantasy film. The experience of the fantastic it generates does not ask Bastian (and, by proxy, the spectator) to simply use phantasy as a necessary tool to comprehend and understand the impossible narrative events or worlds it presents. By demarcating Fantasia from reality and insisting on a separation between its real-life protagonist and high fantasy narrative throughout, the film always offers the spectator the option of rationalizing the impossible events of the narrative as "just a story," just as Bastian tries to do on multiple occasions. The hesitancy the film evokes, then, is not felt as a rupture in the causality of the fiction but a lack of will to rationalize something that can otherwise be rather easily rationalized. If the spectator wishes, they can simply explain away Fantasia as just a story with a story, as the narrative overtly asks them to do. However, if they do so, then they strip it of all meaning and consequence. The film becomes imbalanced and fatuous, giving over a vast component of its narrative to a story that is not real even within the context of its own fiction. However, if the spectator takes the option of responding imaginatively to Fantasia freely, just as Bastian does, and to see the impulse to project onto Fantasia a series of imagined ideas and emotions as a desirable option rather than the only option available, then the high fantasy can become affecting and functional once more. Just as Bastian learns through his experience of Fantasia not to "keep his feet on the ground," as his father instructs him to do at the beginning of the film, but to embrace the book's invitation to "do as he dreams," as he shouts into the sky at the film's climax, the spectator is likewise shifted in their way of approaching the fiction from a desire to rationalize the phantasies it offers to a desire to reject rationality itself. The film becomes an extended meditation on the value of the imagination not as a device that helps to make sense of the world but as a device that helps us to transcend it.

The kind of imaginative desire celebrated in *The NeverEnding Story* is therefore different from the word's usage in regular parlance. In everyday life, wanting something we cannot have is a source of endless frustration and anxiety. Psychotherapists around the world make their living out of attending to just such desires, whether this be a deviant sexual act that the patient's sense of morality or shame will not permit them to enact or a more material desire for something in the world that they are unable to obtain for whatever reasons. Our ability to create such phantasies in the first place is a result of projective phantasy's role in early development. Because we are able to exist in the world at some point without knowing there is a gap between external reality and our internal, projected psyche, it is only as we begin to understand life on a conscious level that desire formulates as something that reveals what we want in the world. Prior to that point, desire functions only to make the outer world into an outward reflection of the inner world of the psyche. However, once we reach the necessary stage in development in which we begin to recognize that there is a world, and that we exist within it, the nature of our phantasy activity shifts. No longer able to just project ourselves onto the world, we must instead project ourselves *into* the world. Phantasy becomes something that negotiates what reality is rather than what we are outside of such a context, changing our capacity to generate phantasies of desire based on our individual and instinctual needs into an ability to desire *for* certain objects and ideas that already exist.

Hollywood cinema typically encourages this latter kind of phantasy activity as part of its ability to encourage the spectator to approach its stories through what Metz refers to as their "perceptual passions."[23] Narrative cinema's ability to get us to desire certain outcomes, to want to see certain things appear onscreen, emerges primarily from a strategy that McGowan refers to as a "structuring absence."[24] An easy example of such a structuring absence might be something like the contents of Marcellus Wallace's (Ving Rhames) briefcase in *Pulp Fiction* (1994). Remaining hidden at all times from the spectator through various framing devices and alluded to but never explained within the plot, the inside of the briefcase becomes something that the spectator wants to see precisely because the filmmaking is structured around evoking its absence onscreen, turning the briefcase into, in effect, an object of desire. Structuring absences do not necessarily have to be contained to single objects or moments onscreen. They can be far more nebulous and far-reaching, whether that be the successful union of a romantic couple in a romcom or the identity of the killer in a detective mystery. The key to their effect, however, is that they create a feeling that you are not just watching cinema but desiring to see more from cinema, allowing your viewing position to be infused with a rush of excitement as desire fuels your engagement with the screen.

On one level, the triangular dynamic established in *The NeverEnding Story* between Bastian, the spectator, and the world of Fantasia functions in a manner akin to a structuring absence. When the narrative first travels from the school attic where Bastian reads a copy of the novel to the world of Fantasia, a series of editing patterns are used to show the contrast between the two worlds. A static image of Bastian's eyes is replaced with a fast-paced, tracking shot traveling through woodland, before revealing the shot of an imagined fantasy creature in the form of a large snail, and the sound of wind and trees replaces Bastian's voice on the soundtrack (figs. 4.4 and 4.5). Reality is evoked as an absence as the film travels into an alternative world, and the spectator is encouraged to see Fantasia not only as a space in and of itself but as a world that in being seen means simultaneously that they are *not seeing* reality. In effect, reality itself become something akin to Marcellus Wallace's briefcase. However, the negation achieved in this moment is very different to the desire to see inside an otherwise mundane object Tarantino's film is able to generate. In *The NeverEnding Story*, the feeling of not being able to see reality does not make the spectator, in turn, want to see it. Instead, the removal of reality generates a desire *to* desire something else in its place, the separation felt causing the spectator not to want things in a preestablished film world but to want to forge a relationship with something fundamentally new and transcendent.

What is occurring in these opening moments in Fantasia is a rerouting of two different types of desire, one of which belongs more firmly to the rational part of ourselves developed in conscious life and another attached to our more primal selves that existed before we even knew there was a thing called reality. McGowan argues that structuring absences typically allow examples of popular cinema to "energize the desire of subjects within the social order."[25] They generate our desire

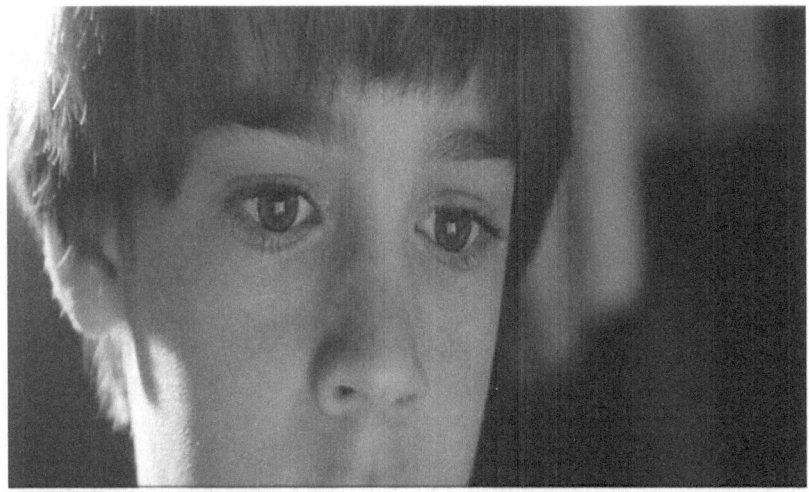

Figures 4.4–4.5. Through a close-up on Bastian's eyes, the film travels into the fictional world of Fantasia.

for things that exist within the world and therefore have the effect of making reality (or at least certain elements within it) more desirable. What occurs in *The NeverEnding Story*, however, is something very different. The experience of the fantastic the film generates allows access to a more primal and creative mode of engagement in which projective phantasy becomes a way not of desiring in a world but expressing our desire onto a world. The spectator's experience of the film amounts to an unleashing of a very different kind of desire, which is uncontained by objective laws or characteristics.

But the film does not stop there. Not satisfied with simply allowing spectators the freedom to desire things that are impossible, *The NeverEnding Story* then asks them to take ownership over those projected phantasies and recognize the role they are playing in bringing this land to life onscreen, a process that mirrors Bastian's own emotional journey throughout the film. Bastian comes to realize that what makes Fantasia desirable as a fantasy world is not some innate equality embedded within the land itself but the values Bastian brings to the world as he negates reality in its favor. This is what makes his relationship with Atreyu so intoxicatingly irresistible. A child warrior, Atreyu seems to represent everything that Bastian is not at the beginning of the film. Not only is he physically strong and capable of looking after himself in a hostile environment, something Bastian struggles to achieve, but the young warrior also seems to exist in a realm that, despite its dangers, is full of friends to help him at key moments when things seem at their most perilous, whether this be in the form of Falkor the luckdragon or the two gnomes Urgl (Patricia Hayes) and Engywook (Sydney Bromley). Atreyu's journey throughout Fantasia is littered with companions who provide good fortune, advice, wisdom, and a nurturing environment with which he can rest, all of which Bastian seems to lack in the real world. The film makes it clear that any admiration Bastian might feel for Atreyu is not merely a result of any external quality the young warrior possesses but is largely to do with Bastian's own subjective desires, something that is revealed explicitly in a scene in which Atreyu is asked to pass through a magic mirror gate in which he will be forced to come face to face with his "true self," only to be greeted with an image of Bastian (fig. 4.6).

Played out without any dialogue, the scene's sense of confusion achieves a quasi-Brechtian dynamic as different levels of dramatic irony serve to distance the spectator from the immediate narrative context. The image of Bastian reading the book is familiar and known to us. It is essentially the same shot that has been interspersed throughout the film, a shot used often to return the spectator to a sense of reality after an extended period in the world of Fantasia. Yet, in this new context, the shot seems to achieve the opposite effect. Instead of restoring reality, it instead creates a sense of distance between the spectator and reality. They occupy Atreyu's perspective rather than Bastian's, and the mirror acts as a screen within a screen to further emphasize a feeling that we

Figure 4.6. Atreyu looks into the magic mirror gate to see Bastian reading the eponymous novel.

are trapped in a world of high fantasy. It is also noteworthy that it is the only moment in which Bastian is seen reading the story without the film providing such images with an accompanying voiceover. Typically, when Bastian is witnessed reading the prose on the page, his voiceover shortly dominates the soundtrack so as to match the sensory information the spectator received with the linguistic information he is decoding. Here, though, Bastian simply reads what we are already watching, further creating a clash of perspectives between what we see and what he reads. When Bastian reacts angrily to what is happening—to the description of himself in the mirror that we are not allowed to see or hear—the film cuts back to the attic abruptly as Bastian tosses the book angrily across the room. Just as we were positioned to feel as deep inside the world of Fantasia as we have ever been, Bastian rejects the fantasy storytelling, ending it suddenly, bringing us back to the real world just when it felt as though we might have left it behind entirely.

The sequence challenges the spectator to recognize that, just like Bastian, their ability to feel as though they are inside Fantasia is brought about by a relationship between phantasy and their own desire. For Bastian, seeing himself in his fantasy world is traumatic because it suggests to him that, despite his wish to eradicate reality altogether, he is unable to fully do so. He may be able to replace the physical world that surrounds him with another world, but he cannot hope to leave himself behind, even if he wishes. Similarly, the spectator is positioned to recognize that finding pleasure in Fantasia is in part a result of their own willingness to be inside the magical land at an imaginative level. They have to take themselves with them to travel to the high fantasy world, and this therefore means that Fantasia becomes, in effect, a product of their desires and phantasies. The specifics of those desires will vary from individual person to person. They may find the exotic nature of the various creatures and lands an opportunity to see a world fresh and anew, in contrast to a realm like reality that, by necessity, needs to maintain order and stability. Alternatively, they may find the rather obvious evil of a creature like the G'mork—a wolflike monster sent to hunt Atreyu—a comfort when compared with the often muddied, complicated, and banal evils we are faced with in reality. But whatever the specific phantasies projected onto Fantasia are, the magical world's capacity to be desired is not a result of anything purely external it possesses but because it exists in a state free from the socialized desire of everyday life. As the spectator is placed in an increasingly self-aware position throughout *The NeverEnding Story*, the film climaxes in a moment toward the end of the story when the childlike empress informs Atreyu that his narrative was necessary not only to engage Bastian in the world of Fantasia but to get others to follow Bastian's story. Those that were "with him when he hid from the boys in the bookstore" are evoked directly, the film nearly breaking the fourth wall not to distance the spectator from the action but to show them that the action cannot exist without their imaginations. They are as much a part of this story as Bastian.

All of these techniques make the experience of the fantastic within the film something akin to a psychoanalytic therapeutic session. In both of their published clinical case studies, Klein and Winnicott show a great deal of care and attention in their clinical reflections of encouraging patients (whether adults or children) to see creative acts like play as useful therapeutic exercises, using such activities to make patients not only use phantasy but see phantasy as something that belongs to them.[26] In everyday life, we often avoid thinking about the phantasies we constantly create out of our own desires, refusing either to project them onto the world or even acknowledge their existence. This act of repression forms the basis for the idea of the unconscious, a term used within psychoanalytic theory to speak to that part of ourselves that we wish to dismiss or deny because we feel it does not allow us to engage properly with the world around us. If I cannot get what I want in life, I have the choice either to be left with an unachievable desire or to somehow restrict or repress that desire so I do not want it anymore. However, in denying myself that phantasy, I am denying aspects of my own existence, creating a relationship with the world that blocks or prevents me from articulating my fullest emotional depths. Well-being is therefore to be found not in denying the existence of our desires but in finding safe environments in which our desires, no matter how transgressive or prohibited they are in reality, are able to be given full voice. It is only by allowing ourselves to desire fully that desire can be responded to, processed, and understood as a part of our conscious, yet still emotional, engagement with the world.

This is the same lesson that Bastian learns in *The NeverEnding Story*. At the beginning of the film, he spends his life drawing pictures of unicorns on his textbook rather than having any emotional relationship to the world around him, the act of phantasy providing him with neither relief nor satisfaction as he seems unable to either stop daydreaming or take ownership over those dreams. But, the story of Atreyu and the Nothing catalyzes him not to retreat into phantasy but to use Fantasia as an invitation to understand what it is he actually wants. The film's external antagonist of the Nothing, then, functions both as narrative device to provide a source of threat and drama to which the protagonists can respond and as a way of awakening and empowering instinctual desire. At the beginning of the film, the Nothing is presented within the narrative as an almost indescribable threat, an abyss of meaning that is ripping its way through the land of Fantasia. It is first introduced by the Rockbiter creature toward the beginning of the narrative, who tells his friends what happened when a lake near his home was engulfed by the strange substance. He says that the lake was simply gone, replaced with "nothing, not even a dried up lake." The fear created in such a description—allowing the Nothing to notably remain off screen and thus unrepresented—is precisely the same fear that prevents Bastian from realizing that he desires not to be in reality. The idea of replacing "something" with "nothing" alludes to the very tensions surrounding the repressive impulses of our psyche, as our consciousness tries to make meaning at the expense of expressing emotional truth, while our emotions try to tell us things that, because we do not understand, we do not want to hear. All of this gives the Nothing a quality of the unconscious, and the way it is presented within the narrative as an antagonistic force within the narrative structure energizes the film with a neurotic energy as the land of Fantasia is split into meaningful and nonmeaningful parts.

Atreyu tries different methods of fighting the Nothing—searching out spells and oracles, and journeying to the furthest parts of Fantasia in an effort to find a cure—but these efforts are all ultimately futile. At the film's climax, as the high fantasy world is ultimately completely swallowed up by the Nothing, what is left is not the abyss of meaning that is suggested throughout the narrative but a serene void of calm. In this moment, the film makes a narrative revelation that transforms the very essence of what the spectator has come to understand the Nothing to be. Transported into the magical land, Bastian is told that the only way to stop the Nothing is not to fear it but to use it. Rather than see its lack of reality as a problem or threat, Bastian is told that the Nothing is something he can use to fill Fantasia with his phantasies rather than someone else's. The transformation the Nothing undergoes in the story from antagonist to vessel for the expression of desire, therefore, narrativizes the spectator's broader engagement with the world of Fantasia. By using projective phantasy, spectators are able not simply to express a desire for Fantasia but to use their desire for Fantasia as a means of expressing their own inner psychic life. It is by giving voice to such desires through phantasy that the film functions as a fantasy blockbuster, providing a unique experience not simply of spectacle but of how such spectacle positions the spectator to engage with the screen in a manner that is not afforded in everyday life.

The true never-ending story of the film's title, then, is not necessarily a high fantasy story about a magical land with fabulous beasts and exotic locations, nor is it a story about Bastian. The true never-ending story alluded to in the film's title is the subject's ability to both phantasize and to desire, as the spectator is positioned to engage in both activities in far less inhibited or repressed ways than in everyday life. It is by giving voice to such desires through phantasy that the film functions as a high fantasy blockbuster, providing a unique experience not simply of frontier spectacle but spectacle we are taught to embrace as belonging to us and desired by us. In *The NeverEnding Story*, what we want is not what we get but something far richer than that. What we want is who we are.

The Fantastic and Infantilization: Projecting Childhood in *Hook*

For the final case study of this chapter, it is perhaps useful to select a film directed by the very individual who helped facilitate the birth of the high fantasy blockbuster, while at the same time being indirectly responsible for its demise. Steven Spielberg's *Jaws* ushered in the first wave of blockbuster filmmaking, the film acting as a template for the industry for the production of similar action-oriented frontier spectacles distributed through block booking strategies during a targeted summer release schedule. Yet, just as quickly as Spielberg helped to invent the blockbuster format, he also managed to subvert it with the success of *E.T. the Extra-Terrestrial* (1982), which became one of the biggest-selling films of the 1980s. In that film, Spielberg combined the kind of effects-driven cinema he had popularized in *Jaws* with a child-centered story set in a domestic setting, fusing frontier action with family melodrama to create a new kind of family-oriented production that yields significant box office returns. The film's commercial success was widely attributed to its ability to appeal to a broad demographic of children and adults alike, a feat that ushered in a new era of ascendency for the "family-film" package, which, as Peter Krämer argues, arose from its somewhat niche and specialist origins within Hollywood's production schedule to become a mode of filmmaking responsible for some of Hollywood's greatest commercial successes of the 1990s and beyond.[27]

The fate of fantasy cinema within the new family-friendly blockbuster market was somewhat mixed. On the one hand, the genre would seem a natural bedfellow for the kind of family-orientated spectacle the success of *E.T.* demanded. Fantasy storytelling has been associated with children's literature arguably since the publication of the Grimm Brothers' *Kinder-und Hausmärchen* (Children's and Household Tales) in 1812, making it an extremely suitable genre for adaptation to this family-friendly commercial model throughout Hollywood's history. Yet, perhaps surprisingly, one of the immediate consequences of the rise of the family-friendly blockbuster was to cause the abrupt curtailment of high fantasy that had previously littered Hollywood's production schedules. Stung by a number of high-profile flops including Disney's *Dragonslayer* (1981) and *Return to Oz* (1985), Ridley Scott's *Legend* (1985), and George Lucas's *Willow*, studios became less convinced that there was a sufficient market to justify the production of high fantasy given the high costs required to create these lavish alternative worlds onscreen. Such efforts attracted a more mature audience of self-declared fantasy fans, while family-friendly fantasy films could seemingly appeal to a broader demographic that more closely matched the commercial expectations of the global media conglomerates who now owned the studios. During the 1990s, fantasy cinema thus became a genre whose commercial potential would be best exploited when aimed at the family-friendly market, utilized as the basis for a number of commercially successful productions including *Beauty and the Beast* (1991), *Aladdin* (1992), *The Santa Clause* (1994), and *Jumanji* (1995), while leaving the science fiction and action genres to target the more mature audience traditionally associated with the blockbuster.

All of these factors make *Hook* a particularly fascinating final case study for examining the types of experiences and pleasures available to the spectator within the high fantasy blockbuster. Conceived as a fanfare effort from Sony's newly acquired Columbia Pictures, *Hook* would be rather self-conscious in its attempts to appeal to a family-friendly demographic through both its marketing and its production history. In 1987, Great Ormond Street Hospital, as part of the legal agreement that saw the charitable body inherit the rights to the *Peter Pan* stories upon the death of J. M. Barrie, lost the ability to refuse permission for adaptation. Capitalizing on this opportunity, Columbia sought to grant Spielberg his lifelong wish to make a version of the *Peter Pan* stories for the big screen, greenlighting the production of a costly venture that would seemingly allow both the high-profile director and studio to trade on the widespread associations the stories themselves had within popular culture with childlike ideals of innocence and the imagination.[28] Reimagining Barrie's Neverland as a spectacle-driven blockbuster, the production team behind *Hook* sought to generate the excitement of audiences of seeing the now iconic images from his famous alternative world complete with pirate ships, fairies, and mermaid coves. In doing so, the film's production team created a work that straddles the era of high fantasy and family-friendly film not only in terms of its production history but in terms of its basic DNA.

A part sequel and part reinterpretation of Barrie's original narrative, *Hook* does not tell the famous story of the boy who never grew up but instead of a man who must learn to be a boy again. Having left Neverland to become a corporate lawyer named Peter Banning (Robin Williams), the now adult Peter has forgotten his adventures among the Lost Boys, thinking instead that he was adopted as a small child by "granny Wendy" (Maggie Smith), an elderly matriarch of a renowned orphanage. In the film's opening act, Peter, his wife Moira (Caroline Goodall), and his two children Jack (Charlie Korsmo) and Maggie (Amber Scott) travel to London to visit Wendy after a long period away, during which time it is made clear that Peter's ascendency into adulthood has meant a severing with anything remotely childlike. His main focus and energy seem to be taken up by dealing with the cutthroat world of corporate mergers and hostile takeovers—as Wendy says to him, he has become a "pirate"—while he finds his children's desire for seemingly pointless games and kinetic activities like baseball to be nothing but irritating distractions from his demanding work schedule. What follows, then, is a journey narrative that interrogates Peter's failings as a father, as well as offering him an opportunity for possible redemption through a form of infantilization. Establishing Peter as a somewhat tragic figure, the film laments the fact that in order for him to grow up, he has had to abandon the very virtues associated with his former life in Neverland, setting up a desire for Peter to return to his former self not necessarily so that he can return to a life of timeless adventure but to become a better father to his children.

The seeming necessity of Peter's emotional return from the Banning figure we are introduced to in the film's opening act to the Pan figure he is more commonly associated with in popular culture is catalyzed through the intrusion into reality of the fantasy world he has left behind. While Peter is out at a charity dinner to celebrate Wendy's accomplishments, his children are snatched in their beds by his old nemesis, Captain Hook (Dustin Hoffman), who leaves a note demanding Peter's return to Neverland. Peter therefore journeys back to his magic alternative world with the help of the returning Tinkerbell (Julia Roberts) who, in a scene that mirrors the original arrival of Peter Pan and Tinkerbell into the Darling nursery, greets Peter only for him to disbelieve what he is seeing and promptly faint. In the original story, Tinkerbell and Peter's arrival into exactly the same nursery was greeted by an enthusiastic set of children who were willing to immediately embrace and believe in the rules of the fantasy world they represented. In *Hook*, Tinkerbell is greeted by a cynical man who refuses either to remember her or even believe she exists. Peter dismisses Tinkerbell as a "complex Freudian hallucination having something to do with [his] mother," trying to rationalize her existence according to some existing principle of reality rather than accept her for what she is, an approach that not only hurts Tinkerbell emotionally and physically (fairies die when people do not believe in them) but causes Peter to faint with shock. While the Darling children in the original story chose willingly to fly to Neverland, an act that prepared them for the idea of an alternative world before they even arrived, Peter remains clinging doggedly to the trappings of reality even as a fairy proves his assumptions about the world to be false, forcing Tinkerbell to literally bundle him up and drag him across the night's sky to facilitate his arrival into the magical world.

These opening exchanges between Peter and Tinkerbell establish the approach Peter will take to Neverland throughout the majority of the narrative, an approach that simultaneously distances him intellectually and emotionally from the sights, sounds, and characters within the alternative world he encounters, as well as from the spectator. Thanks in part to the opening act's attempt to establish Peter's faults as a character and partially by the film's use of visual spectacle upon their arrival into the fantasy land, the spectator is aligned primarily to the adopt the same perspective to this alternative world as they might in a blockbuster like *Conan the Barbarian*. The film offers a vivid invitation to imagine a new world into being onscreen and then places its central character in opposition to the pleasure of being in Neverland that the rest of the characters in the film seem ready and able to enjoy. This is witnessed most profoundly during Peter's arrival. The opening shot of Neverland, seen from Peter's perspective as he rips open a bedsheet to reveal the pirate ship, echoes Dorothy's entrance into Oz rather explicitly (figs. 4.7 and 4.8). Just as in *The Wizard of Oz*, the perspective of the film's protagonist is used to highlight the rupture in space from reality to alternative world, only for the camera to then forgo its main character in favor of a protracted establishing shot used to convey a feeling of excitement in this magical world to the spectator (fig. 4.9). A tracking shot is used to rapidly move around the pirate's docks, taking in a series of vistas thronging with activity, and the rapid tempo of the action in the scene is matched by the orchestral score (fig. 4.10). The feeling of excitement *Hook* offers the spectator in its alternative world creates the necessary conditions to encourage an experience of the fantastic, stimulating an opportunity to project onto the screen a series of phantasies that help them to construct a picture of Neverland out of the spectator's imagination. Yet, the spectacle achieved in these opening few moments is offset against Peter's own refusal to do exactly what the filmmaking invites the spectator to do: to imagine a world unlike reality. For Dorothy, a mere glimpse of Munchkinland was enough to make her realize she was not in Kansas anymore. For Peter, despite everything that he sees, it is as if it all still belonged to reality, a dynamic which quickly becomes a source of humor as he recommends Armani shoes to a hoard of pirates and is immediately chased through the docks to find himself aboard Captain Hook's ship.

Figure 4.7. Peter peers through the ripped bedsheet in *Hook* (1991).

Figure 4.8. Framed from Peter's perspective, a small hole provides access to Neverland.

Figure 4.9. That world is revealed fully.

The contrasting perspective on Neverland achieved between the spectator and by Peter becomes an anchoring point for the rest of the unfolding narrative that stimulates a desire for Peter to learn to be more like his former self. Discovering his kids hanging in a net above the rigging and demanding their safe return, Peter is told by Captain Hook that he need only fly up to the top of the mast and touch his children's hands in order to set them free. Once again, instead of embracing Neverland's otherworldly possibilities, Peter tries to negotiate with the pirate captain as if he were in reality, offering money from his checkbook instead before, eventually, climbing the ship's mast in a vain attempt to reach them that way. Shots of Peter struggling physically are interspersed with the Neverland inhabitants' amusement, before cutting to his children's slow realization that their father will be unable to save them as he too slowly gives up, believing his task to be impossible (fig. 4.11). The somewhat

Figure 4.10. Peter stumbles lost around the world he left behind.

Figure 4.11. Peter Banning/Pan does not believe he can fly.

pathetic image of Peter struggling to reach his children relies on a dramatic irony established between spectator and character over the nature of Neverland as an alternative world. If only Peter would participate in the fun of Neverland, he would remember who he was and be able to fly. Yet, because he clings doggedly to the certainty reality brings him over the possibilities phantasy could provide, he remains a forlorn shadow of the figure who once not only knew how to fly but did so spectacularly.

In this sense, *Hook* represents the epitome of Robin Wood's famously polemical description of the Hollywood blockbuster as a process of cinematic infantilization, positioning "the adult spectator as a child . . . [who] loses him/herself in fantasy."[29] The film equates the joy at being in the world of Neverland with the joy in being a child, mediating the spectator's encounter with the alternative world through a narrative that aims to create a sense of the fantastic not solely out of a desire or need to embrace an exciting and impossible unknown (as was the case with both *Conan the Barbarian* and *The NeverEnding Story*) but by offering a return to a familiar known that has somehow been forgotten or denied by reality. Whether informed by a preexisting familiarity with the *Peter Pan* stories, which the film rewards throughout with numerous references to Barrie's mythology within both the production design and dialogue, or simply by the film's own attempts to present the rules of Neverland and Peter's aversion to them, the spectator is encouraged to recognize that the best way of understanding and appreciating this fantasy land is to reject any concern with rationality or functionality and instead celebrate the setting of Neverland as a quasi-object of play. This applies right down to the film's visual spectacle. The pleasure the film offers from seeing its elaborately constructed sets such as the pirate ship or the home of the Lost Boys onscreen (two locations wherein the vast majority of the narrative action takes place) seems rooted in a relative parade of elaborately constructed games, from the lost boys' skateboard ramp and basketball hoops to Captain Hook's red carpets that are able to disappear and reappear depending on where he steps on his ship. Both locations highlight the enjoyable over the purposeful, a dynamic which is paralleled by the wider topological structures that govern Neverland. Barrie's fantasy world is not one ruled by rationalistic or empiric impulses. It functions to provide a giant playground for the pirates and the Lost Boys, allowing both sides to revel in their antagonistic relationship to one another by enacting a series of "wins" or "losses" in a perennial war that has little overall consequence, purpose, or meaning. What is useful in understanding this world is not the part of our brains that lets us decide what things are and how they should function. What is instead helpful is our ability to imagine alternative usages for objective objects aside from their most obvious or most practical as vessels for play in order that we might create new identities for both the locations and people through our ability to self-consciously project pleasurable phantasies onto them.

The split between an adult and childlike worldview that *Hook* engenders, then, has as much to do with the structuring of individuals within society as it does with any ingrained or biological notion of maturity or immaturity. As Ewan Kirkland argues, much like race and gender, the idea of childhood is more productively thought of as a social rather than a biological category.[30] On an individual basis, children do not possess any innate characteristics or behavioral traits as a direct result of their age, despite what adults might wish to assume or project onto them. Instead, children are assumed to possess certain traits (innocence, a love of games, a closer relationship to the imagination) due to prevailing cultural dynamics that manifest not only within society at large but within psychoanalytic theories of phantasy, particularly in terms of its theories of the imagination. As Freudian theory informs, children learn in later life to become "ashamed" of their early years of phantasy activity, setting aside the pleasure and reassurance they felt in projection both in early life and in play itself in later childhood development in order to become the mature citizens society asks them to be.[31] Yet, this narrative suggests a natural evolution within the psyche from a phantasy of pleasure to one of practicality that, in actuality, is by no means as clear-cut. As many clinical case studies of child patients will attest, children often spend a great deal of time and effort worrying about the effect their phantasy life is having on their understanding of reality. Likewise, adults often feel the need to play in some capacity with the world around them through a variety of cultural forms such as games and art as part of the desire to seek emotional respite from the world's most serious matters. The move from childhood to adult forms of projection, then, is not as biologically as it is sociologically determined. It is because society demands us to let go of pleasures we experienced in childhood that we feel pressured to do so, a situation that proves useful in our attempt to understand the world logically but also repressive to our natural emotional states that might wish to play with the world as much as we might try to understand it.

The pleasure *Hook* offers spectators is therefore not actually a pleasure in returning to a mental state closer to the projective phantasies of early childhood. If that were the case, the kind of process spectators would be required to undergo in order to engage with the fictional events in Neverland would equate to something similar to what is described in Freudian discourse as "regression," a destabilizing or restrictive activity that is often encountered in psychoanalytic treatment as a traumatic symptom that must be worked through if the patient is to progress to the status of well-being.[32] Instead, the experience of the fantastic that *Hook* offers allows the spectator to use projective phantasies to articulate a release from the kind of societal pressures that are bound up with being seen as an adult in a world structured by scientific, rationalistic, and capitalistic impulses that have dominated since the arrival of the enlightenment. It stops the spectator having to use phantasy that is in any way rooted in their ability to be useful or functional citizens, at least beyond the purpose it serves in understanding the fiction onscreen, and to embrace an imaginative activity that *Hook* rewards precisely because it seems to lack an overt objective function. If *Conan the Barbarian* offered spectators an expression of imaginative power and *The NeverEnding Story* an expression of imaginative desire, then *Hook* offers an expression of imaginative freedom. The film offers the spectator freedom from having to think or act in a certain manner that both externally and internally they are pressured to do in everyday life, providing instead a vision of identity associated with their own childhood that, in truth, only ever partially existed, if at all.

Such a dynamic is witnessed within a particular sequence in *Hook* wherein the shift in the function of phantasy from its adult to its childhood connotations is manifested onscreen through a rupture in the mise-en-scène. Living with his forgotten Lost Boys, Peter attempts to learn how to be the person he needs to be in order to return to Hook's pirates in a few days and reclaim his children. After a day of rigorous exercise, the overweight Peter and the Lost Boys gather at the dining table. Peter stares hungrily at the smoke and steam coming from the kitchens, but he soon discovers that what is produced on the table is not the food he craves but instead a series of empty bowls that form the basis of a game in which the Lost Boys pretend to eat and drink their fictional contents. Peter does not want to play a game; he wants "some real food" and so voices his objection in an outburst that leads him into an exchange of insults with the surrogate leader of the group, Rufio (Dante Basco). Replacing Peter Pan as their leader, Rufio has established himself as a very different talismanic figure to that of the boy who never grew up. Instead of leading the Lost Boys through the chaotic fun of play, Rufio seems more concerned with hierarchy and organization. His group activities are often structured around his dominance—his entrance into the film takes place along an elaborate skateboarding ramp as the boys chant his name—while his demeanor is far more serious and hostile than the fun-loving Peter once was. Therefore, while Rufio may be their surrogate leader, he is not a surrogate Pan, and the restoration of Peter's identity is bound up with a restoration of the Lost Boys as playful citizens.

This tension between Peter and Rufio plays out through the verbal exchange at the dinner table. As Rufio shouts various insults, he speaks in a supposedly childlike vernacular, calling Peter a "slug-eating worm," a "puke pot," and a "beef-fart sniffing bubble butt." Rufio's vocal delivery is vicious, gleefully enjoying Peter's hostility and his dominance not because games are fun but because winning is fun. The joy is not in the act of imagination but in the rise in status it might bring among others. As Peter fights back, he gains traction in the game not by matching the level of complexity of Rufio's grotesque imagery or wordplay but because his insults are delivered in such a manner as to indicate that he is enjoying himself. Peter's delivery becomes larger and more theatrical, his vocals more strained and emotive, and his body language more erratic. He brands Rufio a "substitute Chemistry Teacher" and (in a rather crass line) a "near-sighted gynecologist," delivering insult after insult that the Lost Boys seem to enjoy simply because of the fact that Peter seems to be enjoying himself. He is playing with them, at last resembling the fun-loving boy they said goodbye to rather than the man obsessed with not getting mud on his expensive clothes. When Peter shouts his final line to Rufio, "Don't mess with me man, I'm a lawyer," in his most childish of mannerisms, he not only reminds the spectator of the similarities between the vocal contest taking place and Banning's adult occupation but of the blurred lines between adulthood and childhood that exist within his identity, and their own. Proudly proclaiming himself to be lawyer, he shows none of the polished, corporate veneer he has perfected as he has adapted to his adult role. Instead, he is enjoying being himself again.

What Peter achieves in this moment of exuberance is a freedom of self-expression the spectator has not witnessed thus far. His life experience allows him to call out Rufio for what he is—an imposter suffering from "Peter Pan envy"—but it is his reconnection with the kind of gameplay he used to chastise his own children for indulging in that gives him the stimulus to say it. To celebrate his victory, Peter then throws a fake spoonful of food toward Rufio, joining in the game he previously rejected (fig. 4.12). It is at this moment that the rupture occurs within the mise-en-scène and the food that was once just pretend is realized onscreen in all its sensory delights (fig. 4.13). The textures of the individual dishes are emphasized through a close-up and the use of a tracking camera shot

Figures 4.12–4.13. Peter learns to have the imagination to start a food fight.

gives the rich banquet a sense of vitality. The shot now matches a way of approaching the world the film valorizes as childlike, one in which the objective becomes a site for subjective expression rather than the other way around. Phantasy is used to shape and mold the world around them by projecting onto them and the freedom of this process manifests in the pleasure in the food on the table. Peter is "using his imagination," as the Lost Boys exclaim, but this is in fact a misnomer. He has never stopped using his imagination. However, he has now started giving his phantasies the freedom to transcend the restraints society has imposed upon them and project Peter's feelings onto the world. This gives way to a feeling of joyful lawlessness and possibility that ends in a food fight. Food becomes a site of play rather than a vessel for consumption, the thing he so craved at the beginning of the scene but now seems to have forgotten about entirely.

The food fight that follows sets up a change in Peter that climaxes in his return to the iconic role of Peter Pan. At the film's key turning point, Peter learns to fly not by remembering who he was in Neverland but by remembering that he wanted to be a father. It is not a return to childhood that propels him into donning his famous green tights; it is a recognition that his primary motivation to achieve adulthood was to be a father. Remembering the emotional impetus that governs his choices within the world gives Peter the ability to think his happy thought, creating a newly liberated version of his own identity. As he flies off into the sunshine, close-up shots of the Lost Boys are shown one after the other, each turning to glimpse at the pleasurable sight of Peter flying. He has become part of Neverland's visual spectacle rather than being ostracized from seeing it, aligning him finally with the sensibility of being in the alternative world the film has sought to encourage from the spectator. Like Neverland, Peter is now devoid of the adult qualities the film associates with reality. He is not embarrassed by his attire. He is not concerned by perceived danger or fear. Peter is free: free to be among phantasy, free to rid himself of dominant societal structures, and free to save his children.

The commercial and critical failure of *Hook* sounded a temporary death knell for high fantasy onscreen. Even in its infantilized form, Spielberg's *Peter Pan* adaptation was seen as a bloated and extravagant indulgence, creating a "dangerously overextended children's fantasy" (*Newsweek*) "about Steven Spielberg wanting to remain a kid in the worst way" (*Box Office*).[33] The film placed alternative fantasy worlds onto Hollywood's blacklist, where they remained largely untouched until the return of high fantasy in the early 2000s thanks to the success of *The Lord of the Rings*. However, as much as *Hook* became a posterchild for the problems of fantasy filmmaking, its subsequent reappraisal by future generations would offer an alternative take on the film as something far beyond the infantilizing mess it was derided as being on its initial release. As more and more people find in *Hook* a film that managed to generate a highly evocative, imaginative experience, so too the film's thematic and experiential interrogation of the gap between childhood and adulthood as embodied states of being can be reexamined as something far more complex and, potentially, politically nuanced than they might seem at first glance. Far from being fatuous, Neverland's childlike qualities are, in fact, a rejection of a series of predominant societal values. They are a rejection of function, use, and purpose in favor of frivolity and triviality, a shift enacted through the film's positioning of the spectator to experience the alternative world through a series of projected phantasies. They reject a world of phantasies about currency and exchange, commerce and value, credit cards, mortgages, pensions and promotions, and embrace a world of pleasure. They allow a pleasure in being allowed to have pleasure, in "being a child," one that radiates throughout the experience of the fantastic the film offers, turning life from an opportunity to be sensible into a great adventure.

Conclusion: Projecting the High Fantasy Blockbuster

The era of high fantasy was brought about by a series of market considerations unique to 1980s Hollywood. During this era, a selection of fantasy films were made that offered an experience distinct from those favored during previous genre cycles. Focusing the spectator's attention on the alternative world as sight and site of narrative opportunity and visual spectacle, these films generated an experience of the fantastic rooted in the pleasures of projective phantasy, pleasures related to ideas of power (in the case of *Conan the Barbarian*), desire (in the case of *The NeverEnding Story*), and societal pressure (in the case of *Hook*). These films offered spectators opportunities to set aside their worldly concerns and use their imaginations at the expense and defiance of preestablished rules and conventions, constructing worlds out of the information on the screen that spoke to and appeased ingrained tensions about the problems of living in a world of confinements and prefixed meanings when, once, we were all essentially doing what we were asked to do in response to the fantastic in high fantasy cinema: to build a highly imaginative world around us that gives voice to our emotions through it.

The period of the high fantasy blockbuster ultimately proved to be short-lived given the relative commercial failure of many of its productions. Yet, its legacy would continue, its filmmaking patterns finding echoes in future attempts to bring high fantasy back to the screen after its imposed hiatus at the end of the decade. Films like *Wizards of the Demon Sword* (1992) and *Kull the Conqueror* (1997) saw smaller production companies attempt to revive some of the successes of the previous decade, while other productions like *The Last Action Hero* (1993) or *The Pagemaster* (1994) saw studios attempt to reinvent the high fantasy formula by integrating elements of the action film, or by experimenting with the use of cel animation. But it was not until the early 2000s that high fantasy filmmaking would stage a real resurgence among Hollywood studio productions. Thanks to the astonishing commercial and critical success of New Line's *The Lord of the Rings* (2001–2003), a wave of high fantasy franchises followed that seemed to offer up a new kind of fantasy adventure and spectacle to audiences. The techniques perfected during this era, and the new kinds of experiences they offer, will be the subject of the final chapter that is yet to come. Right now, it is important to emphasize that, as much as contemporary fantasy filmmaking differentiates itself from the high fantasy era of the 1980s, it is also indebted to it. Hollywood's first wave of high fantasy blockbusters taught studios what not to do certainly, but they also taught them what to do, meaning that their legacy is not entirely absent from some of the fantasy genre's more recent success stories.

Three key scenes in recent franchises show the debt contemporary fantasy owes to this period of production. The first is the introduction of Hogwarts castle in *Harry Potter and the Sorcerer's Stone* (2001). In a film that is so focused on setting up the stakes of its franchise, its plot almost creaking at the seams as it tries to establish the vast array of characters, settings, and rules surrounding J. K. Rowling's Wizarding World, the film still makes sure to afford time and space to celebrate the presence of its fictional world onscreen, setting aside continuity storytelling practice in favor of an opportunity for the spectator to take part in a process of projection. As Harry steps off the Hogwarts express train and arrives on the edges of the grounds of the Wizarding School for the first time, the camera's sweeping, kinetic movement portrays a sense of excitement and visceral pleasure at being in a fictional space. The castle emerges from the background of the shot, juxtaposed with the intimacy of the foreground as children sit hunched up and tightly packed aboard a set of canoes, and the contrasting sense of space helps place the characters in dialogue with a spectacular vista, much in the same way as a film like *Conan the Barbarian* did beforehand. Pausing to revel in the sight, the spectator's imagination is piqued into projecting onto the castle a set of phantasies about what it might look like inside, phantasies that feel empowering because they cannot, in the moment, be wrong.

The second is the introduction of Narnia in *The Chronicles of Narnia: The Lion, the Witch and the Wardrobe* (2005). Adapting C. S. Lewis's novel, the film depicts Lucy Pevensie's first steps into the magical world through a process of desirable negation. A relatively grim reality is established in the film's opening ten minutes, a world ravaged by warfare and dominated by fear, and Lucy's first steps into the snow-drenched Narnia become palpable in their sense of imaginative release. The entire tone of the film shifts from a sense of tension to relaxation, the orchestration of the score employing high-pitched woodwind instruments to almost lift the film out of its gloomy opening, and the beauty of the white, snow-drenched landscape becomes the focus of the mise-en-scène. Those familiar with Lewis's narrative will no doubt know the darker places its story will go. But, in these opening moments onscreen, Narnia itself becomes a world that allows us to dare to want different things from those in reality, and grants us permission to dream.

The final moment is not so much an introduction but a reacquaintance with a world we have long left behind. Much like the return to Neverland signaled in *Hook*, *Oz: The Great and Powerful* (2013) presents a similar return to the land of Oz, a world familiar to audiences of adults and children alike. Telling a prequel story of the arrival of the wizard into the magical land, and the birth of the Wicked Witch of the West, the film's opening moments back in the land of Oz seem to directly echo the 1939 MGM film, moving as it does from a black and white opening set in Kansas to a Technicolor spectacle in Oz in a single moment. The wizard's arrival into Oz aboard his famous hot-air balloon offers an invitation to the spectator to return, to return to that moment when Oz was first imagined into being both on and off the screen when watching the MGM adaptation, and to use that as a way of mediating the world now presented. Placed in dialogue with the original, *Oz: The Great and Powerful* seems to celebrate its technological differences with the MGM classic, the vast horizon of scenarios feeling more acute at the shot moves from the 4:3 ratio employed in its opening (reminiscent of the original) to the widescreen format favored within the majority of contemporary releases, while at the same time moving from 2D to the digital 3D (at least in its theatrical release). Yet, anchoring that display of technology to a sense of a world once known now forgotten, the film tries to use such a moment to assert a position of childishness on the spectator, a position that gives them license to see this new rendering of Oz as an extension of an imaginative game they have been playing with the screen since their first encounter with MGM's *The Wizard of Oz*, and to return to that game that they might otherwise have lost or forgotten.

All three of these films diverge in many ways from films like *Conan the Barbarian*, *The NeverEnding Story*, and *Hook*. However, the ways they each choose to announce their alternative worlds onscreen are nevertheless reminiscent of the same kind of visual spectacle and same concern with allowing spectators to generate an imaginative response to the diegesis that populated the 1980s high fantasy blockbusters. The demands spectators make for fantasy worlds to feel fully realized are in part a result of the imaginative power these spaces seem to evoke, a power first demonstrated to its full capacity during their initial wave of popularity. In many ways, then, the era of the high fantasy blockbuster demonstrates something that is as ahistorical of fantasy as it is specific to this moment of Hollywood's history. The high fantasy blockbuster created an effective system of visualizing and presenting alternative worlds. But the alternative world is as important to fantasy storytelling as it always has been and always will be.

5

Interpreting the Fantastic

Contemporary Fantasy Cinema and Symbol Formation, 1992–2018

By the end of the 1990s, blockbuster filmmaking had become so ingrained within Hollywood's wider economic model that it no longer made sense to define it as a unique subgenre separated from other forms of commercial filmmaking. Instead, as Jon Lewis argues, the blockbuster has become an industrial phenomenon measured purely by the "cash spent on production and advertising and cash made at the box office."[1] As film studios merged with other multimedia outlets such as Viacom, AT&T, and Sony to create what became known as the contemporary Big Six (Disney, Warner Bros., Sony, Universal, Paramount, and 20th Century Fox—at least until the recent acquisition of Fox by Disney), this definition of the blockbuster would prove to be increasingly significant. Global media companies produced films for a global demographic, and everything about this filmmaking system became larger-than-life—its production costs, advertising budgets, and box office sales soaring to engulf the seemingly antiquated cinema practices of old that relied on the regular production of modest productions for a consistent rather than sporadic audience of cinema-goers. In the age of home-viewing and digital streaming, Hollywood is seemingly required to be bigger if it is to remain better.

Within this macroeconomic climate, fantasy cinema has arisen to become contemporary cinema's most successful form of filmmaking, dominating the yearly box office charts as more and more blockbusters amass vast global profits. The genre's unprecedented levels of commercial success have altered Hollywood's industrial landscape significantly, as film series adapted from well-known examples of fantasy literature such as *The Lord of the Rings* (2001–2003), *Harry Potter* (2001–2011), *The Chronicles of Narnia* (2005–2010), and *The Hobbit* (2012–2014) have helped revolutionize the governing practices of the industry and initiate the now dominant franchise system of production that has given rise to cultural phenomena like the Marvel Cinematic Universe. At the same time, while achieving this commercial success, the fantasy genre has also garnered a level of critical attention and respect among the hierarchical class dynamics of supposedly highbrow, cinephile culture that had spent approximately half a century dismissing the genre's wonder films and blockbusters as derisory and vacuous modes of entertainment. Filmmakers such as Tim Burton (*Edward Scissorhands*, 1990; *Alice in Wonderland*, 2010), Terry Gilliam (*Brazil*, 1984; *The Fisher King*, 1991; *The Imaginarium of Doctor Parnassus*, 2009), David Fincher (*The Curious Case of Benjamin Button*, 2008), and Martin Scorsese (*Hugo*, 2011) have received critical acclaim for making films indebted to the conventions of fantasy storytelling, while films such as *Life of Pi* (2012) and *The Shape of Water* (2017) have been able to garner multiple Oscar nominations and awards by using their parade of Bengal tigers and fishmen to infiltrate Hollywood's most conservative vanguard of taste. All of this is to say nothing about the impact fantasy is currently having on notions of quality television. The success of shows like HBO's *Game of Thrones* (2011–2019) has paved the way for equally complex fantasy stories to be adapted to serial narrations through series like *Good Omens* (2019) and *His Dark Materials* (2019–). Fantasy has therefore become a genre label used by both the consumers of high-, low-, and middle-brow cinema, affording the genre the opportunity to win industry awards and gather favorable newspaper and magazine reviews among respective publications of the traditional intelligentsia, giving it an aura of intellectualism seemingly denied to Hollywood fantasy cinema in previous decades.

For fantasy genre enthusiasts, this latter feat might represent the most noteworthy difference between the contemporary era of fantasy filmmaking and its previous incarnations. Having spent most of the twentieth century having to defend itself against accusations that the fantasy genre was either aimed solely at children or the perpetually adolescent tastes of a certain cultlike subculture, fantasy fans have now taken over the shop. Fantasy fandom has become so intertwined with mainstream popular film culture that it is hard to separate the two, evidenced in the swell in interest in events such as Comic-Con, as well as the domination by fantasy at the global box office. As David Butler argues, "There has also been a belated recognition from the film industry [and its commentators] that fantasy is not just a vehicle for special effects and merchandising opportunities targeted at a juvenile audience."[2] Even at the more commercial end of the spectrum, something as seemingly populist as the superhero film now seems a fruitful ground for the kind of close analysis perfected among the midcentury cine clubs in response to the latest arthouse release, whether this be pondering the political implications of Batman's vigilante nature in *The Dark Knight* (2008) or the distorted utilitarian ethics of Thanos's finger-snap in *Avengers: Infinity War* (2018). While this mode of reception has hardly been universal (there will be, no doubt, many audience members who still find the fantasy genre's unwillingness to rationalize or explain its fanciful surroundings at odds with their cinematic tastes), it is equally true that the past few decades have seen an increase in the public's desire to discuss, debate, and interpret fantasy as offering something else aside from a pleasurable encounter with an impossible event onscreen.

Such attempts to widen the appeal of fantasy filmmaking to incorporate middling-to-highbrow tastes come with a double-edged sword. In seeking to produce fantasy cinema that rewards strategies of interpretation associated with highbrow film criticism, whether self-consciously in an attempt to respond to the genre's low cultural standing at the turn of the twenty-first century or as a more implicit response to the popularity a particular type of fantasy film has received during this era, filmmakers have made fantasy cinema respectable by potentially downplaying its core identity. It is as if writers, producers, and directors recognize that the spectacle of a hobbit and a magic ring is not, in itself, substantial enough to make great cinema, and so they must somehow assure audiences that such fanciful scenarios "mean" something beyond their status as works of fantasy in order to garner praise and traction among audiences. In many ways, then, the spectator is set up much like a Freudian analyst, told to look past the "manifest content" in the fantasy narrative (or, in Freud's case, in the dream) in favor of the more meaningful "latent content" that relates to conscious thought and rational existence.[3] To make fantasy "good," we must supposedly make it operate just like other genres of cinema that appeal toward our desire to make sense of fiction as something that speaks to real-life concerns, turning hobbits into metaphors, dragons into subtext, and magic into a coded illusion that means something different than what it says.

In trying to articulate fantasy cinema's capacity to appeal to traditionally highbrow modes of cultural reception, it is not my intention to repeat or support the embedded cultural hierarchies surrounding this new wave of fantasy appreciation and fandom. Instead, it is my hope that they might be reconciled. Previous eras of fantasy cinema have prioritized the feeling and affect the genre's imaginative creations might produce over the potential opportunities for further intellectualization of the subtextual nuances it makes available. However, this does not mean that such examples of fantasy filmmaking are any worse for that fact. Nor, for that matter, does it mean that contemporary fantasy cinema is now better than its predecessors. On the contrary, my interest is in how these two models of fantasy storytelling can be reconciled as part of the same consistent desire to ask spectators to in respond in some way to the hesitancy of the fantastic. In this sense, I define the act of interpretation in line with the definition of Dudley Andrew, who considers it to be a method of engagement wherein a film's formal and stylistic construction is scrutinized in order to "rectify the confusing, appreciate the subtle, and multiply the thought of the text."[4] Seen in this manner, interpretation can be a way of responding to the fantastic imaginatively, but one that places a particular onus on paying a close enough attention to the nuances of film form and style to perform an act of filmic analysis that has long been aligned with highbrow taste and cinephile culture. My desire is therefore not to find the "something else" in fantasy that, as Richard Dyer argues, theorists of popular cinema often try to locate as means of giving genre cinema a meaning aside from its primary status as entertainment.[5] Instead, I want to examine how a certain brand of fantasy filmmaking popularized after the turn of the twenty-first century entertains through encouraging spectators to participate in an interpretative act of decoding that is in part a response to the experience of fantastic the films provoke.

In thinking through this way of responding to the fantastic, I am drawn to a particular concept discussed in both Kleinian and Winnicottian thought as symbol formation. The term emerges in their respective psychoanalytic theories as a way of describing the act of interpretation that takes place in therapeutic sessions. Like the supposedly highbrow spectator, both analysts and their patients engage in an act of interpretation that encourages both parties to look for the nuances embedded with their acts of communication and their actions in the world in order to expand on something latent, subtle, or nuanced in the patient's psychological behavior that might otherwise go unexplored. Yet, often within Freudian accounts of this phenomenon, interpretation has what François

Sirois refers to as a "mutative" dynamic in that it seeks to transform irrational impulses into rational explanations.[6] In an attempt to avoid this mutative dynamic, Klein's ideas of symbol formation as a therapeutic goal and methodology seek to encourage patients to form interpretations as means of adding value and meaning to their imaginative experience, an idea that was then developed by Winnicott within his playlike therapy sessions through techniques such as the squiggle game.[7] Used on children typically ages five and up, the squiggle game functions to create the necessary conditions whereby symbol formation permits the expression of certain phantasies that are otherwise denied or suppressed by the child's increasing understanding of reality and its underlying symbolism. Drawing a squiggle on a piece of paper, the analyst asks the child to transform the shape into an image with some sort of meaning or value. As the child does this, they express externally the internal life of phantasy they are experiencing through the creation of a symbol, a process enacted due to the failure of the squiggle to function as a symbol in and of itself. The squiggle must be embellished by the child's expression through phantasy, allowing the child not just to use preexisting symbols to express themselves but to create new symbols through the phantasy activity that they bring to the sheet of paper.

Symbol formation is a therapeutic method that encourages interpretation through acts of creativity. As Winnicott states, it is achieved by "bringing the patient from a state of not being able to play into a state of being able to play."[8] Its function is not to provide an interpretation as a means of explaining away the irrational impulses toward phantasy exhibited by patients but to initiate an experience where the patient feels enabled to utilize language and symbols as a way of articulating an experience of the world founded first and foremost in the imagination. If we think of the spectator's relationship to fantasy cinema along similar lines, we can start to understand what the contemporary manifestation of the fantasy genre does that allows it to fulfill its twofold function. By allowing spectators to construct interpretations that seem to emerge out of the imaginative engagement with the film, the genre becomes simultaneously entertainment for traditional genre fans wishing to engage with the genre's capacity toward imaginative pleasure and a means of enhancing appreciation of certain films for new fans who wish to engage in close analysis of film form and style. Like the playing patient within a psychoanalytic therapy session, contemporary fantasy films are designed to offer spectators the ability to interpret their stories as a means of responding to the impossible scenarios they present.

Considering three works of fantasy cinema produced over the past two decades, I will analyze the formal and stylistic conventions of this era as offering opportunities for symbol formation. In doing so, I argue that the desire among contemporary audiences to talk about, discuss, and interpret contemporary fantasy cinema beyond the sheer act of narrative comprehension is not merely a result of shifting cultural dynamics that have realigned popular perceptions of the genre. Instead, it is in part a response to a set of calculated strategies embedded within the films themselves. *The Lord of the Rings* is indicative of the shift in style and technique fantasy filmmaking has undergone in recent years. The trilogy makes a calculated attempt to reframe high fantasy storytelling in response to a perception of how audiences felt about the 1980s cycle of fantasy filmmaking, playing down the alterity and potentially hyperbolic nature of Middle-earth and highlighting instead its ability to speak to both historical and contemporary events and concerns. The trilogy effectively teaches spectators how to channel their experience of the fantastic into a metaphorical exercise more in keeping with the intellectual requirements associated with highbrow cinema. The hesitation felt in response to the impossibility onscreen, once given license to pursue metaphorical solutions, can be channeled into either an appreciation of filmmaking craft (what we might call "poetic" interpretations for reasons that will be clarified later) or an attempt to mirror the events onscreen with real-life events (which suggests instead toward a capacity toward allegory). Considering *Where the Wild Things Are* (2009) and the Fantastic Beasts franchise (2016–), I will look at the shift in how these films seek to code their impossible subject matter in a way that encourages these two alternative modes of interpretative practice and offer new ways of experiencing fantasy fiction.

The Fantastic and Interpretation: Symbol Formation in *The Lord of the Rings*

Peter Jackson's *The Lord of the Rings* trilogy has largely defined the formal characteristics of the fantasy film genre throughout the early twenty-first century, just as its source novel defined the characteristics of popular fantasy literature throughout the second half of the twentieth century. Shot in one large production over a fourteen-month period and released consecutively as three separate films—*The Fellowship of the Ring* (2001), *The Two Towers* (2002), and *The Return of the King* (2003)—New Line Cinema's adaptation of Tolkien's epic novel achieved not only an unprecedented level of commercial success for a fantasy film at the time of its release but was acclaimed by journalists and critics writing in a vast spectrum of newspapers and magazines around the globe. A year prior to the release of the first installment of Jackson's trilogy, fantasy remained a genre struggling for critical legitimacy.[9] *Dungeons and Dragons* (2000) had been released internationally to both critical and commercial disappointment, described by A. O. Scott in the *New York Times* as a "noisy, nerve-racking tedium of contemporary popular culture."[10] Yet, little over a year later, the fairly consistent declaration of *The Fellowship of the Ring* as a "masterpiece" among newspaper and magazine critics was enough to allow the film's marketing department to subsume this critical reverence into its public identity, positioning itself as a new kind of fantasy film for a new kind of audience.[11] The films were lauded as models "for how to bring substance, authenticity and insight to the biggest of adventure yarns" (*Los Angeles Times*),[12] sparking a newfound interest in the fantasy genre among audiences who might otherwise have shunned the genre for its assumed banality and triviality. *The Lord of the Rings* made fantasy Oscar-worthy, tunneling into the heart of Hollywood's critical establishment and planting a tree from which future fantasy films could branch out.

The shift in reception toward fantasy cinema that *The Lord of the Rings* was able to initiate was likely to have been a source of enormous satisfaction for both its financiers and for Jackson's creative team. Kristin Thompson writes at length in her book *The Frodo Franchise* about the consistent desire of both Jackson and his collaborative producers (Barrie M. Osborne, Fran Walsh) and screenwriters (Philippa Boyens, alongside Jackson and Walsh) to avoid associations between *The Lord of the Rings* and the wave of high fantasy films that had come before it during the 1980s.[13] Instead, much work was undertaken within the film's production design to echo Tolkien's own desire for his world of Middle-earth not to be read as an "imaginary land" but as "feigned history," a distinction he makes throughout his private letters and published commentaries on his writing process between an act of pure imaginative speculation and what he conceived of as his attempt to reignite the cultural heritage of the past through fiction.[14] In this vein, the production's design team leaned heavily on real-life historical influences, incorporating elements of both Anglo-Saxon and Viking culture in its design of the civilizations of Rohan and using real-life locations such as Mont St. Michel as reference points for the CGI cityscape and practical sets of the fortress city of Minas Tirith.[15] The design of the weaponry of Sauron's armies was inspired by ancient Middle Eastern and East Asian civilizations, while the architecture of the

City of the Dead was based largely on the ancient city of Petra, Jordan. Frances Pheasant-Kelly has explored this aspect of the trilogy particularly, considering how the design of the films resonate with prevalent racial fears among US and Europe audiences exposed to and expounded by the post-9/11 climate, as well as commenting more broadly only the trilogy's ability to resonate with audiences by telling a story from the perspective of "shared global histories."[16] From the imagery of the Holocaust evoked in the gaunt figure of Gollum to a scene in *The Two Towers* wherein the wizard Saruman (Christopher Lee) delivers a speech to his army of uruk-hai soldiers, a moment reminiscent of Leni Riefenstahl's *Triumph of the Will* (1935), the film presents its fictional circumstances in a way that allows spectators to place onto the film fiction a series of associations and connections with real-life, historic events.

Alongside these visual strategies, *The Lord of the Rings* also manages to further inject a historicized feel into its alternative world of Middle-earth by borrowing filmmaking techniques from contemporary hits like *Braveheart* (1995) and *Gladiator* (2000). The historical epic staged something of a resurgence during the 1990s, producing not only some of the decade's biggest commercial hits but taking advantage of the latest in CGI innovations to set a precedent for a kind of action-oriented spectacle that received critical as well as popular attention. From *Braveheart*, *The Lord of the Rings* inherits a similar focus on the visceral nature of medieval warfare. Action sequences throughout the trilogy deploy a number of techniques to focus the spectator's attention to the bodily impact of swords and arrows, concentrating on the brutality of the weaponry through the use of close-ups, cuts on action, and an intensified soundscape to emphasize the force of each individual impact. From *Gladiator*, the trilogy attempts to emulate a similar kind of visual spectacle in crowd imagery that had made that former film's action sequences within the Colosseum so arresting. Pioneering the Massive software, the technical team at Weta Digital responsible for *The Lord of the Rings* were able to create large CGI crowds and armies onscreen on a scale unrivaled by its predecessors, a feature that would become a key focus within the trilogy's later installments. This focus on spectacular, large-scale warfare allowed Jackson's team to represent the epic war of the ring described in Tolkien's novel by structuring *The Two Towers* and *The Return of the King* around a series of now iconic battle sequences such as Helm's Deep and the Battle of the Pelennor Fields, depicting warfare on a scale that audiences had not seen prior to the trilogy's release, and which has since been redeployed in the action-sequences of films such as *King Kong* (2005), *300* (2007), and *Dawn of the Planet of the Apes* (2014).

Not only is the iconography and source of spectacle in *The Lord of the Rings* more reminiscent of the historical epics of the 1990s blockbuster than the 1980s high fantasy film, but the way the film trilogy approaches the process of adapting Tolkien's story shows a similar commitment to downplaying aspects of the original story that has made it perhaps the quintessential fantasy adventure of the twentieth century. Part of the pleasure of reading *The Lord of the Rings* lay in the extraneous details that sat alongside Tolkien's narrative, its episodic adventures and frequent plot diversions revealing the depths of the world of Middle-earth that Tolkien had developed over decades of writing. Jackson's adaptations, however, streamline this sprawling approach to storytelling into a far more straightforward journey narrative. Frodo's (Elijah Wood) journey to Mordor is given priority over everything else, allowing the films to devote more time that might otherwise be spent revealing the details of its fictional world to focus on their protagonist's descent into existential despair and self-destructive addiction. This technique, described by Gwendolyn A. Morgan as "narrative condensation," functions alongside another adaptive process of "re-characterization."[17] Outside the focus on this main story, secondary characters like Aragorn (Viggo Mortensen) and Faramir (David Wenham) are transformed from the relatively archetypal heroic roles they serve in the novels into characters haunted by angst over the weight of their own responsibility to the story that unfolds, moving it away from Tolkien's own desire to set his story in dialogue with the myths and legends of Anglo-Saxon heroic poetry and toward a story that seems obsessed with promoting its own sense of gravitas. Tolkien's Middle-earth is therefore offered to the spectator for their viewing pleasure, but the kind of richness of detail it exemplifies seems to be revealed most explicitly not through the sheer amount of narrative information the story presents but through the ability of its narrative to feel consequential, weighty, and important.

In making these creative changes to the way they presented Tolkien's world and adapted his narrative for the big screen, Jackson, Boynes, and Walsh were able to emphasize a facet of Tolkien's novel that is perhaps in danger of being forgotten given the perhaps more obvious contribution it has made to the history of high fantasy literature. As well as inspiring numerous imitators and a relative publishing craze, *The Lord of the Rings* was also embraced among certain quarters of the traditional, conservative literary establishment, lending Tolkien's book an air of intellectual credibility that might otherwise have not been available to such a story given the genre in which it belongs. This ability to appeal to a supposedly highbrow sensibility alongside popular literary taste was partially achieved thanks to Tolkien's status as an Oxford professor. Yet, at the same time, his novel was also written in a distinct enough manner for it to read rather differently from that of his fantasy forebearers. In contrast with the economical prose style favored among pulp fantasy fiction at the time, Tolkien's novel is, at times, challenging to read, not least because of its sheer length but also the ambition of its storytelling and complexity of its vision. As Nicholas Burns argues, the story presented is indebted not only to folkloric iconography and myth but "a certain kind of bourgeois social realism" that *The Lord of the Rings* incorporates to infuse its fantasy setting with a quality of modernist literary fiction.[18] Readers are required to invest vast amounts of time and effort into the process of understanding Tolkien's world, carefully examining the nuances of the details it presents to try and construct a cohesive understanding of what all this narrative information might mean. Given the somewhat intimidating nature of such a task (the book is over half a million words in length), it is not surprising to see the sheer wealth of popular interpretations that have surrounded the reception of the book since its initial release. From the 1960s countercultural hippie movement's celebration of *The Lord of the Rings* as an antimaterialist, psychedelic journey through to the critiques often leveled at the novel for its conservative gender attitudes and problematic representation of race, the desire to read, understand, and interpret *The Lord of the Rings* has fed into a huge part of its public reception since the first wave of the novel's popularity, an aspect that the film trilogy tries to replicate by retelling its story through a filmmaking style that was as beholden to recent Oscar successes as it was to the legacy of fantasy fiction onscreen.

All of this means that Jackson's *The Lord of the Rings* seeks to produce a very different kind of experience of being in the alternative world of Middle-earth from the kind invited from previous cycles of fantasy filmmaking. In departing from the formal and stylistic conventions of the 1980s high fantasy cycle, the trilogy creates an experience in which the feeling of the fantastic it generates through the display of their impossible circumstances feels invested with a similar sense of gravitas and importance as the historical epics and psychological dramas that it competed with during their Oscar awards campaign, a feature that transforms the act of deciphering Tolkien's alternative world onscreen undertaken by the spectator into something that contains as much intellectual potential as it does emotional or imaginative value. Compare, for example, the prologue sequence in *The Fellowship of the Ring* with a similar prologue sequence in *Conan the Barbarian* (1981) explored in the previous chapter. Both sequences begin with voiceovers that seem designed to achieve a similar sense of ironic distancing, announcing the presence of an alternative world by barraging the spectator with a large amount of fabricated contextual information. Both describe historical events and places that do not exist in reality, and both do so without explanation but by referring to fictional events in passing as if they were events in history. However, the kind of imaginative response they seem to encourage through the process is markedly different. In *Conan the Barbarian*, the contextual information provided about the world in which the story takes place is brief (less than forty seconds in total), and the information conveyed about the world is largely extraneous to the plot that unfolds. In Jackson's *The Lord of Rings*, however, the opening voiceover in *The Fellowship of the Ring* is not only far more extensive in terms of its duration (lasting approximately seven minutes); it also contains a great deal of information that is pertinent to the story that will shortly unfold. It establishes the origins of the eponymous one ring, the history of Sauron, the trilogy's primary antagonist, and the chronology of ring-bearers to date in order to set up the events of the film's opening act. While the opening of *Conan the Barbarian* creates an impression that the key virtue of its fantasy story is that it negates the concerns of reality in favor of an alternative and imagined set of rules or agendas, *The Lord of the Rings* announces its version of the fantastic through a slightly different sensation. Instead of giving the spectator free license to speculate imaginatively as to what this world might mean, the spectator becomes immediately invested in the act of problem-solving, code-breaking, and, above all else, narrative comprehension. Its impossibility is not an open invitation to phantasize; it is a force that must be reckoned with, understood, and processed intellectually.

The distinction between the experiences these two high fantasy films offer respectively, then, comes down to a distinction in the act of interpretation each encourage from the spectator. As both psychoanalytic and linguistic theory inform us, every thought that we have about cinema, just like every thought we have about the world, is, in effect, an act of interpretation. Ideas, expressed through words, often require us to replace an immediate sensory experience (the image of a tree, for example, or a falling leaf) with a linguistic reflection that provides that event with additional meaning (that is a tree during fall). However, some forms of interpretation feel more intellectually challenging to formulate than others, and this is often to do with how self-conscious we are of the interpretative processes we are asked to perform at any one time. When doing something as basic as recognizing the image of a tree and associating it with the word *tree*, for example, it is not always easy to even notice that there is an act of interpretation taking place. However, when that same image of the tree provides a potential clue as to the right way to progress along the path, the act of interpretation becomes simultaneously more demanding and noticeable. This is because these two examples of interpretation—one seemingly passive and unnoticeable, the other active and self-conscious—require phantasy to play a contrasting role. In the first example, phantasy plays what is refers to in psychoanalytic theory as a metonymic role. By imagining that a tree is the word *tree*, we perform a largely unconscious act of substitution between a signified (the image) and a signifier (the word) as the metonymic displacement of object for symbol helps to give the tree a meaning through an unnoticeable act of imagination. In the second example, however, phantasy plays what is known as a metaphorical role.[19] As you struggle to transform the image of tree into an interpretation that might provide the clue as to your appropriate journey, you are not just performing an act of substitution of a sensory object for a linguistic symbol, you are evading the object altogether in search of its meaning. The interpretation you construct must be played with and forged, its allusive nature emerging because it does not share as close or direct a relationship with the sensory information that sparked it, and the meaning that is thus forged occupies a metaphorical relationship with the original image as a result. While metonymy requires a largely unconscious act of phantasy to make words express meanings in and around reality, metaphorical interpretations are forged through a more creative process of inference and illusion that is far more self-conscious, but no less imaginative.

Either through devices like visual spectacle or through narrative techniques that focus the spectator's attention on the act of story comprehension over other potential interpretive acts that might otherwise be available, Hollywood fantasy films prior to *The Lord of the Rings* largely locate their experience of the fantastic to a metonymic as opposed to metaphorical consideration of impossibility. The hesitation they provoke from the spectator denies them the ability to easily forge metonymic acts of phantasy that displace what is seen with what it might mean because what it might mean is, by its nature, impossible. In *The Lord of the Rings*, however, metaphorical interpretations seem to play an equally important role in the spectator's experience of the narrative events. The act of decoding Tolkien's dense fantasy story onscreen seems to necessitate both consideration of its literal circumstances, while at the same time encouraging the spectator to create more developed, less obvious meanings through a process of inference, allusion, and collision between different ideas, concepts, and images. This latter activity seems to occur particularly in key moments within the storytelling where in the focus within the narrative gives way to a moment of reflection, one which directs attention away from the immediate circumstances taking place toward a postulation about what it might mean at a broader, metaphorical level. These moments of metaphorical allusion are key to stimulating an imaginative response to the film in which part of the pleasure of the film seems to come from articulating different layers of interpretation—speaking not only what the narrative is, but what it might mean.

Take, for example, a memorable scene in *The Fellowship of the Ring* in which the assembled members of the fellowship stop to rest after a day's walking in the underground mines of Moria. Afforded a moment of respite from the long journey, Frodo finds himself talking to the wizard Gandalf (Ian McKellen), to whom he promptly confesses his deep-seated anxieties and concerns over his suitability for the task of being the ring-bearer. He admits to Gandalf that he wishes the "ring had never come to [him]" and "that none of this had happened." Gandalf responds to Frodo's confession by gently telling him, "So do all who live to see such times, but that is not for them to decide. All we have to decide is what to do with the time that is given to us." Gandalf is shot in close-up, staring at the diegetic Frodo but also seemingly beyond the screen as he transcends his status as a character within a story and becomes a force akin to the Greek chorus that acts as a direct interface between audience and narrative (fig. 5.1). The moment of visual excess

Figure 5.1. Gandalf offers Frodo some advice (*The Lord of the Rings: The Fellowship of the Ring*, 2001).

seems to demand something more than merely assigning it an explanation within the immediate context of the narrative, and its repetition later on during the narrative denouement of the film helps to infuse Gandalf's words instead with a sense of grander importance, inviting opportunities for metaphorical as well as metonymic considerations as a by-product of the fictional events depicted onscreen. The resonance of such a line fosters the spectator's ability to forge a cohesive interpretation out of the film, a dynamic evidenced by a popular meme featuring the same line and accompanying image used by social media users as a source of comfort during the COVID-19 pandemic. The imaginative appeal of such a moment is not simply in the impossibility of a wizard speaking to a hobbit, but in finding opportunities for a story that is nominally about completely fabricated peoples living in a completely fabricated world to offer meanings that can resonate beyond such formidable boundaries between Middle-earth and everyday life.

Similar moments as this appear throughout the trilogy, often at key points in the narrative in which the spectator's natural tendency to speculate as to how the events might unfold are directed toward a broader metaphorical consideration as to what the events playing out actually mean. Toward the end of *The Two Towers*, Sam (Sean Astin) compares the journey he and Frodo find themselves undertaking to "the great stories . . . the ones that really mattered," a speech that functions to unite the various strands of the now separated narrative under a wider thematic suggested within Sam's voiceover, and to encourage the spectator to speculate imaginatively on what indeed *matters* about this story being told. Likewise, at the end of *The Return of the King*, Frodo himself is seen writing a copy of *The Lord of the Rings* and reflecting on the nature of the telling of his own story, positing him simultaneously as protagonist and narrator. Once again, the narrative pauses to provide a brief metatextual commentary on the relationship it aims to establish between film and spectator. As the nuances of individual moments onscreen are transcended in favor of an appeal to the narrative's wider thematic resonance, the spectator is cued into a way of experiencing the fiction that fits alongside the standard critical practice of interpretation. Narrative comprehension seems to become part and parcel of a more considered engagement with the film form and style, as *The Lord of the Rings* encourages spectators to find greater meaning in what the film alludes toward rather than what it explicitly presents onscreen.

Once the process of understanding the significance of Middle-earth as a fictional world generates a certain level of interpretative work on the part of the spectator, it begins to mirror a dynamic akin to the therapeutic value of symbol formation within psychoanalytic practice. In interpreting *The Lord of the Rings*, the spectator's response is encouraged first and foremost through a direct engagement with the fantastical nature of what is being told. It is in part because *The Lord of the Rings* fails so acutely to be a valid representation of reality that the spectator is given the necessary time and space through the process of hesitation to forge metaphorical alongside metonymical interpretations, interpretations that emerge out of their imaginative engagement with the events onscreen. In this sense, the trilogy is not unlike other fantasy films like *Conan the Barbarian* that encourage an amount of imaginative speculation through an encounter with an impossible world. The only difference is that, while *Conan the Barbarian* directs this activity largely toward its literal circumstances—it encourages interpretations about the nature of its imagined world—*The Lord of the Rings* encourages equally metaphorical interpretations about what this imagined world means beyond its more immediate context. This gives the act of trying to interpret the film's narrative the quality of an act of play, consisting as it does of an activity in which the spectator is required to try to construct something meaningful out of something that declares itself to be operating outside of objective value. The interpretation is therefore pursued primarily because it allows the means of accessing a pleasure that would otherwise be denied, providing a way of reconciling with the natural hesitancy that comes from watching impossible events unfold, and to view *The Lord of the Rings* as a highly imaginative fantasy film full of ideas, concepts, and creations that resonate emotionally.

Understanding this interpretative process as symbol formation is also important if we are to assess the true function interpretation serves with regard to *The Lord of the Rings*' function as a fantasy film. For symbol formation to provide its therapeutic effect, the patient must be able to take in part in a process of interpretation that, as Klein argues, amounts to "the re-education of the capacity to fantasize."[20] The patient must be provided with either a structured activity designed to encourage such a creative response to the world (painting pictures, playing games, building models with blocks, etc.), or they must be encouraged to participate with the process through a trusting, nurturing dynamic established between patient and analyst. This latter feature is especially true in Winnicottian practice. For Winnicott, play activities are important but not necessarily essential processes that allow patients to engage in symbol formation. Instead, his therapy aims to create a suitable "holding" environment wherein the patient does not seek to censor or suppress the phantasy activity they utilize in both life and in his sessions, and to instead use their creative engagement with the world as the basis for expressing their thoughts and feelings.[21] The patient is metaphorically held by the analyst, and that feeling of being secure enough to abandon the thought processes they require to understand the world literally and instead approach words and symbols as means of externalizing their inner life is offered within the safety of the environment. That potential is also rife within fantasy cinema. The experience of the fantastic has the potential to showcase to the spectator the creative possibilities that surround a film's potential meanings, encouraging them not to find the most direct interpretation that allows the film to be processed as quickly as possible but to find implicit, creative interpretations to the sensory provocations the film offers. But, in order for the spectator to be able to embrace those meanings, they must be similarly "held" by the film, to be made to feel that their interpretation matters, and that it is not simply an act of deciphering a preexisting objective structure but a way of responding imaginatively to the scenario in which they have been placed.

The interplay between *The Lord of the Rings* and its spectator relies on both of these dynamics simultaneously. The more obvious moments within the storytelling in which the spectator seems encouraged to look for the metaphorical interpretations that might be available within the story function akin to the forced structure of a game, allowing symbol formation to emerge in response to the specific circumstances taking place onscreen in any one moment. However, having established this interpretative dynamic, the trilogy is then able to rely on an infusion of this sensibility on the rest of its fictional world. The spectator is "held" by the film's sense of imagination, encouraged to find in the fictional world deeper meanings that resonate on a personal as well as intellectual level that the trilogy nurtures through the safety provided by its impossible subject matter. To interpret Middle-earth is not to try to understand it objectively or rationally, but to articulate how and why stories that seemingly mean nothing are able to mean something to those who experience them depending on the metaphorical allusions and ideas they bring to the screen.

Once the spectator learns to embrace the hesitancy that *The Lord of the Rings* provokes in such a manner, they are allowed access to levels of meaning that might otherwise go unnoticed or unarticulated. The Balrog, for example, Tolkien's beast of the deep released unwittingly by the dwarfs mining into the bowels of the mountains, forms an iconic image from *The Fellowship of the Ring* because of what the creature offers the spectator not just metonymically but metaphorically as well. A creature of fire and darkness born out of the deep mines of the dwarfs, the Balrog may represent a physical manifestation of the avarice of industry, or else possess a more quasi-spiritual dimension given the allusions toward Roman Catholic symbolism both within the film and within Tolkien's source novel. Such allegoric modes of interpretation seek to find a way of articulating the creature's identity by searching for figurative meaning beyond the literal. A similar invitation to interpret the films allegorically is found within their critical reception, with critics praising the trilogy for functioning as everything from an elaborate "metaphor for the Allies' battle against Hitler" (*Time*) to a "morality play [that] will resonate powerfully in these post-Sept. 11 days" (*USA Today*).[22] Likewise, through the focus in the mise-en-scène on the creature's quasi photo-realism (the way the light shimmers through the heat the creature emits, or the immersive soundscape of falling rock employed in the protracted action sequence), it seems equally possible to forgo such thematic considerations and instead ascribe value to the creature through recourse to its status as special effect (fig. 5.2). Again, this is evidenced in the numerous behind-the-scenes and making-of books published during the time of the trilogy's release, as well as the endless features detailing the film's technical production as part of the *Extended Edition* DVDs, and indeed the numerous technical awards the films won. This kind of interpretation we might label as poetic, in that it resides in a focus on the craft and aesthetics of images as images, rather than what the images mean. In either case, both modes of interpretation articulate a response to the feeling of displacement, the sense of the fantastic, generated from the

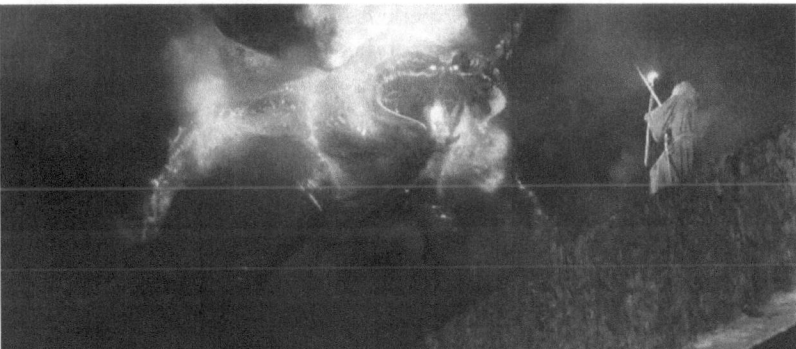

Figure 5.2. Gandalf battles the Balrog.

literal circumstances presented onscreen. The Balrog's impossibility means that it must become a symbol of something, either of technical craft or a manifestation of some figurative function within the wider storytelling.

The reason I have foregrounded these two modes of interpretation in particular—allegoric and poetic—is not solely because they seem to reflect two of the key aspects of the way *The Lord of the Rings* was received by audiences at the time, or because they are necessarily pertinent to the psychoanalytic ideas of symbol formation that I think are useful to consider in assessing the imaginative potential and function of interpretation at large. Rather, poetic and allegorical interpretations have been previously articulated in the context of the fantastic by Tzvetan Todorov, the theorist who first gave us words like *hesitation* to describe the experience of encountering impossible circumstances in fiction. For Todorov, allegory and poetry are ways of describing the potential limitations of the fantastic experience by providing ways of reading impossible events rationality.[23] Allegory transforms the impossible literal to the possible figurative, while poetic readings transform words that denote into words that function as decorative symbols. I do not ascribe to this suggestion. I do not think that the fantastic cannot bear the processes of interpretation, and that it must be experienced only through a purely literal experience of the fiction at the level of comprehension of the events alone. Indeed, as this analysis of *The Lord of the Rings* and the enthusiasm by which fantasy films are interpreted more generally demonstrates, the fantastic can often benefit or be further extended by a process of interpretation that emerges as part of the spectator's attempt to engage with the impossible nature of what is seen. As we move forward to look at other contemporary fantasy films that likewise seem to encourage symbol formation, I will demonstrate precisely how the very same modes of interpretation once dismissed by Todorov as oppositional to the experience of the fantastic—the poetic and the allegoric—can indeed form part of the imaginative response these films are able to conjure, particularly in an age where filmmakers are utilizing techniques like those examined in *The Lord of the Rings* to encourage spectators to establish creative meanings for the film fiction through phantasy.

The Fantastic and Poetry: Emotion and Symbol Formation in *Where the Wild Things Are*

Poetic interpretation offers spectators an opportunity to approach fantasy films through a self-conscious appreciation of filmmaking craft. It is the difference between seeing something impossible and interpreting that impossible thing as a manifestation of an underlying creative impulse, an expression of a certain technique, or as something that finds value and meaning by being considered first and foremost as a constructed work of art. When filmmaker and theorist Pier Paolo Pasolini tried to create a "cinema of poetry," he wanted to develop methods that would allow cinema to reach beyond its photographic capability to capture an objective, pro-filmic event (even a fictional pro-filmic event) in favor of a filmmaking style in which the spectator would be required to view the images as crafted constructions belonging to an author.[24] Likewise, in popular parlance, the term *poetry* is often used by film critics writing in both traditional print and online media outlets as means of both celebrating fantasy cinema's artistic craft and to speak to its ability to do more than simply show us events onscreen. Last year alone, the word was evoked by the *Los Angeles Times* in relation to a recent French fantasy/animation *I Lost My Body* (2019),[25] by *Slate* online magazine to explain the strange delights of the gothic melodrama *The Lighthouse* (2019),[26] and, somewhat disparagingly, by *VOX* magazine as a means of critiquing the deemed-to-be excessively cryptic advertising campaign of *Frozen II* (2019).[27] Poetic interpretation therefore seems to be a key strategy through which contemporary fantasy films are discussed and interpreted by mainstream media and, by extension, its audiences, as well as something we instinctively feel as we perceive certain moments onscreen that seem to display the creative efforts on display as much as they do depict a certain setting or situation.

For a good example of how poetic interpretations can aid a film's identity as a work of fantasy, it is worth turning to a work whose production and distribution was shaped in an expediential manner by the newfound reverence the fantasy film genre had achieved in the years following the success of *The Lord of the Rings* trilogy. Adapted from Maurice Sendak's best-selling picture book, *Where the Wild Things Are* marked the first screenwriting effort in the directing career of Spike Jonze (writing in collaboration with Dave Eggers). It therefore represented an important career milestone for a director who, perhaps unusually among highbrow film circles, was best known for collaborating with the more high-profile screenwriter Charlie Kaufman, namely, with his first two features *Being John Malkovich* (1999) and *Adaptation* (2002). Stepping out from Kaufman's shadow, Jonze was able to use *Where the Wild Things Are* to forge a new identity for himself as a creative individual rather than as a collaborator on Kaufman's absurdist comedies, a reputation he has since cemented through his work on the acclaimed science fiction romance *Her* (2014).

Where the Wild Things Are therefore helped to shape his creative persona as a writer/director, allowing him to present to audiences a distinct, creative sensibility that he sought to achieve by producing a film set in a firmer fantastic mode than his previous absurdist and surrealist efforts.

Jonze's desire to present himself to the world as an artist through his work in fantasy filmmaking was assisted by the cultural transformation the genre had undergone during the early 2000s. Without the success *of The Lord of the Rings* and subsequent international arthouse hits like *Pan's Labyrinth* (2006), it is difficult to see how Jonze would have been given the role of adapting Sendak's source text in the first place, let alone how he would have been afforded a budget of $100 million and the creative freedom through which to do it on his own terms. Sendak's children's picture book had been passed between Disney, Universal, and Warner Bros. in the decades prior to the film's production, as studios struggled to find an appropriate way of adapting the story into the kind of family-friendly fantasy film that might otherwise have seemed appropriate given the target demographic of the book itself. Inspired by fantasy's critical metamorphosis, Warner Bros. performed a shift in commercial strategy by hiring Jonze onto the project in order to target *Where the Wild Things Are* at a mature demographic, hoping the film would achieve a crossover success between mainstream audiences and the more middle-to-highbrow circles who had begun to embrace fantasy cinema in the past decade.

Though the film would ultimately not become the financial success studios were hoping, *Where the Wild Things Are* did manage to resonate strongly with the subsidiary audience demographic to which it was partially intended. Opening to favorable reviews, critics signaled out for particular praise the way the film had managed to bring fresh life and a new perspective on Sendak's beloved children's classic through the manner in which it had been adapted by Jonze. In *USA Today*, Claudia Puig would feel moved to comment that "Jonze's handheld style lends an intriguing immediacy to the dreamscapes . . . [creating] a fiercely innovative film with surprising texture and nuance."[28] Lisa Schwartzbaum of *Entertainment Weekly* likewise described the film as "profoundly beautiful and affecting . . . a breath-taking act of artistic transubstantiation."[29] Aided by "Jonze's ever-graceful direction" (*Wall Street Journal*), *Where the Wild Things Are* managed to be widely acclaimed both as a work of fantasy cinema and as the work of a true auteur.[30] The focus on Jonze's technique as a filmmaker gave individuals license to celebrate the film as a uniquely personal vision from a filmmaker working at the height of his powers. Yet, this focus on Jonze also did not seem to take away from the film's status as a fantasy film. Instead, Jonze's presence as an imaginative creator seemed to give the fantasy film what it needed to thrive, the critical reception intertwining the film's ability to evoke an experience of the fantastic with an appreciation of filmmaking method and style.

This seemingly innate desire to respond to the imaginative and impossible subject matter of *Where the Wild Things Are* by interpreting it as a manifestation of Jonze's creative personality is partially a result of some latent components of the fantasy genre's basic DNA as a form of storytelling. An offshoot of the wider artistic principles of the Romantic movement, the fantasy genre was partially founded on its perceived ability to allow writers a more personal form of expression, allowing individuals, as Kathryn Hume argues, to "assert the importance of things which cannot be measured, seen, or numbered."[31] In the case of *Where the Wild Things Are*, the film's ability to foreground this way of appreciating fantasy fiction is also a result of a number of strategies at play that foreground such an interpretative dynamic. Take, for example, the film's opening credits sequence. Beginning with the now standard presentation of the numerous production companies who have contributed financially to the film, the logos of said organizations are seen to have been scribbled over with a series of childlike drawings (fig. 5.3). With the film contractually obliged to begin with the necessary accreditation of its financial backers, the camera's gaze is imbued with an aura of commercialism, only for that feeling of corporate ennui to be superseded by the vitality of the

Figure 5.3. Doodles and drawings appear over the opening credits (*Where the Wild Things Are*, 2008).

images. The drawings subvert the logos' original intentions, transforming Legendary's logo into a dinosaur's head and Village Roadshow's into an upside down A. In doing so, they create a new way of viewing those images that serves almost as an indicative metaphor for what follows. Rather than finding agency in the film's official producers, or indeed in the ability of the camera to follow conventional representational strategies, the film instead encourages the spectator to locate the source of the images to the child protagonist Max (Max Records), whose name not only appears as a scrawled signature in these opening moments, but he can also be heard humming on the soundtrack. The style of the etching—erratic, jagged, often clumsy—showcases a lack of mastery or knowledge of realistic technique or artistic training but none of these features make the drawing less endearing. Indeed, they are pleasurable because of the way they transcend the somewhat functional, perfunctory nature of a typical opening credits sequence in favor of something that feels personal and original.

These opening moments seem designed to associate the display of fantasy imagery in the film with a long-standing interpretative practice within cinema cultures that goes back to the earliest conceptualization of film authorship. Andrew Sarris argued famously in *The American Cinema*, "The art of the cinema is the art of an attitude, the style of a gesture. It is not so much what as *how*."[32] Most fantasy films seek to deliver an effective vision of an impossible *what*, utilizing the tools of the filmmaking arsenal to present spectators clearly and effectively with the faux, unbelievable reality of what is happening onscreen. We might compare this, say, to a sentence like: *once upon a time there was a human who grew a bull's head and became a minotaur*. The event described is impossible, but the language used to describe it is located to a preestablished lexicon that is perfectly rational and logical. It is in the *what*, not that *how*, where the experience of the fantastic is located. But let us think for a moment about an entirely different sentence, one such as: *the headmaster was angry and his head began snorting like a minotaur's*. In this case, the fantasy imagery that is evoked is used not to offer a break from reality through the sheer nature of what it describes but how what is described is used to embellish or decorate reality within an imaginative sensibility. It is the *how*, not the *what*, that is impossible. This creates an experience in which the fantastic is not communicated through the descriptive power of language to present fantastic notions and ideas. Instead, the description reveals, to use the words of fantasy theorist W. A. Senior, "the fantastic in language."[33] Fantasy poetry makes effective use of just such an experience. Poems like Edward Lear's "The Owl and the Pussycat" (1871) or Lewis Carroll's "Jabberwocky" (1871) offer impossible experiences not just through the circumstances they describe but the way they describe them. The writers create not solely impossible ideas, objects, and creatures but impossible ways of speaking, their exclamations of *'twas brillig* undermining the fixed nature in which we tend to think language operates by somehow meaning something without meaning anything at all. The fantastic becomes a way of relating to the images poetically rather than merely prosaically, becoming a vessel that does not simply claim to present imaginative things but to present things in an imaginative way.

The display of fantasy onscreen within *Where the Wild Things Are* is analogous with this kind of strategy. Adapting Sendak's basic narrative of a boy named Max who is sent to bed without supper only to escape to the island of the wild things, the film not only seeks to present an impossible *what* by retelling the famous story from the picture book but to offer up to audiences an impossible *how* that courts poetic interpretations through the way Jonze both embellishes that story as a screenwriter and chooses to film it as a director. In this effort, Jonze recruits his own onscreen protagonist, Max, to act as a kind of surrogate for the creative sensibility underlying the creative decisions on display within the filmmaking style. Adding a protracted opening section, Max is introduced as a lonely child searching for someone to play with in order that he might find a sense of identity that is otherwise lost. During the day, he attempts to play games with his sister, only to be shunned by her and her friends for being too young, and for not grasping their adolescent desires or tastes. At night, he fights for his mother's (Catherine Keener) attention against her overloaded work schedule and blossoming romance with an unnamed boyfriend (Mark Ruffalo) by dressing up in fantastical outfits and telling her absurd stories to keep her attention, including one in which a bunch of vampires bite some buildings only for their fangs to break off. Max's mother seems to enjoy these stories—feeling the need even to write them down on her computer—and yet the reason why seems to have less to do with the value they have as coherent or developed ideas than what they tell her about her son's personality. They reveal the presence of an incredibly creative mind, one that is not bound by conventional or habitual reasoning but instead responds to the world spontaneously and, therefore, at times, erratically. His inability to function easily within a preestablished set of rules is ultimately the reason he decides to run off to the island of the wild things after one of his games gets too out of hand and he is sent to bed without supper for biting his mother, while at the same time giving him a unique personality that the spectator is encouraged to admire and appreciate during the film's opening act.

The film therefore sets up a dynamic in which Max uses activities like play, storytelling, and fantastical imagery as effective forms of symbol formation, helping to create ways of articulating his own emotions within the safety and security provided through the impossibility of his activities. The same virtues the spectator is encouraged to find in Max, then, become useful in understanding the strategy Jonze adopts as he adapts, alters and adds to Sendak's original ten-sentence story. Unusually, for a Hollywood production, the film's screenwriters were afforded the relative luxury of being able to embellish rather than simply truncate the original source material in order to transform Sendak's relatively slight story into a narrative capable of filling the expected running time of a feature film. And, yet, instead of taking this opportunity to shore up Sendak's fantasy vision, the additions Jonze and Eggers make to the story have almost the opposite effect of making a relatively simple narrative into something that feels far more opaque. An illustrative moment of dynamic occurs during the moment in the film shortly after Max arrives on the island and is given a tour by the wild thing Carol, the group's informal leader. In other examples of fantasy cinema, this moment might serve to introduce the wider world in which the story takes place, allowing the spectator to understand the locations onscreen as part of a coherent spatial logic that they can then imagine into being. Here, though, the film remains true to the deliberately idiosyncratic representation of play established elsewhere. Carol states, "You are the owner of this world and everything you see is yours . . . except that hole, that's Ira's." Carol's statement is not only contradictory, but the claim that Ira possesses a hole is in itself an oxymoron, a linguistic absurdity that is given a visual parallel within the mise-en-scène as Ira's hole is placed in the foreground of the shot (fig. 5.4). The spectator is presented with an image of Ira's hole and sees Max's island through it. These little moments serve as a statement of intention for the rest of the film's sense of geography. As the tour progresses, the island of the wild things is revealed to be a world without coherent rules or laws—the characters pass through forest and desert with little rhyme or reason and at one point a giant dog passes by them only for Carol to dismiss it nonchalantly as an everyday occurrence, adding, "Don't feed it, it'll just follow you around," only for the creature never to appear onscreen again.

Where the Wild Things Are is full of situations like this. As each addition and embellishment to Sendak's simple narrative takes place onscreen,

Figure 5.4. Max is introduced to Ira's Hole.

what is slowly revealed is a coherent strategy among Jonze's storytelling priorities to be as incoherent as possible, offering his version of *Where the Wild Things Are* as almost a mirror reflection of Max's early story about the vampires. The dialogue between Max and the wild things is often willfully illogical, depression can be solved through a "sadness shield that keeps out all the sadness," characters can suffer terrible rage and threaten to "eat their feet off," while the narrative itself often sets up one idea only to then either contradict it or subvert it in a few scenes' time. Perhaps the most audacious example of this comes in a subplot involving Carol and another wild thing named KW. An influential and charismatic member of the group, KW is also often absent from the rest of the wild things as she spends a great deal of time on the other side of the island with her friends Bob and Terry. This causes a great degree of friction among the group, particularly with Carol, who is prone to bouts of rage that end up in destructive and explosive acts of violence whenever Bob and Terry are mentioned. In setting up Bob and Terry as rivals to KW's affection, the film establishes these unseen antagonists as almost Kurtz-like figures, the spectator encouraged to construct a formidable picture of what they must be like out of the wistful anecdotes and descriptions offered by KW on numerous occasions. However, at around halfway through the running time, the film undermines all of these assumptions by presenting Bob and Terry as two rather ordinary-looking owls who proceed to squawk and cluck while barely moving at all (fig. 5.5). In a scene that is played largely for absurdist humor, Max looks on with abject confusion, unable to understand their appeal or indeed what they are even saying, and the moment becomes fantastic not because it makes sense (either within the context of the fiction or

Figure 5.5. Max is introduced to Bob and Terry.

outside of it) but precisely because it does not. After this scene, the threat of Bob and Terry does not really emerge again. The assumed confrontation between Carol and KW never really materializes, and the film detours into a different plot involving the building of a fort. Bob and Terry do not disappear, but they do not seem to function as useful or purposeful characters to the story.

Establishing a general tone in which the impossibility of the film frustrates attempts to make coherent sense of the narrative events, the spectator becomes increasingly aware of the futility of two modes of interpretation that might, in other films, be useful ways of reconciling themselves with the hesitancy caused by the fantastic. The plot can neither be understood on its own terms, allowing the spectator to participate imaginatively in an impossibility that can be experienced outside the trappings and restrictions of reality, nor can it be made into a coherent metaphor for something else. There are some obvious parallels, for example, between this storyline between KW and Max's sister, and Carol seems in many ways to function as a surrogate for Max as he struggles with the rivals for her affections Bob and Terry represent. But their absurdity and ultimate irrelevance within the plot seems to dismiss the validity of such an interpretation. Likewise, there is a temptation throughout to consider the wild things as operating as broad metaphors for aspects of Max's psyche. Carol may represent his rage and his kindness and Douglas his desire to appease and please. But the other wild things are far less simple to understand on these terms, suggesting that any metaphorical reading of the film requires at best a degree of speculation from the spectator that does not ultimately provide a satisfying solution to the illogical impossibility on display. Instead, while watching the film, the only certainty that seems achievable—the only resolution to the hesitancy of the fantastic that the film provides—is to view the creatures as supremely imaginative creations from a uniquely individual mind, just as Max's mother did when she wrote her son's stories down without understanding them.

Once the spectator settles into this mode of interpretation, the impossibility of *Where the Wild Things Are* can be approached through an imaginative exercise that provides access to a pleasure that would otherwise be denied. Like Max's mother, our role is not to make the story make sense, or assign it order on its own terms, but to simply sit back, appreciate it, and gratify the experience with an interpretation that gives shape and validation to that which has been expressed. As in the case with symbol formation, the screen's scenarios become merely vessels that give voice to an emotional relationship forged prior to the idea that objects, people, or places need to mean or do anything consistent or coherent. For Winnicott, symbol formation is important not because it reveals things about the objective world but because it reveals the underlying emotional function of language that is often forgotten or ignored when we use it only to communicate with others. He traces its origins to acts like babbling, singing, and other such vocal phenomena that babies partake in that seem to provide a way of relating to the world without declaring any desire to communicate. These acts of expression are, for Winnicott, the verbal equivalencies of childhood toys like comfort blankets, allowing individuals ways of expressing their inner emotions by taking objective reality and using it as symbol of something internal. *Where the Wild Things Are* creates a similar experience in the way it asks a spectator to interpret the screen. It positions the spectator to perceive its impossible scenarios not so they might be understood as part of a coherent system but as a means of articulating the emotional value these images can possess. The film encourages a critical examination of the interplay between film form and film style as a means of articulating how it feels to watch it, providing not a logical explanation for the film's meaning but a way of understanding how the film addresses the spectator's emotions and phantasies.

The advantage of forging an understanding of the film's fantasy story in this poetic manner, rooting interpretation in the emotional, libidinal aspect of the cinematic mode of address, is witnessed most profoundly in perhaps the film's signature sequence, its "wild rumpus." Featured heavily in the film's trailers, the wild rumpus represents a moment of chaotic celebration in which Max and the wild things unleash their pent-up frustrations by running through the island, shouting, screaming, and playing with one another. There is no set order or reason for each action, and yet the scene feels emotionally cathartic for precisely those same reasons. Not only are the actions befitting of a film that privileges the emotional over the rational throughout, but the filmmaking technique on display seems to add such a sensation as the spectator is cued in to appreciate its implicit poetry. The use of handheld cameras adds a sense of intimacy to the action, the movement framed in such a way that the spectator feels as though they are participating in the rumpus itself, while the decision to shoot on location with naturalistic lighting allows the scene to culminate in a rather beautiful shot of the sunrise (fig. 5.6). The impossibility of fantasy fiction allows for a kind of creative engagement with the screen, one which reframes the function of the camera as a device that does not present information but enacts emotion. It is this privileging of the irrational rather than rational components of cinema's mode of address that forms a key part of the spectator's ability to interpret the film.

While I advocate that such a poetic, interpretative dynamic provides a better means of understanding and appreciating Jonze's film, I also concede that there is certainly a possibility throughout *Where the Wild Things Are* to interpret things differently. The wild rumpus, for those desperate to find some underlying meaning in it, can either be contextualized as a pivotal moment within the story in which Max "tames" the wild things through a display of emotion or else an important moment in his own therapeutic development as he uses phantasy as a vehicle to express his own inner trauma caused by his unsettled family situation. I concede that these interpretations are possible, just as I concede that it

Figure 5.6. A wild rumpus ends.

is always possible to experience fantasy films differently precisely because they allow for so much interpretative space through the very hesitancy they provoke. And, if it is possible for equally imaginative experiences rooted in the metaphorical interpretative process of symbol formation to be found in relation to *Where the Wild Things Are* outside their potential poetic resonance and appeal to a sense of authorship, it is also possible in other fantasy films, both of this era and of any era. As we move on to the final case study of this chapter (and indeed of the book), I wish to highlight one final form of interpretation, that of allegory, and explore its function in the experience invited by a film franchise in which the desire to allegorize seems almost tandem to the pleasure in imagining. It is therefore time to journey to the Hogwarts School of Witchcraft and Wizardry. I hope readers have remembered to pack their brooms.

The Fantastic and Allegory:
Symbol Formation and Estrangement in Fantastic Beasts

Our journey through nearly a century of Hollywood fantasy cinema ends with a film franchise that is currently in the midst of forging a new beginning for a preexisting and extremely popular story. Developed by Warner Bros. in partnership with producer/writer J. K. Rowling, the Fantastic Beasts films are an ongoing attempt to extend both the commercial and narrative potential of what has become known as the Wizarding World franchise, a transmedia fictional universe that consists of the various *Harry Potter* books and films alongside ancillary texts such as the popular West End and Broadway play *Harry Potter and the Cursed Child* (2016/2018). With the Harry Potter film franchise ending in 2011, Fantastic Beasts was conceived as a new multipart saga that would satisfy the demand for new stories set in the same fictional universe, telling a part prequel, part spin-off set during the first half of the twentieth century. Nominally based on Rowling's fictional textbook of the same name (which was originally written as a charity release for the UK-based Comic Relief), the film series took inspiration from the book's title and catalog of fabulous creatures, alongside some references to the backstory of certain characters in *the Harry Potter* novels, to build a narrative that, at the time of writing, is envisioned to span across five films covering the period of wizarding history from 1926 to 1945.

Whether Fantastic Beasts fulfills this promise will depend largely on the commercial performance of its entries. The first two films in the saga have yielded solid, if unspectacular, financial results for the Warner Bros. Studio, taking in worldwide grosses of $841 million and $654 million, respectively (figures that compare unfavorably with the $1.3 billion gross achieved by *Harry Potter and the Deathly Hallows: Part 2*, 2011). This overall downtrend suggests that the goodwill audiences feel toward the Wizarding World is perhaps starting to wane, a dynamic that is also reflected in the critical reception the two films have received thus far. *Fantastic Beasts and Where to Find Them* (2016) opened to positive but hardly glowing reviews, with critics praising its imaginative extension of Rowling's fictional universe but criticizing its episodic pacing and over-complicated storyline. *Fantastic Beasts: The Crimes of Grindelwald* (2018), however, received a more muted reception. The film was criticized for its somewhat expositional narration style, overwhelming number of characters, and overall sense of lackluster, as if the franchise were running out of steam. Further complications surrounding the franchise's future have arisen as a result both of the controversies surrounding Rowling's transphobic remarks on Twitter as well as Johnny Depp's resignation from the franchise following his unsuccessful libel case against the British company News Group for publishing articles relating to his former wife Amber Heard. Yet, despite this overall downward trend in the reception of the films among fans and critics alike and the difficulties future films will face, there were a few notable exceptions to this general paradigm that suggest the franchise might just survive long enough to tell its story to a satisfying conclusion, one that stems partially from the shifting public persona its creator had experienced in the years since writing the original *Harry Potter* novels.

As evidenced by recent controversies, Rowling's success as a writer and producer has not only given her a powerful position within the Hollywood film industry but provided her with a public platform that she has subsequently used to champion a number of social and political causes. Through her popular Twitter profile, Rowling has voiced often vociferous opinions on a number of subjects including the UK-Brexit Referendum, the presidency of Donald Trump, and trans rights. This aspect of her media profile was almost inescapable to many audience members of the Fantastic Beasts franchise and featured heavily in some of the early press coverage on the films. An early preview published by the *New York Times* drew attention to the correlation between Rowling's decision to revisit her Wizarding World and her increasingly politicized public persona, speculating that the films might give her a chance to address the issues she feels passionate about through popular fantasy fiction.³⁴ Telling the story of the rise of an evil wizard advocating a wizard's innate right to rule over nonmagical beings among a receptive population living in a climate of economic and social unease, *Fantastic Beasts* seemed to provide a thinly veiled allegory for a range of concerns that Rowling had expressed opposition to numerous times publicly. Her antagonist Gellert Grindelwald (Johnny Depp), sporting a thin moustache and erratic, peroxide blonde hair, seemed to be mashup of various figures drawn from both the past and the present, resembling not only former US president Donald Trump but, in the UK context, leading Brexit campaigner and future prime minister Boris Johnson, while at the same time echoing the specter of twentieth-century fascism. This aspect was seized upon by high-profile publications like the *Hollywood Reporter* and the *Washington Post* as reasons to celebrate the arrival of the *Fantastic Beasts* films.³⁵ Despite the overwhelmingly apathetic response the films received elsewhere, the franchise was championed by such high-profile publications as fantasy films that spoke through a register of allegory, creating films that were both magical and yet realistic in their concerns.

This desire to allegorize the Fantastic Beasts franchise as a means of both praising it and offering an apologia for its supposed imaginative indulgences has a great deal of precedent. Writing as far back as 1605, Francis Bacon stated that writing imaginative poetry is authorized only "when the secrets and Mistries of Religion, Pollicy, or Philosophy, are involved in fables or parables [sic],"³⁶ and this sense that fantasy fiction is at its most worthy when it is being used to tell stories that have direct consequence or parallel to real-life events has lived on through the history of its popular and academic reception, particularly within the Anglo-European intellectual climate. Historically, fantasy writers have resisted these persistent attempts made by a certain type of reader to consider their works as coded allegories, arguing that such an interpretative practice is limiting the potential of their works to be read and enjoyed as primarily imaginative works.³⁷ However, in the case of the Fantastic Beasts films, allegorical interpretation seems an almost palatable solution to the hesitancy posed by the fantastic experience the franchise offers given some of the narrative and visual techniques at work in the two films. Taking advantage of the preexisting rules established in Rowling's Wizarding World, the narrative of both films adds an additional imaginary dimension to our preexisting reality rather than removing the traces of reality altogether, allowing characters to literally move from settings demarcated as "real" and others belonging to the Wizarding World with the ease of an apparition spell, or by walking through a secret portal.

This allows the franchise to interweave its overt fantasy narrative within a world that otherwise pertains to represent our own, providing frequent opportunities for magical characters to collide with real-life, historical settings, as well as to construct an overall storyline that draws a number of rather clear parallels between the problems this world is facing and our own contemporary sociopolitical climate.

Set in Manhattan in 1926, the first film, *Fantastic Beasts and Where to Find Them*, tells a story of a seemingly affluent and stable society of wizards who are threatened by a rising tide of social anxiety. A fundamentalist sect of "Second Salemers" are tapping into a widespread social unease that seeks to blame deep-seated, structural problems on an unseen, all-powerful, and mysterious controlling body of wizards, thus attempting to stir up a racialized sense of hatred toward a minority of magical folk among the civil majority of nonmagical peoples, all while the wizarding world concerns itself with its own problems as it deals with the disappearance of a notorious dark wizard, Grindelwald. The second film, *The Crimes of Grindelwald*, relocates the action to Paris, losing none of its allegorical potency in the process. This story centers on the attempts made by the now revealed Grindelwald to gather his follows toward his cause, a process he is successful at largely by adopting a benevolent public persona to mask his racial hatred. Grindelwald scalds one of his supporters behind closed doors for espousing racial epithets, claiming "we do not speak like that in public," while using his increasing popularity to spout rhetoric of a wizard's birthright to rule over nonmagical people given their inherent failings as a race. Both plots therefore echo real-life historical events, most notably the rising wave of anti-Semitism throughout the 1920s and 1930s given the era in which the films are set, while also alluding to the recent rise of Islamic fundamentalism within the contemporary Middle East and the alt-right insurgency within Europe and the US.

This echoing between fantasy narrative, real-life history, and post-9/11 politics is also reflected in the film's visual register. The headquarters of the Magical Congress, one of the key set pieces of the first film that introduces a grandiose magical setting to rival that of Hogwarts castle or the Ministry of Magic in the *Harry Potter* films, is centered around a large clock displaying the current threat level to magical peoples, one that looks eerily similar to the now familiar terrorist alerts displayed in and around governmental buildings across the world (fig. 5.7). Likewise, in the second film, Grindelwald's followers become increasingly associated with a raven symbol that functions as a call to arm alerting his followers to his presence, an image that also bears a strong resemblance to the eagle of the Third Reich. This iconographic resemblance to Nazism is further enforced through the narrative events as he relocates to an unnamed mountain retreat in Austria similar to Hitler's own Berghof. Grindelwald tells wizards they are being treated unfairly given their God-given right to rule the world, and he paints a picture of a world in which to not seize power once again is to give over to a chaotic global order run by others, one that echoes recent antiglobalization, as well as anti-Semitic, rhetoric. The attempts to match the Wizarding World narrative to its historical context therefore functions in a manner somewhat akin to the moments in *The Lord of the Rings* that gesture toward the narrative's own thematic substance in order to provoke the spectator into metaphorical alongside metonymical interpretations of the films' events. Interpreting *Fantastic Beasts* as a part-contemporary, part-historical, and part-moral allegory about the potential of the fear caused by economic and social unease to lead to racial hatred becomes not simply a way of viewing the film. It becomes part of the imaginative experience the film seeks to offer the spectator, the films blurring the lines between the experience of the fantastic evoked in its deliberately impossible settings and characters and the sense of unfolding, real-life history that surrounds its storytelling.

Take, for example, a key moment at the end of *The Crimes of Grindelwald*, As the film's protagonists Newt (Eddie Redmayne), Tina (Katherine Waterston), and Jacob (Dan Fogler) find themselves unwitting audience members at a mass rally organized by Grindelwald's followers, a scene that, as it plays out, seems to set out both the literal and figurative stakes that will presumably be at play within the rest of franchise, allowing

Figure 5.7. A magical threat detector displayed in *Fantastic Beasts and Where to Find Them* (2016) closely resembles the real-life terrorist alert signal used in many countries.

for a moment onscreen where the series' antagonist is afforded time to explain his intended actions and justify his decisions (fig. 5.8). As part of this explanation, Grindelwald summons a magical vision of what the future may hold if the so-called muggles (nonmagical peoples) are left to their own devices. What is then seen is a collection of images that will likely be very familiar to spectators, as Grindelwald presents his audience with a vision of ruined cityscapes (fig. 5.9), queues of prisoners being led in chains beside railway tracks (fig. 5.10), and, finally, the mushroom cloud of an atomic bomb (fig. 5.11). These key images of the Holocaust and twentieth-century warfare, images that are seared into the collective memory of audiences given their infamy, serve to distance the perspective of the spectator from that of the characters onscreen, creating an odd feeling of separation between them and the sense of impossibility on display. For the characters onscreen, what they are seeing is a conjured, fabricated illusion in a world where magic is otherwise normalized and real. In contrast, for the spectator, what is seen in Grindelwald's spell is perhaps the first "real" image in the entire film, displaying as it does something that their knowledge of world history is likely to deduce will happen within the context of both the franchise's historical timeframe and has also happened within the real-life past. The immediacy of the action is therefore displaced by a feeling of both foresight and hindsight, not dissimilar to the way a classical Hollywood fantasy film like *It's a Wonderful Life* communicates its sense of the fantastic through a manipulation and hesitation surrounding time onscreen. The spectator knows these images all too well because they have already happened, and thus knows what is inevitably going to come within the context of the Wizarding World. As a consequence, the process of responding to the hesitancy posed by the fantastic requires them to not solely develop imaginative relationship with the characters and settings but to fill in the gaps evoked within the storytelling in order to explain and contextualize what they see.

What occurs in this moment, and throughout the Fantastic Beasts franchise more generally, is a process that theorists of the fantastic refer to as a moment of narrative "estrangement."[38] Coined by Darko Suvin, the term *estrangement* has entered the critical lexicon of studies of fantasy and the fantastic as essentially a counterbalance to the idea of wonder. If wonder is an experience that helps to solve the uncertainty felt in the experience of an impossible moment by drawing people closer to such fictional events through an appreciative sense of curiosity, estrangement functions to push people away from the literal events taking place in order to offer something new and exciting in its place. In short, wonder pulls while estrangement pushes the reader toward the realm of the fantastic,

Figure 5.8. Grindelwald addresses his followers (*Fantastic Beasts: The Crimes of Grindelwald*, 2018).

Figure 5.9. Grindelwald's spell fills the room with WWII-esque imagery.

Figure 5.10. The spell echoes real-life atrocities, including the Holocaust.

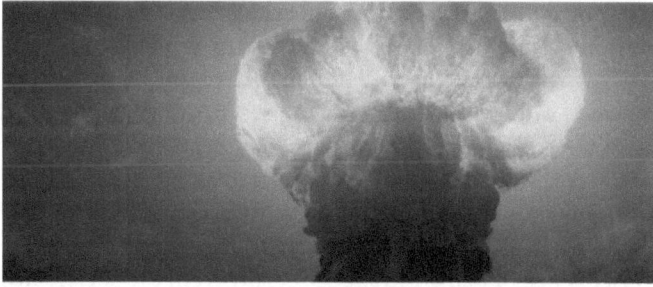

Figure 5.11. Nuclear war is evoked.

creating an experience that has been described by Farah Mendlesohn as "liminal" in that it allows opportunities for imaginative interpretations of a story through the deliberate failings of its own powers of rhetoric.[39] In a cinematic context, such a process occurs through a recalibration of what Metz refers to as the spectator's ability to perform a process of "symbolization as 'bound energy.'"[40] Instead of focusing solely on the interpretative activity of assigning narrative explanations for the literal events taking place onscreen, the spectator instead is encouraged to enter into a new way of viewing the events that allows for considerations of the story's metaphoric, as well as metonymic, potential. In this sense, the pursuit of allegorical interpretation becomes, in effect, another way of allowing for a process of symbol formation. The estrangement felt by the spectator in relation to events taking place in Fantastic Beasts parallels the way Klein describes the child's first attempt to engage with the world through conscious interpretation, emerging, as she argues, out of a state of perception of an "unreal reality."[41] By evoking gaps and slippages in the way it seeks to communicate its imagery as a metonymic replacement for reality, the films create an experience whereby the spectator is estranged from the magical circumstances taking place in such a manner that, to solve the hesitancy posed by the fantastic, the most clear and obvious path toward interpretation is not necessarily the most rewarding.

Fantastic Beasts therefore uses allegory as a device that encourages not just an intellectual response to its fantasy subject matter, giving it an air of highbrow legitimacy, but as a means of guiding the imaginative response its films encourage. The films invite spectators into a particular kind of interpretation practice as a means of shaping the content of their phantasies, directing the kinds of imaginative acts of speculation they make, and the kinds of symbols they are inclined to formulate in response to what they see. Thus far, the franchise seems to be telling a story that espouses the importance in finding value in all living things, particularly in those whom it might be easy to dismiss as either useless or unexceptional. This message is embodied in particular by the series' protagonist Newt Scamander. In the first twenty minutes of *Fantastic Beasts and Where to Find Them*, Newt is presented as a quiet, socially awkward, and somewhat rude individual who refuses to look people in the eye. However, as the story develops, slowly, hidden depths to Newt's personality emerge that we are encouraged to admire, namely, his ability to forge productive and meaningful relationships with the world's population of magical animals in a world openly hostile to their existence. As an almost direct consequence of being estranged socially from the society he lives in,

Newt is able to find value in these so-called beasts that he claims others are "too blinkered to see." His disdain for the world makes it easier for him to see the value in things not deemed to be previously valuable, a quality that then transcends back into the human relationships. Instead of dismissing a working-class nonmagical man like Jacob Kowalski, or a recently demoted auror (essentially a member of the wizarding FBI), these people become budding love interests and confidants because, despite them treating him with a frosty hostility throughout the majority of their early interactions together, Newt's desire to see the best in the world's forgotten and ignored means that he imagines the world differently from most people. Instead of finding the most obvious conclusion to any given moment, he invests time and energy in the imaginative possibilities of what might be or could be, if only it were nurtured into being.

The intended political dimension of this message is clear from the franchise's treatment of the racist ideology espoused by its antagonist Grindelwald. However, by functioning as fantasy films, Fantastic Beasts presents Newt's perspective on the world in a manner that seems equally designed to help align the spectator to a way of approaching its circumstances onscreen, whether directly evoking an allegorical interpretation or not. The very same virtues Newt promotes—open-mindedness, tolerance, and compassion—are also virtues that the film's experience of the fantastic rewards, aligning its imaginative impulse with its ideological impulse to support its allegorical aspirations. Take, for example, a key sequence in *Fantastic Beasts and Where to Find Them* that was signaled out for both praise and criticism within its reviews, one which seems to take a lengthy detour from the plot to allow Newt and Jacob to enter inside Newt's enchanted briefcase and explore the world within. In many ways, then, the scene was viewed as indicative of a wider tonal problem the franchise was perceived to have as a whole in balancing real-life historical parallels with its whimsical side adventures involving spectacular beasts.[42] Yet, if one studies the way these beasts serve as objects of visual spectacle and narrative fascination, it becomes far easier to reconcile these two tendencies of the franchise. It is not that the two films attempt to create a pleasurable, imaginative experience in line with the heritage of popular fantasy fiction that is at odds with its attempt to tell a story that can be interpreted allegorically. Rather, it is that both impulses represent two overlapping attempts to direct the spectator into a particular way of phantasizing, one that both solidifies the allegorical substance of its storytelling and increases the fascination with the film's impossible subject matter at the same time.

The scene in question is not the most overtly estranging in terms of the overall narrative's focus on real-life historical and modern parallels, and it does not seem particularly significant in terms of the film's overall narrative. Jacob is beckoned by Newt to join him inside the briefcase, the non-mag wandering haphazardly into the strange world more out of a sense of curiosity than firm motivation, and the film then utilizes Jacob's reactions as part of a recurring technique throughout fantasy filmmaking history to dramatize the intended reaction it seeks to generate in the spectator from its display of magical imagery. As Jacob looks wide-eyed on a range of magical beasts, each existing in their own unique habitat, he follows in a long line of characters from Dorothy to Jane and Michael Banks (fig. 5.12). Yet, the nature of the imaginative experience Jacob undergoes in this world is worth pausing on. Like the characters that precede him, Jacob is having to undergo a profound shift in his worldview, adjusting in response to the impossibility of what he sees as a set of assumptions about the world. He must learn that briefcases can contain vast animal enclosures, at least this one does, and that Newt—despite being somewhat inept—is actually an incredibly skilled animal trainer. Jacob watches Newt dart from one animal to the next, nursing them, feeding them, and nurturing them, and a sense that the whole world within the briefcase operates as part of a holistic whole is emphasized through a minimal editing pattern that relies on a series of long tracking shots to guide the spectator from one animal environment to another (figs. 5.13 and 5.14). Each beast is seemingly operating in harmony with one another. In the background, giant beetles roll and carry humps of rock in their pincers to help build the environment for yet another beast to live in while, in the foreground, winged animals swoop across the frame to guide characters effortlessly from one location to the next (fig. 5.15). Things that are small become significant, things that might at first go unnoticed become objects of fascination, and every living creature seems to counterbalance the next, as if they all were needed to play their equally important part. The only creature that seems to offer anything other to this dynamic is the obscurus, a magical beast Newt treats with a degree of caution as he revels to Jacob that it exists because of the pain caused by others in damaging a wizard's potential, a creature he is determined to find a function for rather than to simply fear.

This scene serves as a microcosm for the way Newt's fantastic beasts operate throughout the plot. Often introduced as little more than functionless objects of visual spectacle, the film then provides an explanation for their inclusion in the story during a later episode or incident that proves the creature a reason for existing. In *The Crimes of Grindelwald*,

Figures 5.12–5.15. Jacob enters Newt's enchanted briefcase and encounters a menagerie of magical beasts (*Fantastic Beasts and Where to Find Them*, 2016)

Newt encounters a zouwu, a dragonlike beast that seems plucked from the pages of ancient Chinese folklore. At first, this encounter seems to offer little more to the narrative than provide an imaginative diversion from the main storyline. Newt captures the zouwu as part of a wider attempt to trace the movements of Tina, her disappearance helping to providing a key part of the story for at least the first half of the film, and the dragon seems to offer little other than to provide an amusing and spectacular chase sequence set against the Parisian streets. Yet, in the film's denouement, the zouwu once again remerges as a solution to Newt's predicament as he finds himself trapped inside a set of magical archives being pursued by police. Likewise, Newt's Niffler sidekick, a constant source of antagonism throughout the franchise as the creature often escapes from Newt's protection to hunt down shiny, gold objects in a magpie-esque manner, seems to provide the first two films of the franchise with little other than a bit of light comedic relief and occasional distraction from the more serious events that are unfolding. Yet, at the end of *Crimes of Grindelwald*, the Niffler steals the vial of blood shared between Dumbledore and Grindelwald that prevents the former from fighting the latter. The creature's permitted and constant disruption of Newt's aim in two films comes good as he brings about a resolution suggested in the films to come.

In each of these cases, both characters and spectators are rewarded when they approach the various fantastic beasts offered in the film's often episodic narrative style in a particular way. When they dismiss the creatures as irrelevant to the plot, or unhelpful distractions from the serious business of the Wizarding World, they are denied access to the pleasure of being in their company that Newt sees. When they approach the creatures for their imaginative potential, expecting to find value in them even where currently it does not seem to be obvious or clear, they can not only enjoy watching them more but can participate imaginatively in the film's unfolding story. Through some habitual reasoning caused partially by the concurrent plot device of having seemingly "useless" creatures turn out to be of profound value to the story and partially by the wider allegorical estrangement taking placing through the story, spectators are encouraged to imagine possibilities for the creatures and for the world they encounter that are not immediately present or available. The efforts to encourage allegorical interpretation in *Fantastic Beasts* therefore assist a wider function within the franchise. The films allow spectators to forge imaginative interpretations out of what the fiction might be and where the future might go, even if it does not always seems obvious and clear in a franchise whose narrative tension is partially limited by both its status as prequel to an existing story and by its explicit interaction with well-known historical events. Therefore, the spectator's interpretations of the films' literal and figurative meaning serve both the narrative and commercial interests of the franchise. Despite watching a story that nominally we all know where it is going, and despite the franchise clearly testing the patience of some, given its mixed reviews to date, it is by interpreting it is as allegory that Fantastic Beasts become redeemed not just as worthwhile cinematic ventures but exhilarating and imaginative fantasy films.

Conclusion: Symbol Formation and the Contemporary Fantasy Film

This chapter has offered up three examples of contemporary fantasy filmmaking—*The Lord of the Rings*, *Where the Wild Things Are*, and *Fantastic Beasts*—in order to explore the potential of fantasy cinema to be interpreted as well as experienced by its spectator. I have pursued this agenda not because I believe that it is only since the year 2001 that fantasy films have afforded opportunities for spectators to find such metaphorical, poetical, and allegorical interpretations of their literal circumstances, but because this seems to be a particularly prominent feature of contemporary fantasy filmmaking that makes its production and reception different from previous eras. A key moment in the history of the genre took place inside Los Angeles' Kodak Theatre on February 29, 2004. Having already won ten Academy Awards that same evening for achievements in screenwriting and visual effects, *The Return of the King* crowned its success by becoming the first fantasy film to win the coveted Best Picture Oscar. On this occasion, the trilogy's cowriter, coproducer, and director took to the stage to deliver his take on the shift occurring in fantasy's critical recognition. As Jackson stated: "I'm so honored, touched and relieved that the Academy, and the members of the Academy that have supported us have seen past the trolls and the wizards and the hobbits and are recognizing fantasy this year. Fantasy is an F-word that, hopefully, the five second delay won't do anything with." Greeted by warm laughter inside the theater, Jackson's comments reveal an awareness on the part of the creative team behind *The Lord of the Rings* of the somewhat dismissive attitude their choice of genre had received in the years prior to their decision to adapt Tolkien's novel. They also indicate a key strategy by which the films themselves attempted to circumnavigate such opinions, establishing a series of strategies designed to get spectators to "see past" the hobbits onscreen in way that might otherwise have been reserved for middle-to-highbrow arthouse entertainment. In one way or another, we have been *seeing past* hobbits ever since, allowing the fantasy genre to make inroads into all roads of society and all spectrums of culture.

Now that mainstream audiences have been encouraged to interpret fantasy in this way, they would do well to look back on the legacy of filmmaking that has come before it, not in order to erase the power of Hollywood filmmaking to ignite our imaginations but to empower us to find additional means of articulating that power. Films such as *Alice in Wonderland* (1933) can be interpreted with the same gusto and enthusiasm as their literary predecessors, seen as potent satires on prevailing society, metaphors for the chaos and confusion of everyday life, or as poetic relics preserving the artistic sensibilities of their production and costume designers, cinematographers, screenwriters, and directors. Films like *Harvey* can be explored for what they say about the human condition, not at the expense of how we are asked to imagine in response to their stories but in combination with the experience. *The NeverEnding Story* becomes a story about desire. *Hook* becomes a tale of prevailing cultural attitudes toward youth and age. So, in many ways, this book has always been about the challenge of interpreting fantasy. This chapter has simply tried to articulate how such a process might occur not just within the supposedly lofty echelons of academia who are tasked with that job as a professional responsibility but as part of the experience and pleasure the fantasy genre offers its spectator.

The history of fantasy filmmaking is a history of riddles, games and puzzles, one we are invited either to play along with and enjoy for the sake of the act of playing, or to garner intellectual satisfaction in formulating symbols out of nothing, expressing ourselves in the process. If we embrace this, then this will embolden us to continue to interpret fantasy in the future as it responds to ever fluctuating market circumstances, and becomes something new from its predecessors in the process. The last decade has seen the final demise of a series of industrial paradigms that has governed the Hollywood industry since the late 1970s, as the era of single "event" movies gave way to a new series of governing practices upon which commercial success would become reliant. Since then, studio filmmaking has become both increasingly diversified and increasingly convergent. Its commercial strategy relies on ever-growing numbers of co-productions that stretch far beyond the resources of any single national marketplace into a globalized film industry, complete with a globalized demographic. Yet, at the same time as diversifying on an industrial scale, Hollywood's release schedules look increasingly homogenized. They rely on a system wherein the importance of any individual film release is downplayed in favor of its function within an overall franchise system that allows for only a small number of genre cycles. What role fantasy cinema has to play in such a marketplace is still being worked through, particularly as the industry responds to the shockwave caused by COVID-19. Will fantasy expand across multimedia platforms, retreat into the cultural exclusivity and specialism of art house distribution, or continue to fuel our film franchises within traditional public auditoriums as part of a restoration and revitalization of the industry? Whatever happens, the story of the fantastic in Hollywood fantasy cinema will go on, but this particular chronicling of it ends here.

Conclusion

The Fantastic *Beyond* Hollywood Fantasy Cinema?

A LOT OF THE FANTASY FILMS analyzed within the pages of this book have a problem with their endings. In *Alice in Wonderland* (1933), the heroine just wakes up suddenly, with little explanation, without offering any insight as to why the lengthy excursion into the magical land was necessary, worthwhile, or useful, either for her or for the spectator. In *Mary Poppins* (1964), she leaves, despite providing us with so many moments of pleasure, justifying it according to the rationale that she is no longer needed, and yet such an explanation feels a little hollow in a film that seems to celebrate the pleasurable over the necessary at every step of the way. In *The NeverEnding Story* (1984), Bastian ends the tale riding on the back of a luckdragon, shouting euphorically in the sky as the film detours ill-advisedly into the world of reality after spending so much time exploring the nuances of high fantasy. And, finally, *The Lord of the Rings* (2001–2003), famously, just could not stop ending. Its final installment, *The Return of the King* (2003), was almost universally acclaimed among critics who had devoured the first two installments enthusiastically, and the film made history through the number of awards it received. And, yet, there was a pretty solid consensus that the final twenty minutes were some of the weakest in the trilogy as a whole, the film offering scene after scene of possible endings as it worked to bring about a satisfying conclusion to its dense and sprawling narrative, an act that perhaps was always doomed to failure. The act of ending is not always something fantasy storytelling is particularly good at. In a genre that seeks to break down boundaries, open up new possibilities, create alternatives, and bring about the new and different, it seems almost inevitable that the act of closure or containment necessitated by an ending would come across as somewhat distasteful. A conclusion is, perhaps, a closing down of imaginative possibility, something that fantasy fights against at all times through the very manner it seeks to address its spectator.

I have no wish to do that to the fantastic within this book. Like all good fantasy stories, the experience I have articulated is meant to offer readers opportunities for further exploration and imagination, not provide a single and totalizing explanation that merits no further discussion. Journeys cannot go on forever, and I have chosen to end this particular journey, of a particular kind of fantasy storytelling, during a period of history in which the fantasy genre has not only established itself as an extremely profitable form of filmmaking but has demonstrated its impact upon popular culture though a series of globally successful films, critically acclaimed dramas, independent, arthouse sleeper hits and transmedia global franchises stretching across film, television, and gaming. Audiences are embracing the fantasy genre with greater alacrity with each passing day, and this should give many pause for thought as to what new experiences its mode of storytelling might offer, and how we might set about the challenge of putting those experience into words that do not slip into tired clichés or unhelpful banalities. It is time to do away with speaking about fantasy films like they were just like all films or—perhaps worse still—films that cannot be studied because to articulate how they work would be to demystify something magical, ephemeral, and beyond the scope of critical inquiry. It is time instead to talk about fantasy films for the impossible things they are.

I was initially inspired to write this book not just because I was a fan of the fantasy genre—although I do not exclude that from part of my reasoning—but because I felt I did not have the words to explain why, at least not satisfying words. In the theory of the fantastic I have developed ever since, I have reached for a number of different explanations that I think have helped to complicate, develop, and extend our understanding of the type of experience and pleasures this genre offers audiences, and to provide a way of understanding the relationship between phantasy (as a subjective act) and fantasy (as a mode of storytelling). Fundamental to that understanding has been to construct an argument about fantasy cinema that rejects a common narrative told again and again of the power of storytelling to make us believe and instead champion the exciting experiential possibilities available to the spectator when they do not believe.

It is by encountering the impossible, and forging relationships with it nonetheless, that fantasy cinema challenges us to let go of the strategies of meaning-making that we so often prioritize in everyday life—strategies dedicated to understanding the world as an objective, interconnected, and rational sphere—and embrace the desire to feel and to imagine regardless of whether that act of phantasy is real or not. This is the realm of the fantastic, a realm that is uncertain and hesitant, strange and ephemeral, but all the more vivid as a result.

If readers have embraced even some of the ideas I have offered through this book, I hope that they been inspired to go searching for more. If they found my conceptualization of a new way of relating to characters, spaces, and time onscreen as a mode of cathexis offered in chapter 2 compelling, for example, they might wish to seek out other examples of fantasy filmmaking that offer similar opportunities to fuse the subjective will of the spectator with the objective properties of the screen in defiance or transcendence of rational causality. Classics from across the pantheon of world cinema such as *La Belle et La Bête* (1946) might be analyzed for the kinds of imaginative relationships they afford between the spectators and their impossible characters, masterworks like *Ugetsu* (1953) might be considered for the kinds of impossible spaces they create onscreen, while a film like *The Seventh Seal* (1957) might be examined for how it not only explores the theme of existential despair but creates an impossibility of temporal existence that feeds into its thematic content. I have limited my discussion of cathexis to the period of classical Hollywood given the relevance it has to our understanding of the development and implementation of popular narrative filmmaking based on the continuity style. Yet, as many of us know, popular narrative filmmaking, indeed all narrative filmmaking, is a force to be reckoned with around the globe. There is therefore far more work to do to articulate the different kinds of relationships fantasy cinema might invite the spectator to forge with the screen when its genre tropes and conventions are implemented in different national, social, and historical circumstances.

If, instead, the theories of introjection and projection in relation to special effects–driven cycles of fantasy cinema like the wonder film and the blockbuster considered in chapters 3 and 4 spoke to readers with a greater urgency and vitality, then please do go and seek out moments in film history across the globe that might be useful to consider as part of an ongoing discussion of the role of the imagination in the experience of special effects, whether to extend the ideas I have already formulated or in an attempt to evolve and develop them so they might better speak to new films. This exercise might help us to explore crucial staging grounds for both the evolution of both fantasy storytelling and the development of special effects onscreen prior to and preceding the period of filmmaking I have focused upon in my analysis, offering insights into the kind of lavish, if somewhat theatric, spectacle offered by silent epics like *Die Nibelungen* (1924) or *The Thief of Bagdad* (1924), or perhaps even the earliest encounters between fantasy and cinema in the works of Georges Méliès (*Cinderella*, 1899; *Red Riding Hood*, 1900; *The Kingdom of the Fairies*, 1903) or Segundo de Chomón (*The Spring Fairy*, 1902; *Gulliver in the Land of the Giants*, 1903; *The Electric Hotel*, 1908). And if ideas of symbol formation provide a useful means of speaking toward the imaginative content of interpretation itself—an act that defines not just a recent trend in the critical appraisal of popular fantasy cinema but the very essence of what film scholarship attempts to do—then this may ask further questions about when and why we interpret the screen and what kinds of interpretations are out there.

My story has been about Hollywood fantasy filmmaking. I have felt it necessary to tell that story given the prominent role genre plays within that film industry and, indeed, the historical influence Hollywood filmmaking has had on narrative cinema across the globe. However, my story is but one of countless numbers available in the history of the fantasy film that has yet to be told, stories that can transcend the context of a particular industry, filmmaking cycles or historically demarcated periods, and speak to the heart of our imaginative relationship to the screen. I began my academic interest in fantasy cinema as an undergraduate student, writing an assignment on *The Wizard of Oz* (1939) for a course I have long since forgotten. But I remember the moment I discovered what needed to be corrected vividly. Having decided to embark on an analysis of the film from the perspective of fantasy cinema, I entered into the campus library confidently, striding to the genre theory section and taking out a copy of Barry Keith Grant's *Film Genre Reader* (at the time, I believe it was in its third edition).[1] I had discovered the book on a previous project and, in particular, the extremely useful bibliography that Grant provides his readers at the back of his collection, which contains exhaustive lists of scholarship on every film genre an aspiring academic might wish to examine. Flicking through these pages, one is provided with six pages of references detailing studies of the comedy film, nine pages of listings on the western, eleven pages devoted to science fiction, and thirteen chronicling the discussion of horror cinema. In the edition I saw, there was not a single entry on fantasy filmmaking. Now, in its fourth edition, I note that there is still less than one page. I do not point this out to critique Grant's seminal collection. It is for this same reason that fantasy cinema is rarely mentioned in the numerations of seminal genre theorists like Rick Altman or Steve Neale.[2] I do not blame the list-makers, but the lists themselves, highlighting the scarcity of work that has been done on this subject, and how much there is to do. I hope this book plays its part in filling that list, not just by taking up a single line on a single page, but by inspiring future research into the stories, and the experiences, that fantasy films offer.

Fantasy exists, regardless of whether we choose to believe in it. It exists in the hearts and minds of film-goers. It resides in your, and my, sense of imagination. On both an explicit and implicit level, this book is full of fantasy, just as our experience of life is also filtered, mediated, and often consumed by fantasy. If we deny the important role it plays both on and off the screen, then we not only deny the rich legacy of a particular genre of filmmaking but we deny an essential component of how we experience cinema. If we acknowledge the important role that fantasy does play, then we might begin to see how much of both a medium and a genre is predicated on our capacity to dream, and how much dreaming is in fact done while we are wide awake. It is time to accept the truth of fantasy, and deal with the awesome consequences such an acknowledgment brings.

Notes

Introduction

1. David Orr, "Dragons Ascendant: George R. R. Martin and the Rise of Fantasy," *New York Times*, August 12, 2011, accessed June 22, 2018, http://www.nytimes.com/2011/08/14/books/review/george-r-r-martin-and-the-rise-of-fantasy.html.

2. Frances Pheasant-Kelly, *Fantasy Film Post 9/11* (New York: Palgrave Macmillan, 2013), 4.

3. Alec Worley, *Empires of the Imagination: A Critical Survey of Fantasy Cinema from Georges Méliès to "The Lord of the Rings"* (Jefferson, NC: McFarland, 2005), 10; Katherine A. Fowkes, *The Fantasy Film* (Chichester: Wiley-Blackwell, 2010), 2.

4. James Walters, *Fantasy Film: A Critical Introduction* (Oxford: Berg, 2011), 2.

5. Raphaëlle Moine, *Film Genre*, trans. Alistair Fox and Hilary Radner (Malden, MA: Blackwell, 2008), 63.

6. Moine, *Film Genre*, 63.

7. John Fiske, *Understanding Popular Culture* (London: Routledge, 1989).

8. Stanley Fish, *Is There a Text in This Class? The Authority of Interpretative Communities* (Cambridge, MA: Harvard University Press, 1980), 338.

9. Pierre Bourdieu, *Distinction: A Social Critique of the Judgment of Taste*, trans. Richard Nice (Cambridge, MA: Harvard University Press, 1984), 18.

10. Linda Williams, "Gender, Genre, and Excess," *Film Quarterly* 44, no. 4 (Summer 1991): 2–13.

11. Jean Laplanche and Jean-Bertrand Pontalis, *The Language of Psychoanalysis*, trans. Donald Nicholson-Smith (London: Karnac Books, 2006), 315.

12. Bronwen Thomas, *Narrative: The Basics* (London: Routledge, 2015), 1–14.

13. Gary K. Wolfe, *Critical Terms of Science Fiction and Fantasy: A Glossary and Guide to Scholarship* (Westport, CT: Greenwood Press, 1986), 140.

14. W. R. Irwin, *The Game of the Impossible: A Rhetoric of Fantasy* (Urbana: University of Illinois Press, 1976), 4.

15. E. Deidre Pribram, "Spectatorship and Subjectivity," in *A Companion to Film Theory*, ed. Toby Miller and Robert Stam (Malden, MA: Blackwell, 2004), 146.

16. Hugo Münsterberg, *The Photoplay: A Psychological Study*, trans. Alan Langdale (New York: Routledge, 2002); Laura Mulvey, "Visual Pleasure and Narrative Cinema," *Screen* 16, no. 3 (Fall 1975): 6–18; Todd McGowan, *The Real Gaze: Film Theory After Lacan* (Albany: State University of New York Press, 2007).

17. Brian Attebery, *Strategies of Fantasy* (Bloomington: Indiana University Press, 1992), 12.

Chapter 1. What Is the Fantastic?

1. Aristotle, *Poetics*, trans. Richard Janko (Indianapolis, IN: Hackett, 1987), 1.

2. Marina Warner, *From Beast to Blonde: On Fairy Tales and Their Tellers* (London: Chatto & Windus, 1994), 14–16.

3. Samuel Taylor Coleridge, *Biographia Literaria* (London: J. M. Dent & Sons, 1991); J. R. R. Tolkien, "On Fairy Stories," in *The Monsters and the Critics and Other Essays*, ed. Christopher Tolkien (London: George Allen & Unwin, 1983), 109–161.

4. Attebery, *Strategies of Fantasy*, 12.

5. Tzvetan Todorov, *The Fantastic: A Structural Approach to a Literary Genre*, trans. Richard Howard (Ithaca, NY: Cornell University Press, 1975), 46.

6. Todorov, *Fantastic*, 25.

7. See Mark Nash, "*Vampyr* and the Fantastic," *Screen* 17, no. 3 (1976): 29–67; Linda Badley, *Film, Horror and the Body Fantastic* (London: Greenwood Press, 1995); Michael Grant, *The Modern Fantastic: The Films of David Cronenberg* (Westport, CT: Praeger, 2000).

8. Amaryll Beatrice Chanady, *Magical Realism and the Fantastic: Resolved versus Unresolved Antinomy* (New York: Garland, 1985), 9.

9. C. G. Jung, "Archetypes and the Collective Unconscious (1934)," in *The Collected Works: Volume 9*, trans. R. C. Hull (Princeton, NJ: Princeton University Press, 1969); Jacques Lacan, "Seminar on *The Purloined Letter*," in *Écrits: The Complete Edition*, trans. Bruce Fink (New York: W. W. Norton, 2006), 6–48.

10. David Bordwell and Noël Carroll, *Post-Theory: Reconstructing Film Studies* (Madison: University of Wisconsin Press, 1996).

11. Sigmund Freud, "Formulations on the Two Principles of Mental Functioning (1911)," in *The Standard Edition of the Complete Psychological Works of Sigmund Freud Volume XII*, trans. James Strachey (London: Hogarth Press, 1958), 222.

12. Jay R. Greenberg and Stephen A. Mitchell, *Object Relations in Psychoanalytic Theory* (Cambridge, MA: Harvard University Press, 1983), 14.

13. Ian MacRury and Candida Yates, "Framing the Mobile: The Psychopathologies of an Everyday Object," *CM: Communication and Media* 11, no. 38 (January 2016): 41–70; Annette Kuhn, *Little Madnesses: Winnicott, Transitional Phenomena and Cultural Experience* (London: I. B. Tauris, 2013).

14. Melanie Klein, "Love, Guilt and Reparation (1937)," in *Love, Guilt and Reparation and Other Works 1921–1945* (London: Hogarth Press, 1975), 340.

15. Lucie Armitt, *Theorising the Fantastic* (London: Arnold, 1996), 33.

16. Mark Kermode, "*Pan's Labyrinth*—Feature," *The Observer*, November 5, 2006, accessed December 10, 2017, http://www.theguardian.com/film/2006/nov/05/features.review1.

17. Sigmund Freud, "'A Child Is Being Beaten': A Contribution to the Study of the Origin of Sexual Perversions (1919)," in *The Standard Edition of the Complete Psychological Works of Sigmund Freud: Volume XVII*, trans. James Strachey (London: Hogarth Press, 1955), 179.

18. D. W. Winnicott, "The Observation of Infants in a Set Situation (1941)," in *Through Paediatrics to Psychoanalysis: Collected Papers* (London: Tavistock, 1958), 53.

Chapter 2. Continuity and Cathexis

1. Hortense Powdermaker, *Hollywood: The Dream Factory* (Boston, MA: Little, Brown, 1950), 281.

2. Lea Jacobs, *The Decline of Sentiment: American Film in the 1920s* (Berkeley: University of California Press, 2008).

3. David Bordwell, "The Classical Hollywood Style, 1917–1960," in *The Classical Hollywood Cinema: Film Style and Mode of Production to 1960*, ed. David Bordwell, Janet Staiger, and Kristin Thompson (London: Routledge, 1988), 3.

4. Leo Handel, *Hollywood Looks at Its Audience: A Report of Film Audience Research* (Urbana: University of Illinois Press, 1950), 119–120, 127.

5. Richard Allen, *Projecting Illusion: Film Spectatorship and the Impression of Reality* (Cambridge: Cambridge University Press, 1995), 2.

6. Melanie Klein, "On the Development of Mental Functioning (1958)," in *Envy and Gratitude and Other Works 1946–1963* (London: Hogarth Press, 1975), 241.

7. *Variety*, November 28, 1933, 12–13.

8. Bordwell, "Classical Hollywood Style," 12.

9. Donald Crafton, "Pie and Chase: Gag, Spectacle and Narrative in Slapstick Comedy," in *Classical Hollywood Comedy*, ed. Kristine Karnick and Henry Jenkins (New York: Routledge, 1995), 106–119.

10. Christine Roth, "Looking Through the Spyglass: Lewis Carroll, James Barrie, and the Empire of Childhood," in *Alice Beyond Wonderland: Essays from the Twenty-First Century*, ed. Christopher Hollingsworth (Iowa City: University of Iowa Press, 2009), 23.

11. Sigmund Freud, "Group Psychology and the Analysis of the Ego (1921)," in *The Standard Edition of the Complete Psychological Works of Sigmund Freud: Volume XVIII*, trans. James Strachey (London: Hogarth Press, 1955), 105.

12. Christian Metz, *The Imaginary Signifier: Psychoanalysis and Cinema*, trans. Celia Britton, Annywl Williams, Ben Brewster, and Alfred Guzzetti (Bloomington: Indiana University Press, 1982), 70.

13. Murray Smith, *Engaging Characters: Fiction, Emotion and the Cinema* (Oxford: Oxford University Press, 1995).

14. Kamilla Elliot, *Rethinking the Novel/Film Debate* (Cambridge: Cambridge University Press, 2003), 190.

15. A summary of the film's reviews is provided by "Reviews: *Alice in Wonderland*," CaryGrant.net, accessed April 30, 2020, http://www.carygrant.net/reviews/alice.html.

16. See Bonnie Friedman, "Relinquishing Oz: Every Girl's Anti-Adventure," in *The Movies: Texts, Receptions, Audiences*, ed. Laurence Goldstein and Ira Konigsberg (Ann Arbor: University of Michigan Press, 1996), 41–59; Pamela Robertson, "Home and Away: Friends of Dorothy on the Road in Oz," in *The Road Movie Book*, ed. Steve Cohan and Ina Rae Hark (London: Routledge, 1997), 271–286; Corey McCall and Randall E. Auxier, "The Virtues of *The Wizard of Oz*," in *"The Wizard of Oz" and Philosophy: Wicked Wisdom and the West*, ed. Randall E. Auxier and Phillip S. Seng (Peru, IL: Open Court Books, 2008), 19–32; Alexander Doty, "'My Beautiful Wickedness': *The Wizard of Oz* as Lesbian Fantasy," in *Flaming Classics: Queering the Film Canon* (London: Routledge, 2000), 47–78; Lynette Carpenter, "'There's No Place Like Home': *The Wizard of Oz* and American Isolationism," *Film and History* 15, no. 2 (May 1985): 37–45; William Pawlett and Meena Dhanda, "The Shared Destiny of the Radically Other: A Reading of *The Wizard of Oz*," *Film-Philosophy* 14, no. 2 (2010): 113–131.

17. Alexander Sergeant, "Scrutinizing the Rainbow: Fantastic Space in *The Wizard of Oz*," *Alphaville: Journal of Film and Screen Media*, no. 2 (2011): 1–15.

18. Frank Nugent, "The Screen in Review: *The Wizard of Oz*," *New York Times*, August 18, 1939; "Cinema: The New Pictures," *Time*, August 21, 1939, accessed December 9, 2015, http://content.time.com/time/magazine/article/0,9171,762487,00.html.

19. Brian Attebery, *The Fantastic Tradition in American Literature* (Bloomington: Indiana University Press, 1980), 84–85.

20. Attebery, *Fantastic Tradition in American Literature*, 84.

21. James Walters, *Alternative Worlds in Hollywood Cinema* (Bristol: Intellect Books, 2008), 45.

22. Stephen Heath, *Questions of Cinema* (Bloomington: Indiana University Press, 1981), 43–44.

23. Trevor Pateman, "Space for the Imagination," *Journal of Aesthetic Education* 31, no. 1 (Spring 1997): 4.

24. Klein, "Early Analysis (1923)," in *Love, Guilt and Reparation*, 92.

25. D. W. Winnicott, *Playing and Reality* (New York: Routledge, 1991), 55.

26. Winnicott, *Playing and Reality*, 122.

27. Elizabeth Bronfen, *Home in Hollywood: The Imaginary Geography of Cinema* (New York: Columbia University Press, 2004), 74.

28. Gaston Bachelard, *The Poetics of Space*, trans. Maria Jolas (Boston, MA: Beacon Press, 1974), 5.

29. "Film Review: *It's a Wonderful Life*," *Variety*, December 25, 1946, 12; "*Wonderful Life* Gives Stewart Perfect Role, Capra a Perfect Film," *Washington Post*, February 5, 1947, 7.

30. Fowkes, *Fantasy Film*, 62.

31. Peter Valenti, 'The 'Film *Blanc*': Suggestions for a Variety of Fantasy, 1940–45," *Journal of Popular Film* 6, no. 4 (1978): 294–304.

32. Robert B. Ray, *A Certain Tendency of the Hollywood Cinema, 1930–1980* (Princeton, NJ: Princeton University Press, 1985), 200.

33. Gérard Genette, *Narrative Discourse: An Essay in Method*, trans. Jane E. Lewin (Ithaca, NY: Cornell University Press, 1980), 34.

34. Todd McGowan, "Fighting Our Fantasies: *Dark City* and the Politics of Psychoanalysis," in *Lacan and Contemporary Film*, ed. Todd McGowan and Sheila Kunkle (New York: Other Press, 2004), 161.

35. Bliss Cua Lim, *Translating Time: Cinema, the Fantastic, and Temporal Critique* (Durham, NC: Duke University Press, 2009), 1.

36. Christian Metz, *Film Language: A Semiotics of Cinema*, trans. Bertrand Augst (Chicago: University of Chicago Press, 1971), 22.

37. Henri Bergson, *Matter and Memory*, trans. Nancy Margaret Paul and W. Scott Palmer (London: George Allen & Unwin, 1911).

Chapter 3. The Wonder Film

1. David Butler, *Fantasy Cinema: Impossible Worlds Onscreen* (London: Wallflower Press, 2009), 34–36.

2. Michele Pierson, *Special Effects: Still in Search of Wonder* (New York: Columbia University Press, 2002).

3. Kenneth J. Zahorski and Robert H. Boyer, "The Secondary Worlds of High Fantasy," in *The Aesthetics of Fantasy Literature and Art*, ed. Roger Scholbin (Notre Dame, IN: University of Notre Dame Press, 1982), 57.

4. Wolfe, *Critical Terms of Science Fiction and Fantasy*, 140.

5. James Donald, "The Fantastic, the Sublime and the Popular: Or, What's at Stake in Vampire Films?," in *Fantasy and the Cinema* (London: BFI, 1989), 237.

6. Metz, *Imaginary Signifier*, 104.

7. Klein, "The Mutual Influences in the Development of Ego and Id (1952)," in *Envy and Gratitude*, 58.

8. Velma West Sykes, "Invisible Pooka Wins January Blue Ribbon Award," *Box Office*, February 10, 1951, 24; "*Harvey*," *Film Daily*, October 13, 1950, 3; "*Harvey*," *Variety*, October 18, 1950, 6.

9. Christine Brooke-Rose, *A Rhetoric of the Unreal: Studies in Narrative and Structure, Especially of the Fantastic* (Cambridge: Cambridge University Press, 1981), 112.

10. Robert T. Ederwein, *Film and the Dream Screen* (Princeton, NJ: Princeton University Press, 1984).

11. Sigmund Freud, "The Uncanny," in *The Uncanny*, trans. David McLintock (London: Penguin Books, 2003), 121–162.

12. Lia M. Hotchkiss, "The Cinematic Appropriation of Theater: Introjection and Incorporation in *Rosencrantz and Guildenstern Are Dead*," *Quarterly Review of Film and Video* 17, no. 2 (2000): 164.

13. Eric S. Rabkin, *The Fantastic in Literature* (Princeton, NJ: Princeton University Press, 1976), 74.

14. "All-Time Box Office Adjusted for Inflation," BoxOfficeMojo.com, accessed on September 17, 2019, http://boxofficemojo.com/alltime/adjusted.htm.

15. Both *Variety* and the *Washington Post* described *Mary Poppins* in those terms upon its release. "Film Review: Mary Poppins," *Variety*, September 2, 1964, 6; "Miss Poppins' Charges," *Washington Post*, December 22, 1964, B8.

16. See Nicole E. Didicher, "The Children in the Story: Metafiction in *Mary Poppins in the Park*," *Children's Literature in Education* 28, no. 3 (1997): 137–138.

17. Metz, *Imaginary Signifier*, 42–57; Mulvey, "Visual Pleasure and Narrative Cinema," 6–18.

18. Sigmund Freud, *Totem and Taboo*, trans. James Strachey (London: Routledge, 1950), 159.

19. Rosemary Jackson, *Fantasy: The Literature of Subversion* (London: Methuen, 1981), 88–89; Linda Hutcheon, *Narcissistic Narrative: The Metafictional Paradox* (Ontario: Wilfrid Laurier University Press, 1980), 76–77.

20. Klein, "Early Stages of the Oedipus Conflict (1928)," in *Love, Guilt and Reparation*, 193.

21. Jean-Louis Baudry, "Ideological Effects of the Basic Cinematographic Apparatus," trans. Alan Williams, *Film Quarterly* 28, no. 2 (Winter 1974): 45.

22. Fowkes, *Fantasy Film*, 29.

23. Philip Strick, "*The Golden Voyage of Sinbad*," *Monthly Film Bulletin* 41, no. 480 (1974): 8.

24. Joshua David Bellin, *Framing Monsters: Fantasy Film and Social Alienation* (Carbondale: Southern Illinois University Press, 2005), 71.

25. Butler, *Fantasy Cinema*, 59.

26. Marina Warner, *Fantastic Metamorphoses, Other Worlds: Ways of Telling the Self* (Oxford: Oxford University Press, 2002), 2.

27. Jean-Paul Sartre, "*Aminadab* or the Fantastic Considered as a Language," in *Literary and Philosophical Essays*, trans. Annette Michelson (London: Anchor Press, 1955), 65.

28. André Bazin, "The Ontology of the Photographic Image," trans. Hugo Gray, *Film Quarterly* 13, no. 4 (Summer 1960): 4–9.

29. For a more thorough account of the relationship between fantasy cinema and the medium of animation, see Christopher Holliday and Alexander Sergeant, eds., *Fantasy/Animation: Connections Between Media, Mediums and Genres* (New York: Routledge, 2018).

30. Sergei Eisenstein, *On Disney*, trans. Alan Upchurch (New York: Methuen, 1985), 21; Paul Wells, *Understanding Animation* (Abingdon: Routledge, 1998), 69.

31. Winnicott, *Playing and Reality*, 45.

32. Steve Neale, "*Triumph of the Will*: Notes on Documentary and Spectacle," *Screen* 20, no. 1 (Spring 1979): 66.

33. Klein, "On the Development of Mental Functioning (1958)," in *Envy and Gratitude*, 240.

Chapter 4. High Fantasy Blockbusters

1. J. D. Connor, *The Studios after the Studios: Neoclassical Hollywood (1970–2010)* (Stanford: Stanford University Press, 2015), 12.

2. Thomas Schatz, "The New Hollywood," in *Movie Blockbusters*, ed. Julian Springer (London: Routledge, 2003), 29.

3. Edward James, "Tolkien, Lewis and the Explosion of Genre Fantasy," in *The Cambridge Companion to Fantasy Literature*, ed. Edward James and Farah Mendlesohn (Cambridge: Cambridge University Press, 2012), 73.

4. Brian Stableford, *The A to Z of Fantasy Literature* (London: Scarecrow Press, 2009), 198.

5. Geoff King, *Spectacular Narratives: Hollywood in the Age of the Blockbuster* (London: I. B. Tauris, 2000), 18.

6. John Clute, "Alternative Worlds," in *The Encyclopedia of Fantasy*, ed. John Clute and John Grant (London: Orbit, 1999), 21.

7. R. D. Hinshelwood, *A Dictionary of Kleinian Thought* (London: Free Association Books, 1989), 398.

8. Klein, "Weaning (1936)," in *Love, Guilt and Reparation*, 290.

9. Paul Sammon, "*Conan the Barbarian*," *Cinefantastique* 12, no. 4 (1982): 49; Worley, *Empires of the Imagination*, 197.

10. Farah Mendlesohn, *Rhetorics of Fantasy* (Middletown, CT: Wesleyan University Press, 2008), 59.

11. Tom Brown, "Spectacle/Gender/History: The Case of *Gone with the Wind*," *Screen* 49, no. 2 (2008): 159.

12. Brown, "Spectacle/Gender/History," 161.

13. David Bordwell, "Intensified Continuity Visual Style in Contemporary American Film," *Film Quarterly* 55, no. 3 (Spring 2002): 24.

14. V. F. Perkins, "Where in the World? The Horizon of Events in Movie Fiction," in *Style and Meaning: Studies in the Detailed Analysis of Film*, ed. John Gibbs and Douglas Pye (Manchester: Manchester University Press, 2005), 16–31.

15. McGowan, *Real Gaze*, 26–27.

16. Klein, "On the Theory of Anxiety and Guilt (1948)" in *Envy and Gratitude*, 29.

17. Klein, "Mourning and Its Relation to the Manic-Depressive States (1940)," in *Love, Guilt and Reparation*, 347.

18. D. W. Winnicott, "The Deprived Mother (1939)," in *Deprivation and Delinquency*, ed. Clare Winnicott, Ray Shepherd, and Madeline Davis (Abingdon: Routledge, 1990), 31.

19. Roger Ebert, "Conan the Barbarian," RogerEbert.com, January 1, 1982, accessed February 20, 2016, http://www.rogerebert.com/reviews/conan-the-barbarian-1982.

20. See Theodor W. Adorno, *Aesthetic Theory*, trans. Robert Hullot-Kentor (London: Continuum, 2000), 11; Fredric Jameson, *The Political Unconscious: Narrative as a Socially Symbolic Act* (London: Methuen, 1981), 105; Jackson, *Fantasy*, 3.

21. Brian Jacks, "Exclusive: The Never-Before-Told Tale of Steven Spielberg's Involvement in *The NeverEnding Story*," MTV, March 15, 2010, accessed April 20, 2020, http://www.mtv.com/news/2435878/exclusive-the-never-before-told-tale-of-steven-spielbergs-involvement-in-the-neverending-story.

22. Alan Karp, "Reviews: *The Neverending Story*," *Box Office*, September 1, 1984, 120; "Film Review: *The Neverending Story*," *Variety*, July 4, 1984, 16.

23. Metz, *Imaginary Signifier*, 58.

24. McGowan, *Real Gaze*, 70.

25. McGowan, *Real Gaze*, 127.

26. See Melanie Klein, *Narrative of a Child Analysis* (London: Hogarth Press, 1961), 243; D. W. Winnicott, *Holding and Interpretation: Fragment of an Analysis* (London: Hogarth Press, 1986), 96–99.

27. Peter Krämer, "'The Best Disney Movie Never Made': Children's Films and the Family Audience in Cinema since the 1960s," in *Genre and Contemporary Hollywood*, ed. Steve Neale (London: BFI, 2002), 193.

28. See Jacqueline Rose, *The Case of Peter Pan, or the Impossibility of Children's Literature* (Basingstoke: Macmillan, 1992).

29. Robin Wood, *Hollywood from Vietnam to Reagan* (New York: Columbia University Press, 1986), 163.

30. Ewan Kirkland, *Children's Media and Modernity: Film, Television and Digital Games* (Bern: Peter Lang, 2017), 1–26.

31. Sigmund Freud, "The Creative Writer and Daydreaming (1908)," in *The Uncanny*, trans. David McLintock (London: Penguin Books, 2003), 27.

32. Sigmund Freud, "The Psychopathology of Everyday Life (1901)," in *The Standard Edition of the Complete Psychological Works of Sigmund Freud: Volume VI*, trans. James Strachey (London: Hogarth Press, 1960), 47.

33. Newsweek quotation cited in "What the Critics Are Saying about Hook," *Washington Post*, December 15, 1991, G5; Marilyn Moss, "Reviews: *Hook*," *Box Office*, January 1, 1992, 26.

Chapter 5. Interpreting the Fantastic

1. Jon Lewis, *American Film: A History* (New York: W.W. Norton, 2008), 410.

2. Butler, *Fantasy Cinema*, 5.

3. Sigmund Freud, *The Interpretation of Dreams*, trans. Joyce Crick (Oxford: Oxford University Press, 1999), 107.

4. Dudley Andrew, *Concepts in Film Theory* (Oxford: Oxford University Press, 1984), 174.

5. Richard Dyer, "Entertainment and Utopia," in *Only Entertainment* (London: Routledge, 2002), 19.

6. François Sirois, "The Role and Importance of Interpretation in the Talking Cure," *International Journal of Psychoanalysis* 93 (2012): 1379.

7. Winnicott's description of the squiggle emerges out of his various patient commentaries, including "Symptom Tolerance in Pediatrics: A Case Study (1953)," in *Through Paediatrics to Psychoanalysis*, 101–117. For a summary of its technique and underlying psychoanalytic theory, see Michael Jacobs, *D. W. Winnicott* (London: Sage, 1995), 69–73.

8. Winnicott, *Playing and Reality*, 51.

9. See Alexander Sergeant, "Making Fantasy Matter: *The Lord of the Rings* and the Legitimization of Fantasy Cinema," in *The Lord of the Rings: Fan Phenomena*, ed. Lorna Piatti-Farnell (Bristol: Intellect, 2015), 10–17.

10. A. O. Scott, "After D&D You May Need R&R," *New York Times*, December 8, 2000, accessed September 19, 2017, http://www.nytimes.com/2000/12/08/arts/08DUNG.html.

11. Ernest Majithis, "Reviews, Previews and Premiers: The Critical Reception of *The Lord of the Rings* in the United Kingdom," in *"The Lord of the Rings": Popular Culture in Global Context*, ed. Ernest Majithis (London: Wallflower Press, 2006), 121.

12. Kenneth Turan, "Movie Review," *Los Angeles Times*, December 16, 2003, accessed June 17, 2016, http://articles.latimes.com/2003/dec/16/entertainment/et-turan16.

13. Kristin Thompson, *The Frodo Franchise: "The Lord of the Rings" and Modern Hollywood* (Berkeley: University of California Press, 2007), 55; Butler, *Fantasy Cinema*, 84.

14. *The Letters of J. R. R. Tolkien*, ed. Humphrey Carpenter (George Allen & Unwin, 1981), 246.

15. See the various "making of" documentary features accompanying *The Lord of the Rings Special Edition* DVDs.

16. Pheasant-Kelly, *Fantasy Film Post 9/11*, 25.

17. Gwendolyn A. Morgan, "'I Don't Think We're in Kansas Anymore: Peter Jackson's Film Interpretations of Tolkien's *Lord of the Rings*," in *Fantasy Fiction into Film: Essays*, ed. Leslie Stratyner and James R. Keller (Jefferson, NC: McFarland, 2007), 21, 32.

18. Nicholas Burns, "'You Have Grown Very Much': The Scouring of the Shire and the Novelistic Aspects of *The Lord of the Rings*," *Journal of the Fantastic in the Arts* 23, no. 1 (2012): 82.

19. Bruce Fink, *Lacan to the Letter: Reading "Écrits" Closely* (Minneapolis: University of Minnesota Press, 2004), 95–101.

20. Jean-Michel Petot, *Melanie Klein: Volume I*, trans. Christine Trollope (Madison, CT: International Universities Press, 1990), 64.

21. Winnicott, *Holding and Interpretation*, 144–147.

22. Richard Corliss, "Lord of the Films," *Time*, December 17, 2001, accessed July 7, 2016, http://www.time.com/time/world/article/0,8599,188807,00.html;

Claudia Puig, "Middle-earth Leaps to Life in Enchanting, Violent Film," *USA Today*, December 18, 2001, accessed July 7, 2016, http://usatoday30.usatoday.com/life/enter/movies/rings/2001-12-19-rings-review.htm#more.

23. Todorov, *Fantastic*, 58–74.

24. Pier Paolo Pasolini, "The Cinema of Poetry," in *Movies and Methods, Vol. 1*, ed. Bill Nichols (Berkeley: University of California Press, 1976), 542–558.

25. Carlos Aguilar, "How Netflix's 'I Lost My Body' Turns Animation on Its Head, with the Story of a Severed Hand," *Los Angeles Times*, February 6, 2020, accessed April 30, 2020, https://www.latimes.com/entertainment-arts/movies/story/2020-02-06/i-lost-my-body-netflix-oscars-animated-feature.

26. Dana Stevens, "The Lighthouse Is Both Artsy and Fartsy," *Slate*, October 10, 2019, accessed April 30, 2020, https://slate.com/culture/2019/10/the-lighthouse-movie-review-robert-pattinson-horror-farts.html.

27. Constance Grady, "Disney's Latest Frozen II Trailer Is Light on Details, Heavy on Magical Horses," *VOX*, June 11, 2019, accessed April 30, 2020, https://www.vox.com/culture/2019/6/11/18661248/watch-disney-frozen-ii-trailer.

28. Claudia Puig, "Wild Things Will Make Your Heart Sing in Many Ways," *USA Today*, October 15, 2009, accessed May 15, 2016, http://www.usatoday.com/life/movies/reviews/2009-10-15-wild-things-review_N.htm.

29. Lisa Schwartzbaum, "Where the Wild Things Are," *Entertainment Weekly*, October 14, 2009, accessed July 4, 2016, http://www.ew.com/ew/article/0,,20312172,00.html.

30. Joe Morgenstern, "*Wild Things* Delights," *Wall Street Journal*, October 16, 2009, accessed July 4, 2016, http://www.wsj.com/articles/SB10001424052748704107204574475112377652766.

31. Kathryn Hume, *Fantasy and Mimesis: Responses to Reality in Western Literature* (New York: Methuen, 1984), 90.

32. Andrew Sarris, *The American Cinema* (New York: Da Capo Press, 1968), 36.

33. W. A. Senior, "Some Notes on 'The Abyss': The Rhetoric of the Fantastic," *Journal of the Fantastic in the Arts* 16, no. 4 (Winter 2006): 275.

34. Logan Hill, "Rowling Cloaks Politics in a Tale of Magic," *New York Times*, November 6, 2016, accessed April 20, 2020, https://www.nytimes.com/2016/11/06/movies/fantastic-beasts-and-where-to-find-them-preview.html.

35. Michael Sullivan, "*Fantastic Beasts and Where to Find Them* Hits the *Harry Potter* Reset Button," *Washington Post*, November 17, 2016, accessed April 22, 2020, https://www.washingtonpost.com/goingoutguide/movies/fantastic-beasts-and-where-to-find-them-hits-the-harry-potter-reset-button/2016/11/17/c951837 8-ac1d-11e6-977a-1030f822fc35_story.html; John Defore, "*Fantastic Beasts*: Film Review," *Hollywood Reporter*, December 11, 2016, accessed April 22, 2020, https://www.hollywoodreporter.com/review/fantastic-beasts-find-review-946770.

36. Francis Bacon, "The Advance of Learning," in *Critical Essays of the Seventeenth Century: Volume One*, edited by J. E. Springarn (Oxford: Clarendon Press, 1908), 7.

37. Gary K. Wolfe *Critical Terms of Science Fiction and Fantasy: A Glossary and Guide to Scholarship* (Westport CT: Greenwood Press, 1986), 5.

38. Darko Suvin, *Metamorphoses of Science Fiction: On the Poetics and History of a Literary Genre* (New Haven, CT: Yale University Press, 1979), 18.

39. Mendlesohn, *Rhetorics of Fantasy*, 182.

40. Metz, *Imaginary Signifier*, 156.

41. Klein, "The Importance of Symbol-Formation in the Development of the Ego (1930)," in *Love, Guilt and Reparation*, 221.

42. See David Crow, "Fantastic Beasts: The Crimes of Grindelwald Review," Den of Geek, November 22, 2008, accessed April 20, 2020, https://www.denofgeek.com/movies/fantastic-beasts-the-crimes-of-grindelwald-review.

Conclusion

1. Barry Keith Grant, *Film Genre Reader III* and *IV* (Austin: University of Texas Press, 2002 and 2012).

2. Rick Altman, *Film/Genre* (London: BFI, 1999); Steve Neale, *Genre and Hollywood* (London: Routledge, 2000).

Bibliography

Adorno, Theodor W. *Aesthetic Theory*. Translated by Robert Hullot-Kentor. London: Continuum, 2000.
Allen, Richard. *Projecting Illusion: Film Spectatorship and the Impression of Reality*. Cambridge: Cambridge University Press, 1995.
Altman, Rick. *Film/Genre*. London: BFI, 1999.
Andrew, Dudley. *Concepts of Film Theory*. Oxford: Oxford University Press, 1984.
Aristotle. *Poetics*. Translated by Richard Janko. Indianapolis, IN: Hackett, 1987.
Armitt, Lucie. *Theorising the Fantastic*. London: Arnold, 1996.
Attebery, Brian. *The Fantasy Tradition in American Literature*. Bloomington: Indiana University Press, 1980.
———. *Strategies of Fantasy*. Bloomington: Indiana University Press, 1992.
Bachelard, Gaston. *The Poetics of Space*. Translated by Maria Jolas. Boston: Beacon Press, 1974.
Bacon, Francis "The Advance of Learning." In *Critical Essays of the Seventeenth Century: Volume One*, edited by J. E. Springarn, 7. Oxford: Clarendon Press, 1908.
Badley, Linda. *Film, Horror and the Body Fantastic*. London: Greenwood Press, 1995.
Baudry, Jean-Louis. "Ideological Effects of the Basic Cinematographic Apparatus." Translated by Alan Williams. *Film Quarterly* 28, no. 2 (Winter 1974): 39–47.
Bazin, André. "The Ontology of the Photographic Image." Translated by Hugo Gray. *Film Quarterly* 13, no. 4 (Summer 1960): 4–9.
Bellin, Joshua David. *Framing Monsters: Fantasy Film and Social Alienation*. Carbondale: Southern Illinois University Press, 2005.
Bergson, Henri. *Matter and Memory*. Translated by Nancy Margaret Paul and W. Scott Palmer. London: George Allen & Unwin, 1911.
Bordwell, David. "The Classical Hollywood Style, 1917–1960." In *The Classical Hollywood Cinema: Film Style and Mode of Production to 1960*, edited by David Bordwell, Janet Staiger, and Kristin Thompson, 1–87. London: Routledge, 1985.
———. "Intensified Continuity Visual Style in Contemporary American Film." *Film Quarterly* 55, no. 3 (Spring 2002): 16–28.

Bordwell, David, and Noël Carroll. *Post-Theory: Reconstructing Film Studies*. Madison: University of Wisconsin Press, 1996.

Bronfen, Elizabeth. *Home in Hollywood: The Imaginary Geography of Cinema*. New York: Columbia University Press, 2004.

Brooke-Rose, Christine. *A Rhetoric of the Unreal: Studies in Narrative and Structure, Especially of the Fantastic*. Cambridge: Cambridge University Press, 1981.

Brown, Tom. "Spectacle/Gender/History: The Case of *Gone with the Wind*." *Screen* 49, no. 2 (2008): 157–178.

Bourdieu, Pierre. *Distinction: A Social Critique of the Judgment of Taste*. Translated by Richard Nice. Cambridge, MA: Harvard University Press, 1984.

Burns, Nicholas. "'You Have Grown Very Much': The Scouring of the Shire and the Novelistic Aspects of *The Lord of the Rings*." *Journal of the Fantastic in the Arts* 23, no. 1 (2012): 83–101.

Butler, David. *Fantasy Cinema: Impossible Worlds on Screen*. London: Wallflower Press, 2009.

Carpenter, Lynette. "'There's No Place Like Home': *The Wizard of Oz* and American Isolationism." *Film and History* 15, no. 2 (May 1985): 37–45.

Chanady, Amaryll Beatrice. *Magical Realism and the Fantastic: Resolved versus Unresolved Antinomy*. New York: Garland, 1985.

Clute, John. "Alternative Worlds." In *The Encyclopedia of Fantasy*, edited by John Clute and John Grant, 21–22. London: Orbit, 1999.

Coleridge, Samuel Taylor. *Biographia Literaria*. London: J. M. Dent & Sons, 1991.

Connor, J. D. *The Studios after the Studios: Neoclassical Hollywood (1970–2010)*. Stanford, CA: Stanford University Press, 2015.

Crafton, Donald. "Pie and Chase: Gag, Spectacle and Narrative in Slapstick Comedy." In *Classical Hollywood Comedy*, edited by Kristine Karnick and Henry Jenkins, 106–119. New York: Routledge, 1995.

Didicher, Nicole E. "The Children in the Story: Metafiction in *Mary Poppins in the Park*." *Children's Literature in Education* 28, no. 3 (1997): 137–149.

Donald, James. "The Fantastic, the Sublime and the Popular: Or, What's at Stake in Vampire Films?" In *Fantasy and the Cinema*, 233–251. London: BFI, 1989.

Doty, Alexander. "'My Beautiful Wickedness': *The Wizard of Oz* as Lesbian Fantasy." In *Flaming Classics: Queering the Film Canon*, 47–78. London: Routledge, 2000.

Dyer, Richard. "Entertainment and Utopia." In *Only Entertainment*, 19–35. London: Routledge, 2002.

Ederwein, Robert T. *Film and the Dream Screen*. Princeton, NJ: Princeton University Press, 1984.

Eisenstein, Sergei. *On Disney*. Translated by Alan Upchurch. New York: Methuen, 1985.

Elliot, Kamilla. *Rethinking the Novel/Film Debate*. Cambridge: Cambridge University Press, 2003.

Fink, Bruce. *Lacan to the Letter: Reading "Écrits" Closely*. Minneapolis: University of Minnesota Press, 2004.

Fish, Stanley. *Is There a Text in This Class? The Authority of Interpretative Communities*. Cambridge, MA: Harvard University Press, 1980.
Fiske, John. *Understanding Popular Culture*. London: Routledge, 1989.
Fowkes, Katherine A. *The Fantasy Film*. Chichester: Wiley-Blackwell, 2010.
Friedman, Bonnie. "Relinquishing Oz: Every Girl's Anti-Adventure." In *The Movies: Texts, Receptions, Audiences*, edited by Laurence Goldstein and Ira Konigsberg, 41–59. Ann Arbor: University of Michigan Press, 1996.
Freud, Sigmund. "'A Child Is Being Beaten': A Contribution to the Study of the Origin of Sexual Perversions (1919)." In *The Standard Edition of the Complete Psychological Works of Sigmund Freud: Volume XVII*, translated by James Strachey, 175–204. London: Hogarth Press, 1955.
———. "The Creative Writer and Daydreaming (1908)." In *The Uncanny*, translated by David McLintock, 23–34. London: Penguin Books, 2003.
———. "Formulations on the Two Principles of Mental Functioning (1911)." In *The Standard Edition of the Complete Psychological Works of Sigmund Freud: Volume XII*, translated by James Strachey, 218–226. London: Hogarth Press, 1958.
———. "Group Psychology and the Analysis of the Ego (1921)." In *The Standard Edition of the Complete Psychological Works of Sigmund Freud: Volume XVIII*, translated by James Strachey, 65–143. London: Hogarth Press, 1955.
———. *The Interpretation of Dreams*. Translated by Joyce Crick. Oxford: Oxford University Press, 1999.
———. "The Psychopathology of Everyday Life (1901)." In *The Standard Edition of the Complete Psychological Works of Sigmund Freud: Volume VI*, translated by James Strachey. London: Hogarth Press, 1960.
———. *Totem and Taboo*. Translated by James Strachey. London: Routledge, 1950.
———. "The Uncanny." In *The Uncanny*, translated by David McLintock, 121–162. London: Penguin Books, 2003.
Genette, Gérard. *Narrative Discourse: An Essay in Method*. Translated by Jane E. Lewin. Ithaca, NY: Cornell University Press, 1980.
Grant, Barry Keith. *Film Genre Reader III and IV*. Austin: University of Texas Press, 2002 and 2012.
Grant, Michael. *The Modern Fantastic: The Films of David Cronenberg*. Westport, CT: Praeger, 2000.
Greenberg, Harvey K. "*The Wizard of Oz*—Little Girl Lost—And Found." In *The Movies on Your Mind*, 14–17. New York: Saturday Review Press, 1975.
Greenberg, Jay R., and Stephen A. Mitchell. *Object Relations in Psychoanalytic Theory*. Cambridge, MA: Harvard University Press, 1983.
Handel, Leo. *Hollywood Looks at Its Audience: A Report of Film Audience Research*. Urbana: University of Illinois Press, 1950.
Heath, Stephen. *Questions of Cinema*. Bloomington: Indiana University Press, 1981.
Hinshelwood, R. D. *A Dictionary of Kleinian Thought*. London: Free Association Books, 1989.
Holliday, Christopher, and Alexander Sergeant, eds. *Fantasy/Animation: Connections Between Media, Mediums and Genres*. New York: Routledge, 2018.

Hotchkiss, Lia M. "The Cinematic Appropriation of Theater: Introjection and Incorporation in *Rosencrantz and Guildenstern Are Dead*." *Quarterly Review of Film and Video* 17, no. 2 (2000): 161–186.

Hume, Kathryn. *Fantasy and Mimesis: Responses to Reality in Western Literature*. New York: Methuen, 1984.

Hutcheon, Linda. *Narcissistic Narrative: The Metafictional Paradox*. Ontario: Wilfrid Laurier University Press, 1980.

Irwin, W. R. *The Game of the Impossible: A Rhetoric of Fantasy*. Urbana: University of Illinois Press, 1976.

Jackson, Rosemary. *Fantasy: The Literature of Subversion*. London: Methuen, 1981.

Jacobs, Lea. *The Decline of Sentiment: American Film in the 1920s*. Berkeley: University of California Press, 2008.

Jacobs, Michael. *D. W. Winnicott*. London: Sage, 1995.

James, Edward. "Tolkien, Lewis and the Explosion of Genre Fantasy." In *The Cambridge Companion to Fantasy Literature*, edited by Edward James and Farah Mendlesohn, 62–78. Cambridge: Cambridge University Press, 2012.

Jameson, Fredric. *The Political Unconscious: Narrative as a Socially Symbolic Act*. London: Methuen, 1981.

Jung, C. G. "Archetypes and the Collective Unconscious (1934)." In *The Collected Works: Volume 9*, trans. R. C. Hull. Princeton, NJ: Princeton University Press, 1969.

King, Geoff. *Spectacular Narratives: Hollywood in the Age of the Blockbuster*. London: I. B. Tauris, 2000.

Kirkland, Ewan. *Children's Media and Modernity: Film, Television and Digital Games*. Bern: Peter Lang, 2017.

Klein, Melanie. *Envy and Gratitude and Other Works 1946–1963*. London: Hogarth Press, 1975.

———. *Love, Guilt and Reparation and Other Works 1921–1945*. London: Hogarth Press, 1975.

———. *Narrative of a Child Analysis*. London: The Hogarth Press, 1961.

Krämer, Peter. "'The Best Disney Movie Never Made': Children's Films and the Family Audience in Cinema since the 1960s." In *Genre and Contemporary Hollywood*, edited by Steve Neale, 185–200. London: BFI, 2002.

Kuhn, Annette. *Little Madnesses: Winnicott, Transitional Phenomena and Cultural Experience*. London: I. B. Tauris, 2013.

Lacan, Jacques, *Écrits: The Complete Edition*. Translated by Bruce Fink. New York: W.W. Norton, 2006.

Laplanche, Jean, and Jean-Bertrand Pontalis. *The Language of Psychoanalysis*. Translated by Donald Nicholson-Smith. London: Karnac Books, 2006.

Lewis, Jon. *American Film: A History*. New York: W.W. Norton, 2008.

Lim, Bliss Cua. *Translating Time: Cinema, the Fantastic, and Temporal Critique*. Durham, NC: Duke University Press, 2009.

MacRury, Ian, and Candida Yates. "Framing the Mobile: The Psychopathologies of an Everyday Object." *CM: Communication and Media* 11, no. 38 (January

2016): 41–70.
McCall, Corey, and Randall E. Auxier. "The Virtues of *The Wizard of Oz*." In *"The Wizard of Oz" and Philosophy: Wicked Wisdom and the West*, edited by Randall E. Auxier and Phillip S. Seng, 19–32. Peru, IL: Open Court Books, 2008. 19–32.
McGowan, Todd. *The Real Gaze: Film Theory After Lacan*. Albany: State University of New York Press, 2007.
———. "Fighting Our Fantasies: *Dark City* and the Politics of Psychoanalysis." In *Lacan and Contemporary Film*, edited by Todd McGowan and Sheila Kunkle, 145–171. New York: Other Press, 2004.
Mendlesohn, Farah. *Rhetorics of Fantasy*. Middletown, CT: Wesleyan University Press, 2008.
Metz, Christian. *Film Language: A Semiotics of Cinema*. Translated by Bertrand Augst. Chicago: University of Chicago Press, 1971.
———. *The Imaginary Signifier: Psychoanalysis and Cinema*. Translated by Celia Britton, Annywl Williams, Ben Brewster, and Alfred Guzzetti. Bloomington: Indiana University Press, 1982.
Moine, Raphaëlle. *Film Genre*. Translated by Alistair Fox and Hilary Radner. Malden, MA: Blackwell, 2008.
Morgan, Gwendolyn A. "I Don't Think We're in Kansas Anymore: Peter Jackson's Film Interpretations of Tolkien's *Lord of the Rings*." In *Fantasy Fiction into Film: Essays*, edited by Leslie Stratyner and James R. Keller, 21–34. Jefferson, NC: McFarland, 2007.
Mulvey, Laura. "Visual Pleasure and Narrative Cinema." *Screen* 16, no. 3 (1975): 6–18.
Münsterberg, Hugo. *The Photoplay: A Psychological Study*. Translated by Alan Langdale. New York: Routledge, 2002.
Nash, Mark. "*Vampyr* and the Fantastic." *Screen* 17, no. 3 (1976): 29–67.
Neale, Steve. *Genre and Hollywood*. London: Routledge, 2000.
———. "*Triumph of the Will*: Notes on Documentary and Spectacle." *Screen* 20, no. 1 (Spring 1979): 63–86.
Pasolini, Pier Paolo. "The Cinema of Poetry." In *Movies and Methods, Vol. 1*, edited by Bill Nichols, 542–558. Berkeley: University of California Press, 1976.
Pateman, Trevor. "Space for the Imagination." *Journal of Aesthetic Education* 31, no. 1 (Spring 1997): 1–8.
Pawlett, William, and Meena Dhanda. "The Shared Destiny of the Radically Other: A Reading of *The Wizard of Oz*." In *Film-Philosophy* 14, no. 2 (2010): 113–131.
Perkins, V. F. "Where in the World? The Horizon of Events in Movie Fiction." In *Style and Meaning: Studies in the Detailed Analysis of Film*, edited by John Gibbs and Douglas Pye, 19–41. Manchester: Manchester University Press, 2005.
Petot, Jean-Michel. *Melanie Klein: Volume I*. Translated by Christine Trollope. Madison, CT: International Universities Press, 1990.
Pheasant-Kelly, Frances. *Fantasy Film Post 9/11*. New York: Palgrave Macmillan, 2013.

Pierson, Michele. *Special Effects: Still in Search of Wonder*. New York: Columbia University Press, 2002.
Powdermaker, Hortense. *Hollywood: The Dream Factory*. Boston, MA: Little, Brown, 1950.
Pribram, E. Deidre. "Spectatorship and Subjectivity." In *A Companion to Film Theory*, edited by Toby Miller and Robert Stam, 146–164. Malden, MA: Blackwell, 2004.
Rabkin, Eric S. *The Fantastic in Literature*. Princeton, NJ: Princeton University Press, 1976.
Ray, Robert B. *A Certain Tendency of the Hollywood Cinema, 1930–1980*. Princeton, NJ: Princeton University Press, 1985.
Robertson, Pamela. "Home and Away: Friends of Dorothy on the Road in Oz." In *The Road Movie Book*, edited by Steve Cohan and Ina Rae Hark, 271–286. London: Routledge, 1997.
Rose, Jacqueline. *The Case of Peter Pan, or the Impossibility of Children's Literature*. Basingstoke: Macmillan, 1992.
Roth, Christine. "Looking Through the Spyglass: Lewis Carroll, James Barrie, and the Empire of Childhood." In *Alice Beyond Wonderland: Essays from the Twenty-First Century*, edited by Christopher Hollingsworth, 23–36. Iowa City: University of Iowa Press, 2009.
Sarris, Andrew. *The American Cinema*. New York: Da Capo Press, 1968.
Sartre, Jean-Paul. "*Aminadab* or the Fantastic Considered as a Language." In *Literary and Philosophical Essays*, translated by Annette Michelson, 56–72. London: Anchor Press, 1955.
Schatz, Thomas. "The New Hollywood." In *Movie Blockbusters*, edited by Julian Springer, 15–42. London: Routledge, 2003.
Senior, W. A. "Some Notes on 'The Abyss': The Rhetoric of the Fantastic." *Journal of the Fantastic in the Arts* 16, no. 4 (Winter 2006): 273–276.
Sergeant, Alexander. "Making Fantasy Matter: *The Lord of the Rings* and the Legitimization of Fantasy Cinema." In *The Lord of the Rings: Fan Phenomena*, edited by Lorna Piatti-Farnell, 10–17. Bristol: Intellect, 2015.
———. "Scrutinizing the Rainbow: Fantastic Space in *The Wizard of Oz*." *Alphaville: Journal of Film and Screen Media*, no. 2 (2011): 1–15.
Sirois, François. "The Role and Importance of Interpretation in the Talking Cure." *International Journal of Psychoanalysis* 93 (2012): 1377–1402.
Smith, Murray. *Engaging Characters: Fiction, Emotion and the Cinema*. Oxford: Oxford University Press, 1995.
Stableford, Brian. *The A to Z of Fantasy Literature*. London: Scarecrow Press, 2009.
Suvin, Darko. *Metamorphoses of Science Fiction: On the Poetics and History of a Literary Genre*. New Haven, CT: Yale University Press, 1979.
Thomas, Bronwen. *Narrative: The Basics*. London: Routledge, 2015.
Thompson, Kristin. *The Frodo Franchise: "The Lord of the Rings" and Modern Hollywood*. Berkeley: University of California Press, 2007.

Todorov, Tzvetan. *The Fantastic: A Structural Approach to a Literary Genre*. Translated by Richard Howard. Ithaca, NY: Cornell University Press, 1975.
Tolkien, J. R. R. "On Fairy Stories." In *The Monsters and the Critics and Other Essays*, edited by Christopher Tolkien, 109–161. London: George Allen & Unwin, 1983.
———. *The Letters of J. R. R. Tolkien*. Edited by Humphrey Carpenter. London: George Allen & Unwin, 1981.
Valenti, Peter. "The 'Film Blanc': Suggestions for a Variety of Fantasy, 1940–45." *Journal of Popular Film* 6, no. 4 (1978): 294–304.
Walters, James. *Alternative Worlds in Hollywood Cinema*. Bristol: Intellect Books, 2008.
———. *Fantasy Film: A Critical Introduction*. Oxford: Berg, 2011.
Warner, Marina. *Fantastic Metamorphoses, Other Worlds: Ways of Telling the Self*. Oxford: Oxford University Press, 2002.
———. *From Beast to Blonde: On Fairy Tales and Their Tellers*. London: Chatto & Windus, 1994.
Wells, Paul. *Understanding Animation*. Abingdon: Routledge, 1998.
Williams, Linda. "Gender, Genre, and Excess." *Film Quarterly* 44, no. 4 (Summer 1991): 2–13.
Winnicott, D. W. *Deprivation and Delinquency*. Edited by Clare Winnicott, Ray Shepherd, and Madeline Davis. Abingdon: Routledge, 1990.
———. *Holding and Interpretation: Fragment of an Analysis*. London: Hogarth Press, 1986.
———. *Playing and Reality*. New York: Routledge, 1971.
———. *Through Paediatrics to Psychoanalysis: Collected Papers*. London: Tavistock, 1958.
Wolfe, Gary K. *Critical Terms of Science Fiction and Fantasy: A Glossary and Guide to Scholarship*. Westport, CT: Greenwood Press, 1986.
Wood, Robin. *Hollywood from Vietnam to Reagan*. New York: Columbia University Press, 1986.
Worley, Alec. *Empires of the Imagination: A Critical Survey of Fantasy Cinema from Georges Méliès to "The Lord of the Rings."* Jefferson, NC: McFarland, 2005.
Zahorski, Kenneth J., and Robert H. Boyer. "The Secondary Worlds of High Fantasy." In *The Aesthetics of Fantasy Literature and Art*, edited by Roger Scholbin, 56–81. Notre Dame: University of Notre Dame Press, 1982.

Index

Page numbers in **bold** refer to case study films

action/action cinema, 6, 81, 114, 122, 132, 144, 147, 159–160, 171, 182, 191
adaptation, 18, 20, 33, 35, 39, 49–50, 101–102, 132, 134, 160, 173–174, 180, 183–184, 193
Adaptation (2002), 193
Aladdin (1992), 160
Alexander, Lloyd, 131
Ali Baba and the Forty Thieves (1918), 115
Alice in Wonderland (1933), **38–49**, 69, 76, 149, 216, 219
Alice in Wonderland (2010), 176
Alice's Adventures in Wonderland (1865), 38. *See also* Carroll, Lewis
allegory, 180, 192, 203, 205, 207, 210, 215
alternative worlds, 74, 129–133, 135, 137–139, 142, 145–146, 150, 152, 159–162, 165, 170–171, 173–174, 182, 184–185, 215
ambiguity, 15–16, 30, 90, 149. *See also* hesitation
Angel on my Shoulder (1946), 66
angels, 66–69. *See also* religion
animation, 5, 100, 111–114, 116–118, 120–121, 122–124, 171, 193. *See also* computer-generated imagery (CGI); special effects; stop-motion animation
Aristotle, 12, 30, 35, 50
audience(s), 12–13, 18, 31, 33–35, 49–51, 66–67, 75–76, 80, 82, 87, 100, 114, 119–120, 129–130, 135, 146, 150, 160, 172–173, 175, 177, 180–182, 187, 192–194, 197, 204, 207–208, 216, 220
and their distinction from spectators, xiii–xiv
and their relationship with genre theory, 3–5
See also spectatorship theory
Avatar (2009), 126
Avengers: Infinity War (2018), 177

Babes in Toyland (1934), 35
Back to the Future: Part III (1990), 5
Badlands (1973), 129
Barrie, J. M., 8, 160, 165
Baum, L. Frank, 19, 50–51, 56
Beastmaster, The (1982), 131
Beasts of the Southern Wild (2012), 77
Beauty and the Beast (1991), 160
Bedknobs and Broomsticks (1971), 125
Being John Malkovich (1999), 193
Belle et La Bête, Le (1946), 221
Ben Hur (1959), 81

Beyond Tomorrow (1940), 66
Big Fish (2003), 77
Black Cauldron, The (1985), 131
blockbusters, 77, 127, 129–138, 145–146, 158–160, 162, 165, 171–174, 175–176, 183, 221
Boot, Das (1981), 146
Braveheart (1995), 182
Brazil (1984), 176
Bridge to Terabithia (2007), 77
Brigadoon (1954), 80
body genres, 6
Burton, Tim, 176

Canterville Ghost, The (1944), 35
Capra, Frank, 66, 69
Carroll, Lewis, 8, 38–40, 46, 48–49, 197
cathexis, 36–38, 43–44, 46, 48–49, 57, 60–61, 65, 74–77, 221
childhood
  cultural concepts of, 166–167, 216
  and infantilization, 159, 161, 165, 170
  and its relationship to adult identity, 165, 168, 170–171, 173
  and its relationship to nostalgia, 31
  as a concept within psychoanalytic theory, 22, 23 44, 59–60, 74. 103, 110, 133, 135, 166
children's films. *See* childhood
Christianity, 3, 12. *See also* religion
Christmas Carol, A (1938), 35
Chronicles of Narnia, The (franchise), 1, 176
Chronicles of Narnia: The Lion, the Witch and the Wardrobe, The (2005), 172
Chronicles of Prydain, The (1964–1968), 131
cinephiles/Cinephilia, 176, 178
Cinderella (1899), 33, 222
Citizen Kane (1941), 25, 69, 139
Clash of the Titans (1981), 132
clinical psychology, 7

cognitive psychology, 20
Columbia Pictures, 114, 160
comedy, 40, 49–50, 76–77, 85–86, 90, 162, 199, 214, 222
Company of Wolves, The (1984), 15–16
computer-generated imagery (CGI), 126, 181–182
Conan the Barbarian (1982), **135–145**, 162, 165, 167, 171–173, 184–185, 189
Conan the Destroyer (1984), 135
Connecticut Yankee in King Arthur's Court, A (1931), 35
Constantin Film, 146
continuity filmmaking, 35–37, 45, 49, 56, 64, 70, 77–78, 81, 117, 172, 221
Cooper, James Fenimore, 51
costume design, 46, 48, 50, 60, 80, 137, 216
creativity, xiii, 23, 60, 93, 98, 100, 193
Cronenberg, David, 15
Curious Case of Benjamin Button, The (2008), 176

Darby Gill and the Little People (1959), 76
Dante, Joe, 125
Dark Crystal, The (1982), 131
Dark Knight, The (2008), 177
Dawn of the Planet of the Apes (2014), 182
De Chomón, Segundo, 222
delusions, 14–15, 26–27, 82, 86–87, 93
disbelief, 9, 16–17, 25, 29, 72, 101–102, 118
  suspension of, 13
Disney Studios, 2, 50, 99, 101–102, 117, 159, 175, 194
Doctor Dolittle (1967), 80
Dragonslayer (1981), 159
dreams, xiii, 1, 6, 11–12, 16, 19, 20–21, 26, 29, 34, 44, 56, 60,

63–64, 67, 82–83, 94–95, 100, 108–110, 115, 120, 124, 133–134, 145, 150–151, 157, 173, 177, 223. See also psychoanalysis
Dungeons and Dragons (roleplaying game), 131
Dungeons and Dragons (2000), 181
Dynamation, 114, 117, 121–122

Edward Scissorhands (1990), 125, 176
Eggers, Dave, 193, 198
Electric Hotel, The (1908), 222
Empire Strikes Back, The (1981), 132
Enchanted Cottage, The (1945), 35
estrangement, 208, 210, 214
E.T.: The Extra-Terrestrial (1982), 159
Excalibur (1982), 131

fairy tales, 12, 15, 19, 25, 33, 146. See also folklore
Fall of the House of Usher, The (Poe), 15, 90
fandom, 160, 176
fantastic, 9, 13–16, 19, 23–25, 29, 32–34, 42–43, 50, 53, 57, 63, 65, 70–71, 74, 77, 82, 85, 87, 90, 93, 102, 108, 116, 118, 121, 124, 126, 130, 134, 138–139, 140, 153, 156, 162, 165, 167, 171, 178, 180, 184–185, 191–192, 194, 196–197, 198–201, 208, 210, 217, 220. See also hesitation; Todorov, Tzvetan
Fantastic Beasts (franchise), 180, **203–215**. See also Wizarding World Franchise
Fantastic Beasts and Where to Find Them (2016), 204, 206, 210–211
Fantastic Beasts: The Crimes of Grindelwald (2018), 204, 206–207, 212, 214
fantasy. See adaptation; alternative worlds; creativity; fairy tales; fantastic; film blanc; folklore; high fantasy; fantastic; imagination; magic; metamorphosis; monsters; myth; orientalist fantasies; phantasy; trick films; wonder films
film blanc, 66–67, 73
Fincher, David, 176
Fisher King, The (1991), 176
5,000 Fingers of Dr. T, The (1953), 80
folklore, 11–12, 14, 19, 130, 132, 184, 214
Francis (1950), 86
Freaky Friday (1976), 76
Freud, Sigmund, 19–22, 27, 29, 36, 42, 103, 122, 161, 166–167, 177–178
Frozen II (2019), 193

Game of Thrones (2011–2019), 176
Geisel, Theodor Seuss, 80
gender, xiv, 107, 166, 184. See also representation
General, The (1926), 4
genre, as a method of classification, 4–5
Ghost (1990), 77
Ghost and Mrs. Muir, The (1947), 35
Gilliam, Terry, 176
Gladiator (2000), 182
Godfather, The (1972), 129
Golden Blade, The (1953), 80
Golden Voyage of Sinbad, The (1973), 85, **113–124**, 125–126, 149
Gone with the Wind (1939), 138
Good Omens (2019), 176
Gremlins (1984), 76
Grimm Brothers, 159
Groundhog Day (1993), 77
Gulliver in the Land of the Giants (1903), 222
Gulliver's Travels (1902), 33
Guy Named Joe, A (1943), 66

hallucinations, 14, 26, 82, 86, 92, 124, 161

Harryhausen, Ray, 113–117, 122, 125, 132. *See also* Dynamation
Harry Potter (franchise, 2001–2011), 2, 176, 203, 206. *See also* Wizarding World (franchise)
Harry Potter (novels), 203–204
Harry Potter and the Cursed Child (2016 play), 203
Harry Potter and the Deathly Hallows: Part 2 (2011), 204
Harry Potter and the Sorcerer's Stone (2001), 1, 172
Harvey (1950), **85–99**, 100, 102, 125, 216
Hawthorn, Nathaniel, 51
Helen of Troy (1956), 80
Her (2014), 193
Here Comes Mr. Jordan (1941), 66
hesitation/hesitancy, 14–19, 23–24, 27, 29–30, 44, 47, 50, 69–70, 82, 84, 108, 118, 122, 140, 150, 180, 186, 189–190, 192, 200–201, 203, 205, 208, 210
high fantasy, 77, 130–136, 139, 144–150, 155–156, 158–160, 170–174, 181, 183–185, 190, 219
His Dark Materials (2019–), 176
His Majesty, the Scarecrow of Oz (1914), 50
Hobbit, The (2012–2014), 176
Hoffman, E. T. A., 12, 15
Hollywood. *See* blockbusters; continuity filmmaking; Columbia Pictures; Disney Studios; MGM Studios; naturalism; new Hollywood; Paramount Studios; Sony Pictures; 20th Century Fox; Warner Bros
Hook (1991), 135, **159–171**, 173, 216
horror, 6, 12–16, 19–20, 24, 82, 222
Howard, Robert E., 135
humor. *See* comedy

idealization (idealized objects), 106–108, 110, 113, 117, 125–126. *See also* Klein, Melanie
identification, 36, 38, 42–44, 46–49, 76, 103, 106, 124
ideology, 99, 143–144, 211
I Lost My Body (2019), 193
Imaginarium of Doctor Parnassus, The (2009), 77, 176
imagination, 6–8, 11–12, 19–21, 24, 26, 29, 34, 36, 51, 82–84, 90–92, 95, 98, 100–101, 106, 108, 111, 115, 126, 132, 134, 139–140, 142, 145, 148, 150–151, 156, 160, 162, 166, 168–169, 171–172. *See also* creativity; play; Winnicott, D. W.
I Married a Witch (1942), 35
imperialism, 115, 131
indecision, 28, 102. *See also* hesitation
Indiana Jones series (1981–1989, 2008), 132
infantilization. *See* childhood (and infantilization)
internal objects, 120–122. *See also* Klein, Melanie
interpretation, 50, 90, 177–180, 184–193, 195–197, 200–203, 205, 207, 210–211, 214–215, 222. *See also* symbol formation
introjection/introjective Phantasy, 83–86, 91–94, 99, 102, 106–111, 113, 115, 118, 120–122, 124–126, 133, 221. *See also* Klein, Melanie
Irving, Washington, 51
It's a Wonderful Life (1946), **65–75**, 76–77, 85, 149, 208

Jabberwocky (1871), 197
Jack and the Beanstalk (1902), 33
Jack the Giant Killer (1962), 80
Jackson, Peter (director), 180–185, 215
Jason and the Argonauts (1963), 114

Jaws (1975), 125, 129, 159
Jonze, Spike (director), 193–195, 197–199, 202
Jordan, Neil (director), 15
Jumanji (1995), 126, 160

Kafka, Franz, 14
Kaufman, Charlie (screenwriter), 193
Kingdom of the Fairies, The (1903), 222
King Kong (1933), 35, 81, 125
King Kong (2005), 182
King of Kings (1927 & 1961), 3
Kiss for Cinderella, A (1925), 38
Klein, Melanie, 21–23, 36–37, 74, 84, 106, 120–121, 134, 141–142, 156, 178–179, 189, 210. *See also* object relations
Krull (1983), 131
Kull the Conqueror (1997), 171

Lacan, Jacques, 20–21
Last Action Hero, The (1993), 171
Last of the Mohicans, The (1841), 51
Lear, Edward, 197
Le Guin, Ursula, 8
Legend (1985), 159
Lewis, C. S., 130, 172–173
Life of Pi (2012), 176
Lighthouse, The (2019), 193
Lion, the Witch and the Wardrobe, The (novel), 130
Lord of the Rings, The (novel), 130–131, 176, 183–184, 215
Lord of the Rings, The (1978 animation), 131
Lord of the Rings, The (2001–2003), 2, 20, 144, 170, 172, **180–192**, 193–194, 207, 215, 219
Lost Horizon (1937), 35
Lost World, The (1924), 125
Love Actually (2003), 4
Lucas, George, 129, 159

MacDonald, George, 12
magic
 as force/spell, 12, 67, 69, 90, 101, 106–107, 114, 116–117
 as mode of address, 3, 13, 51, 71, 101, 117, 137, 205, 208, 220.
 beings and characters, 16, 26, 76, 86, 94, 99–100, 114, 122, 125, 205–206, 210–212
 circumstances, 102, 210
 effects 126. *See also* special effects
 imagery, 110, 117, 212
 lands/settings/worlds, 53, 56, 63, 137, 139, 148, 150, 154–156, 158, 161–162, 172–173, 206, 214, 219. *See also* alternative worlds
 objects, 5, 130, 177
 shows, 81–83
 visions, 87, 94, 110, 208. *See also* delusions; hallucinations; perception
Magic Cloak of Oz, The (1914), 50
Magic Sword, The (1962), 80
Marble Faun, The (1861), 51
Marvel Cinematic Universe, 2, 176
Mary Poppins (1964), 85, **99–113**, 115, 117, 125–126, 139, 149, 219
Mary Poppins Returns (2018), 126
mass media, 4
Mean Streets (1973), 129
Méliès, Georges, 33, 115, 222
metamorphosis, 116–118, 120, 124, 126
metaphor, 73, 95, 150, 177, 180, 186–191, 196, 200, 203, 207, 210, 215–216
MGM Studios, 50–51, 66, 77, 129, 130, 132, 173
Midsummer Night's Dream, A (1935), 35
mimesis, 11–12, 137. *See also* naturalism; realism
Mr. Smith Goes to Washington (1939), 66

monsters, 16, 25, 32, 35, 60, 76, 83, 114–115, 122, 124, 149, 156. See also magic (beings and creatures)
musicals, 56, 80, 99–100, 108, 112, 117
Mysterious Island (1961), 114
myth, 3, 20, 77, 80, 116, 130–132, 136, 140, 165, 183–184

narcissism, 103–104, 106–108, 110
narrative theory, 69–70, 90, 131–132, 139, 151
naturalism, 6, 9, 34–36, 56, 69–70, 76, 78, 118, 202
NeverEnding Story, The (1984), 135, 145–158, 165, 167, 171, 173, 216, 219
NeverEnding Story, The (1995, TV Series), 146
NeverEnding Story II: The Next Chapter, The (1990), 146
NeverEnding Story III: Escape from Fantasia (1994), 146
new Hollywood, 130. See also blockbusters
Niebelungen, Die (1924), 222
Nutcracker and the Mouse-King (1816), 15

object relations, 21, 45–46, 57, 121
O'Brien, Willis, 125
orientalist fantasies, 35, 115
Owl and the Pussycat, The (1871), 197
Oz: The Great and Powerful (2013), 173

Pagemaster, The (1994), 171
Palace of the Arabian Nights, The (1905), 115
Pan's Labyrinth (2006), **25–30**, 194
pantomime, 35
Paramount Studios, 38, 45, 49, 79, 125, 130, 175
Patchwork Girl of Oz, The (1914), 50

perception, 48, 56, 82, 84–85, 90–91, 93, 95, 98–99, 102, 109–111, 115, 127, 180, 210
performance, 39, 46, 48, 92
Peter Pan (1924), 18, 38
Peter Pan (2004), 18
Peter Pan stories, 160, 165, 170. See also Barrie, J. M.
Peterson, Wolfgang, 146
phantasy. See cathexis; creativity; dreams; delusion; Freud, Sigmund; hallucinations, introjection/introjective phantasy; Klein, Melanie; narcissism; play; projection/projective phantasy; psychoanalysis; symbol formation; Winnicott, D.W
phenomenology, 20
Pirates of the Caribbean franchise, 1
play, 8, 20–21, 23, 29–31, 38, 42, 44–47, 60, 98, 100–101, 120, 131, 156, 165–169, 179, 189, 197–198, 216. See also creativity
pleasure, 4, 6–7, 16, 18, 20, 31, 38–39, 41, 48, 57, 60, 64, 71, 76, 81–82, 85, 90, 92–93, 95, 101–103, 110, 113, 115, 121, 132, 134–135, 137–138, 142, 144–145, 156, 160, 162, 165–166, 169, 171–172, 179, 183, 187, 189, 201, 203, 214, 216, 219–220
Poe, Edgar Allan, 15, 90
poetry, 11, 29, 72, 93, 180, 183, 191–192, 193, 196–197, 201–203, 205, 215–216
popular culture, 4, 50, 77, 130–131, 160–161, 176, 181, 220
Porter, Edwin S, 33
Potocki, Jan, 14
Princess Bride, The (1987), 77, 145
Prince Valiant (1954), 80
production design, 40, 50, 165, 181
projection/projective phantasy, 133–135, 139–142, 144–145, 151,

153, 156, 158, 162, 166–167, 169, 171–172, 221
psychoanalysis, xiii, 6, 16, 19–24, 29, 36, 42, 74, 83, 92, 103, 120–121, 141, 156–157, 166–167, 178–179, 185–186, 189, 192. See Freud, Sigmund; Klein, Melanie; Winnicott, D. W.
psychology. See clinical psychology; cognitive psychology
Pulp Fiction (1994), 151
pulp literature, 80, 132, 135, 184

race, 115, 166, 184, 206, 211. See also representation
realism, 3, 8, 12, 37–38, 108, 111, 117, 118, 184, 191. See also mimesis; naturalism
Red Riding Hood (1900), 33, 222
Red Sonja (1985), 135
religion, 3, 12, 66–68, 71, 99, 135, 191
representation, 11, 34, 51, 92, 95, 98, 111, 117, 120, 126, 184, 189, 196, 198
Return to Oz (1985), 159
Rip Van Winkle (1819), 51
romance (film genre), 35, 71, 76–77, 152, 193
romanticism, 13, 14, 51, 71, 82, 95, 102, 195
Rowling, J. K., 172, 203–205

Santa Clause, The (1994), 160
Saragossa Manuscript (Potocki), 14
Saving Mr. Banks (2013), 102
science fiction, 5, 12–14, 20, 24, 80, 82, 160, 193, 222
Scorsese, Martin, 176
Sendak, Maurice, 193–194, 197–198
set design, 51, 53, 85, 137, 165, 181
Seuss, Doctor. See Geisel, Theodor Seuss
7 Faces of Dr. Lao (1964), 76

Seventh Seal, The (1957), 221
Seventh Voyage of Sinbad, The (1958), 113
Shape of Water, The (2017), 176
Singin' in the Rain (1952), 4
Snow White and the Seven Dwarfs (1937), 50
Sony Pictures, 160, 175. See also Columbia Pictures
Sound of Music, The (1965), 17
special effects, 33, 47, 80–82, 84, 86, 99–101, 103, 110, 114–115, 117, 125–127, 131, 177, 191, 221–222. See also animation; computer-generated imagery (CGI)
spectacle, 50, 81, 106, 112, 116, 121, 124, 131–132, 137–138, 141, 144, 158–160, 162, 165, 170–173, 177, 182–183, 186, 211–212, 222
spectatorship theory, 6–8, 30, 37, 42, 56, 72, 91, 92, 103, 107, 139, 151
critical definitions of, xiii–xiv, 9
See also identification; fantastic; naturalism; realism
Spellbound (1945), 56
Spielberg, Steven, 125, 129, 146, 159–160, 170
Spring Fairy, The (1902), 222
Star Wars (1977), 5, 129, 135
stop-motion animation, 113–118, 122, 125
supernatural, 14–15, 19, 35, 75, 90, 100
Sword and the Sorcerer, The (1982), 131
sword and sorcery, 80. See also high fantasy
symbol formation, 178–180, 189–190, 192, 198, 201, 203, 210, 215, 222

Tales from the NeverEnding Story (2001), 146
taste, 5, 176–178, 183
Technicolor, 51, 53, 63, 66, 80, 100, 173

technology, 80–81, 115, 120–121, 173
television, 66, 79, 146, 176, 220
Thief of Baghdad, The (1924), 115, 222
300 (2007), 182
thrillers, 6
Through the Looking Glass and What Alice Found There (1871), 38. See also Carroll, Lewis
Thousand and One Nights, A (1945), 35
Todorov, Tzvetan, 14–16, 19, 24–25, 50, 192
Tolkien, J. R. R., 13, 130, 180–184, 186, 190–191, 215
Tom Thumb (1958), 76
Topper (1938), 35
Travers, P. L. 101–102
trick films, 81
Triumph of the Will (1935), 182
20th Century Fox, 175
20,000 Leagues Under the Sea (1870), 147

Ugetsu (1953), 221
uncanny, 15, 92, 124. See also Freud, Sigmund; Todorov, Tzvetan
unconscious, 19–20, 22, 30, 145, 157–158, 186
Universal Studios, 135, 175, 194

Vampyr (1932), 15–16
vaudeville, 40, 50
Verne, Jules, 147
Vertigo (1958), 56
Videodrome (1983), 16

Warner Bros, 146, 175, 194, 203–204

well-being, 21–22, 157, 167
westerns, 5, 222
Where the Wild Things Are (2009), 180, **192–203**, 215
Where the Wild Things Are (picture book), 193–194. See also Sendak, Maurice
Who Framed Roger Rabbit? (1988), 126
widescreen, 80, 173
Willow (1988), 131, 144, 159
Willy Wonka and the Chocolate Factory (1971), 125
Winnicott, D. W., 21–23, 29–30, 36, 60–61, 74, 120, 142, 156, 178–179, 189, 201
Wizarding World (franchise), 172, 203–208, 214
Wizard of Oz (1925), 50
Wizard of Oz, The (1939), 1, 18, 20, 38, **49–65**, 66, 69, 75–77, 138–139, 149, 162, 173, 222
Wizards (1977), 131
Wizards of the Demon Sword (1992), 171
wonder, 27, 81–86, 99–100, 102–103, 106, 110–114, 124–127, 208
wonder films, 81, 85, 112, 124–125, 127, 129–130, 132, 147, 176, 221
Wonderful World of the Brothers Grimm, The (1962), 77
Wonderful Wizard of Oz, The (book), 19–20
world-building, 139. See also alternative worlds

You Can't Take It With You (1938), 66

THE SUNY SERIES

MURRAY POMERANCE | EDITOR

Also in the series

William Rothman, editor, *Cavell on Film*

J. David Slocum, editor, *Rebel Without a Cause*

Joe McElhaney, *The Death of Classical Cinema*

Kirsten Moana Thompson, *Apocalyptic Dread*

Frances Gateward, editor, *Seoul Searching*

Michael Atkinson, editor, *Exile Cinema*

Paul S. Moore, *Now Playing*

Robin L. Murray and Joseph K. Heumann, *Ecology and Popular Film*

William Rothman, editor, *Three Documentary Filmmakers*

Sean Griffin, editor, *Hetero*

Jean-Michel Frodon, editor, *Cinema and the Shoah*

Carolyn Jess-Cooke and Constantine Verevis, editors, *Second Takes*

Matthew Solomon, editor, *Fantastic Voyages of the Cinematic Imagination*

R. Barton Palmer and David Boyd, editors, *Hitchcock at the Source*

William Rothman, *Hitchcock: The Murderous Gaze, Second Edition*

Joanna Hearne, *Native Recognition*

Marc Raymond, *Hollywood's New Yorker*

Steven Rybin and Will Scheibel, editors, *Lonely Places, Dangerous Ground*

Claire Perkins and Constantine Verevis, editors, *B Is for Bad Cinema*

Dominic Lennard, *Bad Seeds and Holy Terrors*

Rosie Thomas, *Bombay before Bollywood*

Scott M. MacDonald, *Binghamton Babylon*

Sudhir Mahadevan, *A Very Old Machine*

David Greven, *Ghost Faces*

James S. Williams, *Encounters with Godard*

William H. Epstein and R. Barton Palmer, editors, *Invented Lives, Imagined Communities*

Lee Carruthers, *Doing Time*

Rebecca Meyers, William Rothman, and Charles Warren, editors, *Looking with Robert Gardner*

Belinda Smaill, *Regarding Life*

Douglas McFarland and Wesley King, editors, *John Huston as Adaptor*
R. Barton Palmer, Homer B. Pettey, and Steven M. Sanders, editors, *Hitchcock's Moral Gaze*
Nenad Jovanovic, *Brechtian Cinemas*
Will Scheibel, *American Stranger*
Amy Rust, *Passionate Detachments*
Steven Rybin, *Gestures of Love*
Seth Friedman, *Are You Watching Closely?*
Roger Rawlings, *Ripping England!*
Michael DeAngelis, *Rx Hollywood*
Ricardo E. Zulueta, *Queer Art Camp Superstar*
John Caruana and Mark Cauchi, editors, *Immanent Frames*
Nathan Holmes, *Welcome to Fear City*
Homer B. Pettey and R. Barton Palmer, editors, *Rule, Britannia!*
Milo Sweedler, *Rumble and Crash*
Ken Windrum, *From El Dorado to Lost Horizons*
Matthew Lau, *Sounds Like Helicopters*
Dominic Lennard, *Brute Force*
William Rothman, *Tuitions and Intuitions*
Michael Hammond, *The Great War in Hollywood Memory, 1918–1939*
Burke Hilsabeck, *The Slapstick Camera*
Niels Niessen, *Miraculous Realism*
Alex Clayton, *Funny How?*
Bill Krohn, *Letters from Hollywood*
Alexia Kannas, *Giallo!*
Homer B. Pettey, editor, *Mind Reeling*
Matthew Leggatt, editor, *Was It Yesterday?*
Merrill Schleier, editor, *Race and the Suburbs in American Film*
Neil Badmington, *Perpetual Movement*
George Toles, *Curtains of Light*
Erica Stein, *Seeing Symphonically*